HANDBOOK OF INTERNATIONAL DISASTER PSYCHOLOGY

Recent Titles in
Contemporary Psychology

HANDBOOK OF INTERNATIONAL DISASTER PSYCHOLOGY

Volume 3
Refugee Mental Health

Edited by Gilbert Reyes and Gerard A. Jacobs

Preface by Charles D. Spielberger

Foreword by Benedetto Saraceno

Praeger Perspectives

Contemporary Psychology
Chris E. Stout, Series Editor

PRAEGER

Westport, Connecticut
London

Library of Congress Cataloging-in-Publication Data

Handbook of international disaster psychology / edited by Gilbert Reyes and Gerard A. Jacobs ; preface by Charles D. Spielberger ; foreword by Benedetto Saraceno.
     p.   cm. — (Contemporary psychology, ISSN 1546–668X)
    Includes bibliographical references and index.
    ISBN 0-275-98315-3 ((set) : alk. paper) — ISBN 0-275-98316-1 ((vol. I) : alk. paper) — ISBN 0-275-98317-X ((vol. II) : alk. paper) — ISBN 0-275-98318-8 ((vol. III) : alk. paper) — ISBN 0-275-98319-6 ((vol. IV) : alk. paper) 1. Disaster victims—Mental health. 2. Disaster victims—Mental health services. 3. Disasters—Psychological aspects. 4. Disaster relief—Psychological aspects. 5. Humanitarian assistance—Psychological aspects. 6. Community psychology. I. Reyes, Gilbert. II. Jacobs, Gerard A. III. Contemporary psychology (Praeger Publishers)
    RC451.4.D57H36   2006
    362.2'2—dc22   2005018786

British Library Cataloguing in Publication Data is available.

Library of Congress Catalog Card Number: 2005018786
ISBN: 0-275-98315-3 (set)
        0-275-98316-1 (vol. 1)
        0-275-98317-X (vol. 2)
        0-275-98318-8 (vol. 3)
        0-275-98319-6 (vol. 4)

ISSN: 1546–668X

First published in 2006

Praeger Publishers, 88 Post Road West, Westport, CT 06881
An imprint of the Greenwood Publishing Group, Inc.
www.praeger.com

Printed in the United States of America

The paper used in this book complies with the Permanent Paper Standard issued by the National Information Standards Organization (Z39.48–1984).

10 9 8 7 6 5 4 3 2 1

DEDICATION

The *Handbook of International Disaster Psychology* would not have been possible without the compassion and commitment of the international humanitarian community. In a world where millions are killed or harmed each year, either by natural hazards or because of the intentional and accidental actions of humankind, legions of caring people rise to these occasions, determined to relieve the suffering and protect the welfare of people who are in the most dire of circumstances.

The recent history of humanitarian operations has seen a surge of violence directed against these most charitable and nonpartisan individuals who have sacrificed the safety of their homes and families, and who have risked their lives to comfort distant neighbors and to promote peace in the face of force.

Those of us living in zones of relative safety, passing our days and nights in homes and workplaces equipped with modern conveniences, and having plentiful access to clean water, should feel humbled by the courage, dedication, and resilience of those who journey unarmed to enact the values and embody the virtues of our better nature.

In light of these things, it is a small thing indeed to dedicate this book to the international humanitarian personnel who are its inspiration.

Gilbert Reyes

Contents

SET FOREWORD

As I write this, the media are filled with video footage and written accounts of survivors and relief workers in the aftermath of "The Tsunami." For many this is a word newly added to their vocabulary, along with words like "al Qaeda" or "anthrax" that were added a few years ago—formerly foreign and unknown, now sadly popular and common in use, as is "tsunami." But disasters—whether man-made or nature-born—share the common thread of victims in need. Historically the psychological and emotional impacts of disasters, regardless of genesis, on those impacted were largely left unconsidered. Thankfully, this has changed, and these books demonstrate another critical step in this evolving process and area of endeavor—a global consideration.

Too often, once psychological aspects of a phenomenon were considered, they were done so through a narrow lens of exclusively Western or Northern perspectives. Such work, while of definite merit, rigor, and additive benefit to knowledge, was limited in its generalizability. I very much enjoyed the turn of phrase that a reporter for the *Wall Street Journal* used in citing coeditor Gerard Jacobs: "Care for traumatic stress," he warns, "can't be delivered by Western experts parachuting into affected cultures without an appreciation of the cultures infused with strong Islamic, Hindu, and Buddhist beliefs." So true in so many additional ways, and yet so often unwittingly ignored—but thankfully changing.

At this point in time there is a growing appreciation, understanding, and grateful application of the adage that one size does not always fit all. Reyes and Jacobs have woven together a group of authors whose perspectives and work clearly demonstrate the differential aspects of dealing with the trauma of disasters from a global, diverse set of perspectives. Such is a major step forward, and I congratulate them.

For some reason still a mystery to me, it is very easy for most observers to consider post-disaster aid and relief efforts to exclusively include food, shelter, and medical attention. But what cameras cannot capture as well as food stations, vaccination lines, and pitched tent encampments are the psychological wounds that without intervention (when called for) can become scars at best, or risk the infection of apathy or stigma, and result in the deadly consequences of suicide, substance abuse, and other manifest ills. Perhaps this inability for many to "see" fosters a concomitant inability to understand. People can see grain being trucked in and food stations preparing and distributing it, but they cannot see those who cannot eat it for lack of will.

Still More to Do

Much of my work involves medication distribution and medical interventions in areas of need. And again, and thankfully, while there is still a massive amount to be done globally in the battle for treating HIV/AIDS and getting retrovirals distributed, it is equally important to distribute culturally based and relevant psychosocial support for those who need such care. Both are necessary to save their lives. Both.

It is said that there are often opportunities in crises. Perhaps we may see some as a result of the current worldwide focus on the region impacted by the tsunami. Many had never heard of or cared about Aceh prior to the disaster, but there had already been a 15-year-long "disaster" when the water hit that the world had ignored—an often brutal Indonesian military dominion that has resulted in deaths of over 10,000 in Aceh alone, resulting from guerrilla skirmishes with separatist rebels. Along with this loss of lives are comorbid human-rights abuse allegations of torture and rape at the hands of the troops. Now with Kofi Annan's pronouncement that "the UN is the lead in the coordination of the humanitarian effort," there is renewed hope that a side effect will have a kindling influence for the end of such political violence. Likewise, in Sri Lanka then U.S. Secretary of State Powell visited vis-à-vis relief efforts, and it is hoped that the tsunami will also be a catalyst for restarting the stalled peace talks between the government and the ethnic-based insurgency known as the Liberation Tigers of Tamil Eelam (ETTE), or Tamil Tigers.

Psychologically trained researchers and clinicians obviously have much to offer, as evidenced in this set of books. It is a positive evolution that such psychological professionals are now considered along with other colleagues when the proverbial yellow tape is strung in the aftermath of a catastrophe. It is also important to have like involvements in preparation—be it in conflict resolution, resilience training, or other related aspects.

Irony?

Perhaps it is the psychology of indifference or just irony, but last year the United Nations proclaimed that the world's "worst humanitarian disaster" was . . .? The tsunami? No, in fact they were referring to the mass killings in the Darfur region of Sudan by militias. This appears on few television screens or newspaper front pages, and thus is not on many people's minds or touching many people's hearts. Not that there is some morbid competition for compassion, response, and intervention between tsunami victims and the Sudanese, but it certainly is easier to offer relief to an area after a natural catastrophe than it is to intervene in an armed combat situation. The ghosts of Rwanda come to mind, however, and many mental health professionals are focusing efforts there a decade after the genocide, and it makes me wonder what the psychological aftermath will be in Sudan.

Most of the world has empathetically responded to those impacted by the tsunami—they have contributed, volunteered, prayed, and shed tears. And this is how it should be. But such is not so for Darfur today or Kigali a decade ago. Perhaps psychology and mental health professionals should add to their already overburdened to-do lists to work on how to move the world away from such indifference. I remain hopeful based on the work of those herein.

Chris E. Stout
Series Editor

FOREWORD

Every day millions of people in the world are affected by disasters. For many reasons, people in resource-poor countries tend to be hit especially hard by disasters. Data from Red Cross and Red Crescent societies suggest that resource-poor countries tend to be confronted with more conflict and more natural disasters compared to countries that are rich. Resource-poor countries tend to have weaker physical infrastructures that are less likely to withstand extreme conditions, such as earthquakes or cyclones. Also, resource-poor countries tend to have fewer financial resources to prepare for and respond to disaster. Most resource-poor countries often invest relative few resources in their health systems. Most resource -poor areas in the world hardly invest in mental health services and do not have well-functioning community-based mental health systems through which a post-disaster mental health response may be organized.

Disaster psychology is a complex field. Disaster psychology deals with psychological trauma (i.e., an extreme stressor that is likely to elicit a strong acute anxiety and/or dissociation reaction in most people) as a risk factor for mood and anxiety disorders and for nonpathological physical and emotional distress. Psychological trauma is an area that is generating rich research in the areas of anthropology and sociology, child protection and social work, epidemiology and health economics, history and philosophy, neuroscience and pharmacology, clinical and social psychology, psychiatry and psychotherapy, public health and health services research, political science and social policy, and alcohol and other substance abuse management. Thus, disaster psychology practitioners need to be able to think beyond their discipline. Disaster psychology deals not only with psychological trauma but also with enormous losses, which often tend to be forgotten. Affected persons may have lost family members, community support structures, employment and valued material possessions during the disaster. Like trauma, loss is a well-known risk factor for mood and anxiety disorders, for nonpathological distress as well as social problems. Thus, a disaster psychology practitioner needs to be not only an expert on psychological trauma but also an expert on loss and community change. Moreover, the practitioner needs to know how to work in and with communities in a culturally appropriate way. Also, the practitioner needs to know how to work in a collaborative and coordinated manner with others, because uncoordinated aid responses are not in the best interest of disaster survivors.

Concern for people's mental health after disasters is a relatively recent phenomenon. Disaster psychology is a young field; practitioners and researchers alike need to learn from one another. We all need to learn from one another on how to achieve meaningful objectives in a culturally appropriate and sustainable manner in order to reduce avoidable mental and social suffering without causing harm. This handbook provides a rich collection of writings by many of the world's experts on disasters. Reading these chapters will prepare both novice and experienced practitioners for a better response. This is an important book.

Benedetto Saraceno
Director
Department of Mental Health and Substance Abuse
World Health Organization

PREFACE

Catastrophic events causing great damage and destruction have been a part of human life since the beginning of world history. The earth-shaking, cataclysmic eruption of Mount Vesuvius in 79 AD, which wreaked terrible destruction and loss of life, and completely destroyed the Roman city of Pompeii, continues to be reflected in recent excavations. The devastation caused last year by four hurricanes in Florida during a period of less than six weeks and the great seawave produced by the tsunami in the Indian Ocean and Southeast Asia have received major recent attention. Hundreds of people in Florida are not yet back in their homes nearly a year after the fourth hurricane; victims who lost their lives in the tsunami disaster are still being identified and survivors are still searching for them months later.

Not so visible or readily recognized are the psychological effects of disasters for survivors, effects that can linger large and long in the minds of even those with no apparent physical injuries. Effects from the horrific and huge loss of life. Loss of home. Loss of identity. Loss of nearly all that was familiar. Sometimes, too, loss of dignity, faith, or even the will to live.

The development of theory, research, and professional practice by psychologists and other mental health specialists evaluating and helping the victims of such catastrophic events is relatively new, and much needed. This four-volume *Handbook of International Disaster Psychology* provides a solid foundation to facilitate understanding of the terrible effects of traumatic disasters. Vital information is also provided on assessment of disaster victims, and on interventions to help those who are directly affected to deal with their resulting emotional distress and physical injuries.

The general goals of these volumes are to provide information for furthering the assessment of the psychological impact of disasters, and to report procedures for developing, implementing, and evaluating the effectiveness of these programs. Many contributors to this set have been deeply involved in projects to reduce the suffering of disaster victims, and to help them adapt to life circumstances substantially and adversely altered. The editors here have remarkable experience in disaster psychology, reflected in the chapters that they have contributed. Professor Gilbert Reyes is a tireless activist and educator in the field and Professor Gerard Jacobs was recently appointed to coordinate the activities of the American Psychological Association in providing assistance for victims of the recent tsunami.

The chapters first focus on fundamental issues pertaining to international disasters. Significant political and philosophical issues are also examined, and the need for effective collaboration among culturally diverse groups providing assistance is emphasized. The critical importance of understanding the particular needs and interests of populations indigenous to a disaster site is also spotlighted, along with the necessity of assessing available resources. Several contributors show us community-based models for assessment and intervention, as opposed to Western-oriented clinical approaches. Clearly, providing effective, culturally appropriate psychosocial support requires a great deal of skill and flexibility in programs that are delivered under very difficult circumstances.

We also come to understand, with these volumes, programs and practices that have been carried out in diverse geographical and cultural settings in Europe, Latin America, and Africa. In most, the interventions have focused on small groups, along with individuals and families, as the basic targets of intervention. The critical impact of national disasters in parts of the world where poverty, disease, and civil strife have weakened the capacity for coping with adversity is especially difficult to navigate, due to a persistent sense of danger that interferes with the healing process. Yet excellent examples of interventions are described, demonstrating why organizations such as the International Red Cross and the Red Crescent are considered best suited for dealing with disasters.

Reading in these books of interventions with refugees and "special needs" populations, we see that cultural diversity compounds the difficulty of developing effective programs. A prevailing climate of hatred and violence in many refugee populations further impairs effectiveness. And special emphasis is given to interventions that address the psychosocial needs of women and children, and to crisis interventions with military and with emergency services personnel.

These four volumes on international disaster psychology will be of great interest to psychologists, mental health workers, and other professionals working with disaster victims and their families. Trauma researchers, those interested in topics such as post-traumatic stress disorder (PTSD) and related disorders, will also find a wealth of useful information here. Indeed, these books will also well serve all students, scholars, and general readers focused on understanding how the most horrific, trying, and torturous of events can tear at psychological health, and how we all might play a role in helping heal the wounds.

For the past 30 years, I have personally worked in collaborative cross-cultural research with colleagues from more than 50 countries, and in developing adaptations of our anxiety and anger measures. I have also enjoyed and greatly benefited from participation in international meetings and conferences. While international psychology has addressed a wide range of topics, including stress and emotions, which have been the major focus of my work, these volumes pioneer new directions in psychological research and professional practice. Tsunamis, earthquakes, and other worldwide disasters are frequently encountered in modern life. Effective clinical and community interventions are urgently needed to help people cope. These volumes provide both a solid foundation for the emerging field of international disaster psychology and important guidelines for future research.

Charles D. Spielberger, Ph.D., ABPP
Distinguished Research Professor
University of South Florida, Tampa
Past President, American Psychological Association

ACKNOWLEDGMENTS

It goes without saying that the writing and editing of such an extensive book as this takes a great deal of effort and patience on the part of all concerned. What is perhaps less evident is that it also takes a great deal of trust and respect. As first-time editors undertaking a project of this scope and complexity, we required the trust of our publisher that we could indeed complete what we started. In this regard, we were extremely fortunate to be working with Debbie Carvalko at Greenwood Publishing, who came at this project with such infectious enthusiasm and confidence that she inspired the same in us. She also gently but firmly guided us through the unfamiliar process of delivering an edited book in four volumes consisting of over 40 chapters by authors from around the world. Without her patience, persistence, and professionalism, it is doubtful that this project could have proceeded so successfully.

We also required a great deal of trust from our colleagues, the authors who toiled for months over these chapters, that their efforts would not be in vain and that our work as their editors would prove commensurate to their investment in us. Many of these humanitarians and scholars knew us personally, but several did not, and all had only our word that the project would be completed as promised. We thank them sincerely for their confidence in our ability to make worthy use of their contributions.

The editors also wish to acknowledge the work of Mary E. Long, Ric Monroe, Sandra Schatz, and Tina Waldron, graduate research assistants who helped us to organize and process an almost unmanageable amount of information. Particular gratitude is owed for the editorial assistance supplied by Sandra Schatz, who labored tirelessly and diligently over the final drafts to detect and correct any errors or omissions. The efforts of these assistants are greatly appreciated and are reflected in the quality of these volumes.

Overview of the International Disaster Psychology Volumes

Gilbert Reyes

The four volumes that constitute the *Handbook of International Disaster Psychology* are composed of chapters addressing most of the pressing issues being confronted in this relatively new and expanding area of research and practice. Each volume and the chapters it contains are designed to inform a diverse audience of readers about the activities that have been undertaken around the globe to improve the psychological and emotional well-being of people affected by disasters. Many of the authors are deeply involved in developing programs and projects designed to relieve the psychological suffering of people exposed to disasters. They are mostly citizens of the Western nations, though the editors have attempted to attract contributions from colleagues residing in Asia, Africa, and South America. The objectives pursued by these authors in their humanitarian roles include, among other things, the assessment of the psychosocial impacts of disasters, implementation of prevention and intervention programs, and the development of strategies for improving the effectiveness of their programs. This in turn requires a sophisticated appreciation of factors that exert influence on the success of these operations. The authors have drawn from their own experience and what they have learned from other sources to share the key ideas and practices with the greatest promise of succeeding under the least favorable conditions. Their dedication to serving the psychosocial needs of people coping with terrifying and debilitating circumstances is deserving of the highest respect and admiration. Each is a humanitarian in the truest sense.

Volume 1: Fundamentals and Overview

The first volume of the *Handbook of International Disaster Psychology* provides readers with an orientation to the field of international disaster psychology

(Reyes, 2006) and an overview of the fundamental issues that pertain across most disasters and humanitarian emergencies. Toward that aim, the contributors identify and discuss many of the political and philosophical issues and assumptions involved in the humanitarian "therapeutic" enterprise and the "psychosocial" lens that magnifies the existence and importance of trauma to suit Western expectations (Pupavac, 2006). These matters cannot be easily dismissed, disputed, or ignored and reflect a perception among some that an intentional or inadvertent cultural imperialism comparable to "White Man's Burden" is at work.

The recent blending of military operations with humanitarian relief services has further complicated these issues by blurring the boundaries between partisan use of force to coercively serve national interests and impartial initiatives compelled by empathy and compassion (Wessells, 2006). Sadly, at the same time that agents of humanitarianism are accused of having sacrificed their fundamental principles to political expediency (Rieff, 2002), the casualty rates among relief personnel have skyrocketed, leading even the most courageous of NGOs to withdraw in the face of mounting dangers (Burnett, 2004; Gall, 2004; Kelly, 2004). And while few question the benefits and necessity of providing the tradition "survival" supplies, the value of psychosocial support has been a more contentious issue than most and remains unresolved. As a matter of conscience and ethics, anyone involved in promoting services of questionable benefit under conditions of mortal danger must acknowledge and respond respectfully to these concerns (Beech, 2006).

In order for psychosocial programs to be implemented successfully, effective collaboration among culturally diverse groups of people must take place (Peddle, Hudnall Stamm, Hudnall, & Stamm, 2006). Perhaps the most distinct intercultural partnership is that which forms between the populations indigenous to the disaster-affected areas and the relief agencies that are foreign to those regions. International humanitarian agencies employ expatriate (ex-pat) staff from around the world, so there is also a great deal of cultural diversity among their personnel. However, it is an undeniable reality of the hierarchical structure of these agencies that most of the managerial staff are of European or North American origin, while middle- and lower-level personnel comprise a more diverse assembly representing the less wealthy nations. Providing culturally appropriate psychosocial support under these conditions requires considerable skill and flexibility at every level, since the people with the most useful cultural knowledge and insight are often not those who decide policies and practices. Development of approaches that could be applied in any event and context is perhaps a desirable goal, but an unlikely one given the diversity of situations, values, cultures, and customs. Nevertheless, there are similarities across events that allow for construction of flexibly structured templates based on tested principles of good psychosocial practices (Ager, 2006).

A basic necessity for any relief operation is to assess the needs and resources of the affected populations, and in this regard psychosocial programs are not substantively different. Supplies and services based entirely on typical assumptions are unlikely to accurately match the types, levels, and characteristics of what is truly required in a specific context. Moreover, this profile of needs and resources is a moving target and must be persistently assessed and modified to remain pertinent (Dodge, 2006a). Among the many options for efficiently matching needs and services and making them available and useful to those who are most likely to benefit, the preference has shifted strongly toward community-based models, both for assessments and for intervention designs. Consequently, psychosocial planners and implementing personnel are less concerned with "clinical" training and skills because of the growing importance of methods associated with community psychology (Dodge, 2006b). The roles of ex-pat personnel are also increasingly educational in nature, with direct human services often being reserved for local staff, who are more likely to have the requisite language skills and cultural knowledge to work effectively within the communities where needs are greatest.

Communities constantly gather information to inform their decisions and guide the actions of their members. Thus, the importance of public information in disaster management should never be ignored. The mass news and entertainment media, especially television and increasingly the Internet, provide a critical resource in disasters, and the effective use of these media may spell the difference between success and failure in some instances (Kuriansky, 2006). Inaccurate rumors can have destructive consequences, and urgent transmission of vital information can save lives. And given the education components of psychological support, the print and electronic media are crucial to the mission of disseminating information that can help to reduce distress and direct survivors toward resources that are most likely to meet their needs. Therefore, it is important to make effective use of these techniques and technologies, in the interest of public education and according to well-proven public health models (Cohen, 2006).

Volume 2: Practices and Programs

The second volume of the *Handbook of International Disaster Psychology* addresses various psychosocial programs and the practices they employ to provide services to a variety of populations under difficult circumstances. The contributors describe not only what they do and with whom, but also the underlying reasons for certain decisions and activities. The approaches employed in designing effective intervention programs vary according to the types of problems being targeted and the types of people being helped. Some interventions are designed to work with people one at a time, though most are conducted with small groups or across entire communities. For instance, faculty at Massey University in New Zealand have developed and refined a model for providing optimal psychosocial care to youth and families (Ronan, Finnis, & Johnston, 2006). Their approach identifies the family as the basic unit of intervention, but it also makes optimal use of community resources such as schools and the news media. Under very different conditions, however, adaptations to cultural and sociopolitical conditions such as those encountered in Southeast Asia may require very different and innovative approaches (Armstrong, Boyden, Galappatti, & Hart, 2006). As is clear in these two examples, the approaches to such interventions are also profoundly influenced by the operational assumptions made by the designers and practitioners involved.

Ongoing violent conflicts produce perhaps the most difficult situations in which to implement such services, but the psychosocial needs that became evident during the collapse of the former Yugoslavia were urgent and could not wait until more peaceful times (Kapor-Stanulovic, 2006). The fact that hostilities have not ceased creates a perpetual sense of danger and dread, making it almost impossible to promote hope and healing with any sincerity. Similar horrors have been experienced across the African continent, whether stretched out over decades in such places as Uganda (Agger, 2006), or compressed into genocidal rampages as in Rwanda (Neugebauer, 2006). Although there are many important differences between conditions of persistent violence and singular events such as the terrorist bombing of the U. S. embassy in Nairobi (Ndetei, Kasina, & Kathuku, 2006), the psychological impact on survivors and the principles of psychosocial support are mostly similar.

Natural disasters can also wreak tremendous havoc, and they often occur in parts of the world where poverty, disease, and civil strife have already weakened the local capacity for coping with adversity. Latin American countries provide an example of such conditions (Cohen, 2006), with a recent string of major earthquakes and deadly storms having killed tens of thousands and left many times that number homeless and destitute. The prime example can be found in the recent history of Venezuela. That country was overwhelmed in 1999 by flooding and mudslides that killed over 30,000 people (Blanco, Villalobos, & Carrillo, 2006) and has since experienced a military junta, rioting, a disputed election, and extreme economic hardships. Given these worsening conditions, the psychosocial interventions initially mobilized for the flood survivors taught lessons about the need for developing long-range plans to deal with a succession of crises.

Among the organizations best suited for developing such capacities are the International Federation of Red Cross and Red Crescent Societies (IFRC), which has played an important role in teaching its member societies how to develop and sustain a national program of psychological support. An exemplary application of the IFRC model took place recently in Cuba, which had invited the psychosocial training director of the Danish Red Cross to provide a "training-of-trainers" for local Red Cross staff and volunteers. Those receiving the training then became trainers of others until, in just one year's time, they had disseminated the information and skills to every corner of their country (Atherton & Sonniks, 2006). The Cuban Red Cross has sustained and implemented its psychological support activities with great success as Cuba has endured a series of hurricanes and other disasters. More recently, the IFRC has published a manual consisting of six modules that is used to train its national societies in community-based principles of psychological support (Simonsen & Reyes, 2003). Training-of-trainers workshops employing that manual were field tested in Eastern Europe, Southeast Asia, and the Middle East and have since been conducted in several other regions around the world.

Concurrently, a number of other humanitarian NGOs have developed their own training procedures and begun to proliferate them wherever such a need is identified. Additional sources of training exist across various academic and clinical institutions scattered around the globe. Some of these institutions take a general approach to disaster mental health, while others specialize in assisting with a particular problem or population. What works best in any given instance is still an open question requiring further examination and resolution. What is clear, however, is that people and institutions interested in learning about the psychosocial programs and practices employed with disaster survivors now have access to more information and training options than ever before.

Volume 3: Refugee Mental Health

The third volume of the *Handbook of International Disaster Psychology* addresses several key issues confronted by those who have been involved in mental health work with refugees. Among the most persistently troubling aspects of international affairs in the twentieth century was the sharp increase in forced international migrations, which created refugee crises on a massive scale. This was one of the earliest and most pressing issues facing the fledgling United Nations, and it led to the creation of the United Nations High Commissioner for Refugees (UNHCR) in 1951. Worldwide estimates from international relief organizations indicate that there are more than 10 million refugees and twice that number of internally displaced persons (IDPs) at this time. The psychosocial impact of the countless horrific events that characterize the refugee experience are sometimes temporary and manageable, but can also be enduring and disabling. Among survivors of war, the prevalence of psychological distress and mental disorders is often strikingly elevated, as studies of Vietnamese and Cambodian refugees demonstrated over two decades ago (Kinzie, 2006).

To accurately assess the mental health needs of displaced and transient populations is a difficult task under the best of circumstances, and to do so during the emergency phase is in some ways the most difficult option (Jacobs, Revel, Reyes, & Quevillon, 2006). However, if we are to respond with immediacy and accuracy to refugee mental health needs, such an option must be explored and developed. Furthermore, it is important to conduct research that clarifies not only the most prevalent psychopathologies seen among refugees following migration, but also the risk and protective factors that differentiate the most resilient outcomes from those requiring clinical intervention. Culturally diverse perspectives and assumptions compound the difficulty of such research, which is most often conducted in Western industrialized nations to which large populations of refugees have migrated. However, since most people displaced by forced migrations return to their regions of origin, it is important to conduct culturally sensitive research that is congruent with local customs, rather than erroneously imposing a Western psychiatric perspective (Bolton, 2006). Moreover, if we are to fully comprehend how psychosocial healing can best be supported across varying conditions and cultures, we must find ways to study the most important factors with simultaneous sensitivity and responsiveness to the needs of the survivors.

Programs serving the mental health needs of refugees are often located in the Western nations where they have settled. Europe, Australia, and North America are the most popular destinations for refugees, and nearly all of the published studies evaluating intervention programs originate from these regions. Sweden and other Scandinavian countries are among the most welcoming of refugees, and many excellent programs have been developed to help relieve postmigratory distress and improve the adjustment of forced migrants to cultural conditions that are entirely foreign to their experience (Ekblad, 2006). Australia has also experienced an influx of refugees fleeing persecution and violence, many of whom arrived from neighboring Asian nations. Innovative and culturally sensitive programs have been implemented in response to trauma and torture that can serve as models of blending individual and community intervention strategies into a more integral whole (Silove, 2006). The United States also receives large numbers of refugees and has become home to many who fled the wars and persecution across the Balkan republics following the disintegration of the former Yugoslavia. An abundance of intervention programs have been implemented in major American cities to assist refugees with psychosocial concerns, some of which have become particularly influential examples of innovation. Among those is a program in Chicago that employs family therapy and other techniques to apply a framework of intervening with groups composed of multiple families (Raina et al., 2006).

The work with refugees taking place in postmigration countries is often enhanced by experiences working with corresponding populations that remained in their country of origin. Several researchers and clinicians who work with postmigratory refugees in the West also invest great effort in working with former IDPs in the countries from which refugees have recently fled. The mental health infrastructures of such countries were often poorly developed and are typically overwhelmed and underfunded for meeting the needs of their postconflict population. International collaborations between mental health professionals from poorly resourced and highly resourced settings offer countless opportunities for improvement on both ends of such partnerships (Weine, Pavkovic, Agani, Ceric, & Jukic, 2006). Of particular merit is the movement to assign the same level of human rights, commitment to healing, and compassionate regard for mental illness as that which is felt toward those with physical ailments and injuries.

As wars and other levels of massive violence continue to erupt in repetitious cycles in many parts of the world, some patterns and principle are clear. Among those is that hatred and revenge have long memories and can reemerge after extended periods of apparent peace. One approach to breaking the cycle of violence has been to seek social justice through human rights instruments and international criminal tribunals. Another approach emphasizes rapprochement through community processes of communicative expression, such as the Truth and Reconciliation Commissions in South Africa, Peru, East Timor, Sierra Leone, and elsewhere. Unfortunately, the idealistic goals of such an undertaking often run headlong into the sheer force and brutality of the hatred they are created to alleviate. Moreover, for many who continue to endure an ever-present pain borne of atrocities that can never blend into an innocuous past, forgiveness seems like a form of betrayal that joins victims with perpetrators in a profane alliance belying all truth. Nevertheless, without forgiveness, complete psychosocial health cannot be achieved and the transmission of violence is more likely continue across generations as children enact themes of revenge in a perverse pursuit of honor and retribution (Borris, 2006).

Volume 4: Interventions with Special Needs Populations

The fourth volume of the *Handbook of International Disaster Psychology* addresses populations whose needs differ in some critical way from more general expectations. There are many reasons why this might occur, including that the "special" population is at elevated risk of harm or that key aspects of what they have endured differ from the experiences of most disaster survivors. Another reason may be that the group's needs are not well matched to the practices that are typically effective with people. Groups with "special needs" have been identified in regard to several variables, including developmental characteristics (e.g., children, the elderly), gender, types of traumatic experiences (e.g., torture, sexual assault), and occupational roles (e.g., relief workers, military personnel, journalists). Although several elements of good psychosocial practice reliably combine to form a strong core that can be applied across most populations and conditions, it is important to take special needs into account and not to expect any approach to be universally effective.

The manner in which different groups of people are treated in disasters and humanitarian crises usually reflects how they are treated under more normal circumstances. That is, if categories of people are less privileged in general, they are unlikely to receive better treatment in the worst of times. If anything, the social destabilization characteristic of most crises tends to amplify disparities in power and encourage opportunistic exploitation of the weak and vulnerable. Among the populations most often targeted for exploitation are women and children. Gender inequities are prevalent in most societies and, from a global perspective, the gains resulting from social justice movements such as feminism have been meager and fragile. Thus, while women have made remarkable progress on some issues in some nations, the worldwide economic and human rights advances for women have been shamefully slow and sporadic in their progress. Therefore, to understand the special needs of women in disasters, wars, and other crises, one must grasp the conditions and obstacles with which women are faced even in the best of times (Hudnall & Lindner, 2006).

Among the many ways in which women and girls are demeaned and exploited, one of the most humiliating and pernicious is widespread sexual violence (Reis & Vann, 2006). Sexual coercion and assault are all too commonplace in women's lives, and the protection of women and girls against such violations is pathetically inadequate. When war and social upheaval are entered into this equation, the levels of sexual depravity against women achieve sickening proportions. Tenuous social restrictions designed to at least postpone the exploitation of female children until they have reached sexual maturity are easily swept aside in times of lawlessness and war. Civilian women have historically suffered under the domination of conquering armies, who have subjected them to systematic rapes and sexual slavery. The history of these atrocities has been disputed and denied by governments unwilling to take responsibility for the heinous acts that transpire under cover of war.

Given that, there is perhaps some comfort to be taken behind international human rights protections when governments war against one another. No such restrictions exist for outlaw bands of militia and other paramilitary fighters that dominate many regions of conflict in today's world. Therefore, while the member states of the UN enact resolutions and other instruments, such as the Convention on the Rights of the Child, to protect children from harmful practices such as child labor, sexual exploitation, early marriage, and premature military service, these problems persist and worsen in the darkest corners of civilization. Wherever societies crumble into chaos and bitter conflict, children are exposed to countless hazards and may also be drawn into battle, either as fighters or as captive workers to support the troops (Boyden, de Berry, Feeny, & Hart, 2006).

While the prototypical child soldier is a young boy armed with a light machinegun, girls too are forcibly ensnared into service (McKay. 2006). In such instances, girls are used as porters, domestic servants, sexual slaves, and "wives." Whether they are boys or girls, once these children escape captivity or are otherwise returned to civilian lives, the process of reunion and reintegration is often one of stigma, rejection, and shame. Girls in particular may be viewed as damaged goods and never regain the status and opportunities that were once within reach.

The type and intensity of traumatic events can also create differential impact characteristics that translate into unique needs for certain kinds of survivors. For instance, the impact of torture on the mind can be uniquely complex and intractable, thus requiring exquisitely precise skills unlike those which suffice for other types of disaster and trauma interventions (Holtz, 1998). In response to this need, dozens of excellent facilities, such as the Rehabilitation and Research Centre for Torture Survivors in Copenhagen, have developed noteworthy expertise in helping people who have suffered terribly at the hands of others (Berliner & Mikkelsen, 2006).

A paradoxical aspect of disasters and humanitarian emergencies is that, while most people flee from these zones of mayhem and destruction, others rush into the breach to assist survivors and pursue altruistic ends. The impact of facing death and other gruesome consequences of disasters fall particularly hard upon humanitarian aid workers, emergency services personnel, members of the military, and other occupations who perform heroic services. International humanitarian organizations (Ehrenreich, 2006), civilian fire and police departments (De Soir, 2006), and other agencies have recently come to recognize the importance of responding to the psychosocial needs of their employees and volunteers. Managing occupational stress among their personnel challenges these organizations not only to add a psychosocial component to their existing employee health services, but also to modify their systems so that they are less likely to create the stress that must then be managed. It is at least ironic, if not hypocritical, that humanitarian organizations charged with the mission of relieving the suffering of any and every unfortunate soul whom they encounter often fail to treat their own staff and volunteers with comparable compassion and regard for their dignity and well-being.

As noted earlier, the role of the news media in providing reliable information about crises and relief operations has become a critically important component of marshaling resources and public opinion in helpful directions. In viewing the "media" as a mammoth multinational corporate operation involving cameras, satellites, and high technology, it is easy to overlook the fragile human elements. International correspondents and their coworkers, many of whom are poorly paid local citizens, sometimes cover these stories at great risk to their own lives. In recent events it has become clear that journalists reporting from war zones and humanitarian crises are being killed and injured at historically high rates, sometimes due to their own risky decisions, though often at the hands of military forces they had trusted to protect them. Perhaps in part because the status of war correspondents in the journalistic community is so high, they are expected to shake off the ill effects of their occupation without complaint and bask in the glory they have earned through daring deeds. But recent collaborative projects have been initiated between journalists and psychologists that examine the psychological effects of covering traumatic stories, assess the mental health needs of journalists exposed to trauma, and design proactive interventions to reduce the negative psychosocial impact on those who inform the public about these critically important events (Newman & Shapiro, 2006).

Appendix of NGO Profiles (Volume 4)

The international humanitarian relief community that developed over the past century was pioneered by a small number of organizations dedicated to serving victims of war, disease, famine, and other natural calamities. Paramount among these was the Red Cross movement, which began in Switzerland in 1863 and slowly spread throughout most of the world over the next several decades. The red cross on a white background came to be recognized as a symbol of neutrality and compassion in the face of conflict and brutality. Hospitals, ambulances, and personnel marked with the Red Cross emblem earned a status as noncombatants that allowed them to function in war zones and other dangerous places with few direct attacks upon their operations. This philosophy of mercy within a context of violence eventually led to the Geneva Conventions and other international accords designed to provide limited protection for civilians and military prisoners as an ever widening swath of war engulfed the world. As the Red Cross movement proliferated, national societies were founded in dozens of countries and a new emblem, the Red Crescent, was approved to accommodate societies in regions where Islam was the predominate faith.

The founding of the United Nations at the end of World War II fostered a period of growing humanitarian aid through both governmental agencies and nongovernmental organizations (NGOs). Several agencies within the UN system, such as the United Nations Children's Fund (UNICEF), the United Nations High Commissioner for Refugees (UNHCR), and the World Health Organization (WHO), developed programs and policies that saved millions of lives and improved the quality of life for untold numbers of the world's most vulnerable citizens. The scourges of war, disease, and disaster were never abolished, but a countervailing force of hope and compassion was established, and hundreds of NGOs have been founded to serve the needs of people who might otherwise perish or wither.

Perhaps the most recent of humanitarian relief activities is the formal provision of psychosocial support, though this is certainly an element of any compassionate care to the afflicted. The story of international disaster psychology cannot be fully told without repeated reference to the humanitarian NGOs that have developed and disseminated psychosocial support training and services with great dedication and determination. Moreover, volunteers who aspire to work in this field of endeavor will almost certainly work closely with several of these NGOs and will benefit from obtaining at least a cursory knowledge of their missions, philosophies, histories, and activities.

Therefore, the editors of the *Handbook of International Disaster Psychology* have included an appendix consisting of brief profiles that describe some of the prominent humanitarian organizations operating in the world today. The information contained in these profiles was gathered from public sources and may contain accidental inaccuracies. Given the rapidly evolving nature of the NGOs profiled, it is also quite likely that some of the information will soon become outdated. However, these profiles are substantially accurate, and the contact information given for each agency makes it possible for interested readers to obtain more current and detailed information.

References

Ager, A. (2006). Toward a consensus protocol for psychosocial response in complex emergencies. In G. Reyes & G. A. Jacobs (Eds.), *Handbook of international disaster psychology, Vol. 1. Fundamentals and overview.* Westport, CT: Praeger Publishers.

Agger, I. (2006). Approaches to psychosocial healing: Case examples from Lusophone Africa. In G. Reyes & G. A. Jacobs (Eds.), *Handbook of international disaster psychology, Vol. 2. Practices and programs.* Westport, CT: Praeger Publishers.

Armstrong, M., Boyden, J., Galappatti, A., & Hart, J. (2006). Participatory tools for monitoring and evaluating psychosocial work with children: Reflections on a pilot study in Eastern Sri Lanka. In G. Reyes & G. A. Jacobs (Eds.), *Handbook of international disaster psychology, Vol. 2. Practices and programs.* Westport, CT: Praeger Publishers.

Atherton, J., & Sonniks, M. (2006). Implementation of a training of trainers model for disseminating psychological support in the Cuban Red Cross. In G. Reyes & G. A. Jacobs (Eds.), *Handbook of international disaster psychology, Vol. 2. Practices and programs.* Westport, CT: Praeger Publishers.

Beech, D. R. (2006). Peace-building, culturally responsive means, and ethical practices in humanitarian psychosocial interventions. In G. Reyes & G. A. Jacobs (Eds.), *Handbook of international disaster psychology, Vol. 1. Fundamentals and overview.* Westport, CT: Praeger Publishers.

Berliner, P., & Mikkelsen, E. (2006). Serving the psychosocial needs of survivors of torture and organized violence. In G. Reyes & G. A. Jacobs (Eds.), *Handbook of international disaster psychology, Vol. 4. Interventions with special needs populations.* Westport, CT: Praeger Publishers.

Blanco, T., Villalobos, M., & Carrillo, C. (2006). The psychological support network of the Central University of Venezuela and the Venezuelan floods of 1999. In G. Reyes & G. A. Jacobs (Eds.), *Handbook of international disaster psychology, Vol. 2. Practices and programs.* Westport, CT: Praeger Publishers.

Bolton, P. (2006). Challenges in international disaster mental health research. In G. Reyes & G. A. Jacobs (Eds.), *Handbook of international disaster psychology, Vol. 3. Refugee mental health. Westport,* CT: Praeger Publishers.

Borris, E. (2006). The healing power of forgiveness and the resolution of protracted conflicts. In G. Reyes & G. A. Jacobs (Eds.), *Handbook of international disaster psychology, Vol. 3. Refugee mental health.* Westport, CT: Praeger Publishers.

Boyden, J., de Berry, J., Feeny, T., & Hart, J. (2006). Children affected by armed conflict in South Asia: A regional summary. In G. Reyes & G. A. Jacobs (Eds.), *Handbook of international disaster psychology, Vol. 4. Interventions with special needs populations.* Westport, CT: Praeger Publishers.

Burnett, J. S. (2004, August 4). In the line of fire. *The New York Times*, Late Edition–Final, p. A17, col. 1.

Cohen, R. (2006). Implementation of mental health programs for survivors of natural disasters in Latin America. In G. Reyes & G. A. Jacobs (Eds.), *Handbook of international disaster psychology, Vol. 2. Practices and programs.* Westport, CT: Praeger Publishers.

De Soir, E. (2006). Psychosocial crisis intervention with military and emergency services personnel. In G. Reyes & G. A. Jacobs (Eds.), *Handbook of international disaster psychology, Vol. 4. Interventions with special needs populations.* Westport, CT: Praeger Publishers.

Dodge, G. R. (2006a). Assessing the psychosocial needs of communities affected by disaster. In G. Reyes & G. A. Jacobs (Eds.), *Handbook of international disaster psychology, Vol. 1. Fundamentals and overview.* Westport, CT: Praeger Publishers.

———. (2006b). In defense of a community psychology model for international psychosocial intervention. In G. Reyes & G. A. Jacobs (Eds.), *Handbook of international disaster psychology, Vol. 1. Fundamentals and overview.* Westport, CT: Praeger Publishers.

Ehrenreich, J. (2006). Managing stress in humanitarian aid workers: The role of the humanitarian aid organization. In G. Reyes & G. A. Jacobs (Eds.), *Handbook of international disaster psychology, Vol. 4. Interventions with special needs populations.* Westport, CT: Praeger Publishers.

Ekblad, S. (2006). Serving the mental health needs of postmigratory adult refugees in Sweden: A transitional augmentation approach. In G. Reyes & G. A. Jacobs (Eds.), *Handbook of international disaster psychology, Vol. 3. Refugee mental health.* Westport, CT: Praeger Publishers.

Gall, C. (2004, June 3). Aid agency halts operations in Afghanistan. *The New York Times*, Late Edition–Final, p. A5, col. 3.

Holtz, T. H. (1998). Refugee trauma versus torture trauma: A retrospective controlled cohort study of Tibetan refugees. *Journal of Nervous & Mental Disease, 186,* 24–34.

Hudnall, A., & Lindner, E. (2006). Crisis and gender: Addressing the psychosocial needs of women in international disasters. In G. Reyes & G. A. Jacobs (Eds.), *Handbook of international disaster psychology, Vol. 4. Interventions with special needs populations.* Westport, CT: Praeger Publishers.

Jacobs, G. A., Revel, J. P., Reyes, G., & Quevillon, R. P. (2006). Development of the Rapid Assessment of Mental Health: An international collaboration. In G. Reyes & G. A. Jacobs (Eds.), *Handbook of international disaster psychology, Vol. 3. Refugee mental health.* Westport, CT: Praeger Publishers.

Kapor-Stanulovic, N. (2006). Implementing psychosocial programs in the Federal Republic of Yugoslavia: Was it really mission impossible? In G. Reyes & G. A. Jacobs (Eds.), *Handbook of international disaster psychology, Vol. 2. Practices and programs.* Westport, CT: Praeger Publishers.

Kelly, A. (2004, December 15). Caught in the crossfire. *The Guardian Weekly.* Retrieved March 4, 2005, from http://society.guardian.co.uk/societyguardian/story/0,,1373410,00.html

Kinzie, J. D. (2006). Personal reflections on treating traumatized refugees. In G. Reyes & G. A. Jacobs (Eds.), *Handbook of international disaster psychology, Vol. 3. Refugee mental health.* Westport, CT: Praeger Publishers.

Kuriansky, J. (2006). Working effectively with the mass media in disaster mental health. In G. Reyes & G. A. Jacobs (Eds.), *Handbook of international disaster psychology, Vol. 1. Fundamentals and overview*. Westport, CT: Praeger Publishers.

MacDonald, C. M. (2003). Evaluation of stress debriefing interventions with military populations. *Military Medicine, 168*, 961–968.

McKay, S. (2006). How do you mend broken hearts? Gender, war, and impacts on girls in fighting forces. In G. Reyes & G. A. Jacobs (Eds.), *Handbook of international disaster psychology, Vol. 4. Interventions with special needs populations*. Westport, CT: Praeger Publishers.

Ndetei, D., Kasina, R., & Kathuku, D. (2006). Psychosocial responses to the bombing of the American Embassy in Nairobi: Challenges, lessons, and opportunities. In G. Reyes & G. A. Jacobs (Eds.), *Handbook of international disaster psychology, Vol. 2. Practices and programs*. Westport, CT: Praeger Publishers.

Neugebauer, R. (2006). Psychosocial research and interventions after the Rwanda genocide. In G. Reyes & G. A. Jacobs (Eds.), *Handbook of international disaster psychology, Vol. 2. Practices and programs*. Westport, CT: Praeger Publishers.

Newman, E., & Shapiro, B. (2006). Helping journalists who cover humanitarian crises. In G. Reyes & G. A. Jacobs (Eds.), *Handbook of international disaster psychology, Vol. 4. Interventions with special needs populations*. Westport, CT: Praeger Publishers.

Peddle, N., Hudnall Stamm, B., Hudnall, A. C., & Stamm, H. E. (2006). Effective intercultural collaboration on psychosocial support programs. In G. Reyes & G. A. Jacobs (Eds.), *Handbook of international disaster psychology, Vol. 1. Fundamentals and overview*. Westport, CT: Praeger Publishers.

Pupavac, V. (2006). Humanitarian politics and the rise of international disaster psychology. In G. Reyes & G. A. Jacobs (Eds.), *Handbook of international disaster psychology, Vol. 1. Fundamentals and overview*. Westport, CT: Praeger Publishers.

Raina, D., Weine, S., Kulauzovic, Y., Feetham, S., Zhubi, M., Huseni, D., & Pavkovic, I. (2006). A framework for developing and implementing multiple-family groups for refugee families. In G. Reyes & G. A. Jacobs (Eds.), *Handbook of international disaster psychology, Vol. 3. Refugee mental health*. Westport, CT: Praeger Publishers.

Reis, C., & Vann. B. (2006). Sexual violence against women and children in the context of armed conflict. In G. Reyes & G. A. Jacobs (Eds.), *Handbook of international disaster psychology, Vol. 4. Interventions with special needs populations*. Westport, CT: Praeger Publishers.

Reyes, G. (2006). International disaster psychology: Purposes, principles, and practices. In G. Reyes & G. A. Jacobs (Eds.), *Handbook of international disaster psychology, Vol. 1. Fundamentals and overview*. Westport, CT: Praeger Publishers.

Rieff, D. (2002). *A bed for the night: Humanitarianism in crisis*. New York: Simon & Schuster.

Ronan, K. R., Finnis, K., & Johnston, D. M. (2006). Interventions with youth and families: A prevention and stepped care model. In G. Reyes & G. A. Jacobs (Eds.), *Handbook of international disaster psychology, Vol. 2. Practices and programs*. Westport, CT: Praeger Publishers.

Silove, D. (2006). The impact of mass psychological trauma on psychosocial adaptation among refugees. In G. Reyes & G. A. Jacobs (Eds.), *Handbook of international disaster psychology, Vol. 3. Refugee mental health*. Westport, CT: Praeger Publishers.

Weine, S., Pavkovic, I., Agani, F., Ceric, I., & Jukic, V. (2006). Mental health reform and assisting psychiatric leaders in postwar countries. In G. Reyes & G. A. Jacobs (Eds.), *Handbook of international disaster psychology, Vol. 3. Refugee mental health*. Westport, CT: Praeger Publishers.

Wessells, M. G. (2006). Negotiating the shrunken humanitarian space: Challenges and options. In G. Reyes & G. A. Jacobs (Eds.), *Handbook of international disaster psychology, Vol. 1. Fundamentals and overview*. Westport, CT: Praeger Publishers.

CHAPTER 1

THE IMPACT OF MASS PSYCHOLOGICAL TRAUMA ON PSYCHOSOCIAL ADAPTATION AMONG REFUGEES

Derrick Silove

The Challenge of Trauma

The notion that extreme events such as torture and armed conflict lead to mental disturbances has been imprinted on the public mind, at least in Western countries. Mental health professionals have been more divided on the issue, with some critics noting that exposure to violence is normative and that throughout history societies have been exposed to mass persecution, armed conflict, and forced displacement (Summerfield, 1999). Is it reasonable then to assume that all members of affected populations are traumatized, and that they suffer from disabling mental conditions as a consequence of these experiences (Silove, 1999b)? Over the course of my work with refugees and populations exposed to mass violence and displacement, I have remained preoccupied with this question: To what extent do large-scale human-engendered disasters lead to psychiatric disability? Deliberating answers to this question leads to the next one: What is the appropriate mental health response both in the acute, humanitarian phase and in the longer-term postconflict phase?

I have worked with communities affected by discrimination, persecution, and organized violence since the 1970s, first in general hospital and primary care settings in South Africa, and then, while embarking on my early psychiatric career in Australia, with indigenous persons, Holocaust survivors, and exiled anti-Apartheid militants. In the mid-1980s a multidisciplinary group established a refugee torture and trauma rehabilitation service in Sydney known as Service for the Treatment and Rehabilitation of Torture and Trauma Survivors (STARTTS) (Reid, Silove, & Tarn, 1990). Similar services were initiated in all the states and territories of Australia in response to the needs of the large number of trauma-affected refugees arriving in the country from many parts of the world. The torture and refugee trauma movement of the 1980s coincided with the growing wave of interest in traumatic stress in general, itself an outgrowth of the inclusion of post-traumatic stress disorder (PTSD) in the third edition of the *Diagnostic and Statistical Manual* (DSM-III) (American Psychiatric Association, 1980).

The Introduction of PTSD and the Growth of Psychiatric Traumatology

The adoption of PTSD was a unifying factor that provided a simplified and easily understood model for diagnosis and intervention across diverse fields relevant to trauma and abuse. The linear causal model implied by PTSD indicated that exposure to certain extreme events (now more clearly defined by DSM-IV as life threatening events; American Psychiatric Association, 1994) predicts risk of PTSD, a condition defined by three clusters of symptoms: upsetting intrusive memories (flashbacks, nightmares); avoidance of environmental triggers that bring back these memories, including emotional numbing and social withdrawal; and heightened arousal manifested by physiologic reactions (sweating, trembling, increased heart rate, startling easily, poor sleep, irritability, and cognitive disturbances such as concentration and memory difficulties).

The Influence of the Trauma Model on Refugee Mental Health

The emerging trauma model had several consequences for the way rehabilitation services for refugees were designed and implemented (Reid et al., 1990; Somnier & Genefke, 1986). PTSD was seen as a clinical syndrome, and treatments were framed in those terms, that is, provided by health experts applying individual or small group therapies. Even in the early days, however, it was recognized that an excessively clinical setting could provoke fears by reminding survivors of torture chambers or settings in which medical personnel were implicated in the abuses they had suffered (Reid et al., 1990).

When refugee services were first established, there was a dearth of population-wide studies examining the mental health effects of torture and refugee trauma (Goldfield, Mollica, Pesavemto, & Faraone, 1988) so that clinicians tended to draw theoretical inferences about these issues from the cases seen in clinics. As a consequence, we were all prey to what is known as the "clinician's delusion"; that is, we assumed that the cases we saw in clinics accurately reflected the psychosocial status of refugee populations in general. The cases we saw often had chronic, disabling mental health and psychosocial problems, and the first small, mostly clinic-based studies appeared to support these characterizations (Gold-field et al., 1988).

What was easy to overlook was that the patients we saw in clinics were special in that they were a minority who had sought treatment from a professional for severe symptoms and related disabilities. Although we recognized the importance of culture and the stress of migration and resettlement on refugees (Reid et al., 1990), there still tended to be an underlying belief that exposure to trauma was the core problem and that probing into trauma memories in psychotherapy was the most important task (Somnier & Genefke, 1986).

The conviction that most members of refugee populations were "traumatized" led to certain frustrations in our clinical work. At one time, STARTTS was based in offices overlooking the central business district of a densely multicultural suburb, Fairfield, situated in the west of Sydney, where large numbers of Southeast Asian refugees were resettled. I remember distinctly staring out of the window between consulting patients and feeling some frustration that I was only able to treat 10 Vietnamese, Cambodian, or Lao refugees on any one day, when the streets were thronging with their compatriots who were receiving no treatment. Experience showed that severe, chronic post-traumatic stress reactions can be highly disabling, requiring the application of multimodal and multidisciplinary interventions involving psychologists, psychiatrists, interpreters, bicultural counsellors, physiotherapists, occupational therapists, and a range of agencies assisting with legal, resettlement, language, and acculturation issues (Reid et al., 1990). Even then, interventions often yielded only slow and incremental therapeutic effects over prolonged periods of time. In other words, the optimal treatment for these complex trauma-related conditions appeared to demand a high level of skills and input from a multidisciplinary team, making interventions costly in terms of human resources, funding, and time. If indeed, whole populations were traumatized, it was difficult to conceive of a model in which such intensive treatments could be offered at the population-wide level.

Tensions between General Traumatology and Concepts of Refugee Torture and Trauma

Yet, in spite of cross-fertilization, the refugee trauma field never fully integrated within the broader field of traumatology whose main focus was on civilian trauma (sexual assault, road and technological accidents, natural disasters) or military psychiatry. The distinctness of the refugee trauma field arose for some self-evident reasons, namely the additional issues arising from displacement, migration, and resettlement, as well as the obvious salience of working in a transcultural and multilingual arena (Reid et al., 1990).

Nevertheless, discontent with the standard trauma model ran deeply (Summerfield, 1999), with critics in the refugee and postconflict area arguing that the labelling of refugees with diagnoses such as PTSD "medicalized" problems best understood within the frameworks of human rights and cultures. Some commentators (Summerfield, 1999) rejected the trauma model altogether, claiming that PTSD was a Western invention that encouraged a focus on the individual rather than on the community and that the notion of PTSD arose in response to a context-specific, social imperative in the United States, mainly as a platform for advocacy for stigmatized Vietnam combat veterans. An added concern was that trauma counseling imported by international agencies into postconflict settings may be alien and unwelcome in cultures with their own traditions for overcoming adversity.

The trauma critique has influenced policy makers in leading international agencies, including the United Nations framework. In a sense then, ironically, a new battleground has opened up over trauma, dividing those who adhere to the notion of PTSD and focus on developing treatments for that disorder and a contingency within the refugee field who either reject the concept altogether or who have reservations about it. Much of the ensuing debate has occurred without comprehensive reference to the growing research literature in the field. I will attempt to draw on that literature together with my own impressions from working with two communities, the Vietnamese and the East Timorese, in order to propose an adaptive framework for conceptualizing mass trauma.

Questions about Trauma

To begin to unravel the debate about PTSD, several interrelated questions need to be asked: (1) Can PTSD symptoms be identified across cultures? (2) How prevalent are these symptoms, what is their course, and are they always disabling? (3) Is it possible to develop a model of psychosocial adaptation that encompasses issues of trauma but that extends the focus to include wider challenges faced by refugees and other populations exposed to mass violence? (4) How do answers to the foregoing questions guide strategies for clinical interventions?

My colleagues and I at STARTTS have treated refugees arriving in Australia from over 100 countries. This experience has been supplemented by work in postconflict countries in Africa and Asia, most recently in East Timor. Such exposure to a multiplicity of cultures leaves me in no doubt that the broad features of PTSD can be identified across societies, suggesting that the core symptoms associated with traumatic stress, with some cultural variation, may represent a universal psychobiological response pattern to life threatening experiences. Furthermore, the majority of large-scale epidemiological research studies (e.g., Modvig et al., 2000; Mollica et al., 1999; Shrestha et al., 1998) undertaken in the past decade among refugees and postconflict populations, suggested that PTSD symptoms are highly prevalent across these groups.

Normative versus Pathological Responses to Trauma

A key question, however, is what PTSD symptoms signify in relation to mental health, psychosocial disability, and need for clinical assistance. One of the potential problems of including a category such as PTSD in a psychiatric diagnostic system is that it implies that the relevant response pattern is always pathological. An important question is whether symptoms that are typical of PTSD may reflect normative psychobiological survival responses to life threatening experiences, particularly in the earlier post-traumatic phase. I have speculated (Silove, 1998) that post-traumatic responses may make evolutionary sense, particularly if we think back to the time when primitive hominids lived precarious lives in small bands roaming the savannah of Africa, a period that played a substantial role in shaping human adaptation and survival behaviors. Early hominids had poorly developed cerebral hemispheres and hence had a limited capacity for complex problem solving, communication, and the capacity to consciously predict future danger. In contrast, their limbic system (or archaic brain) was well developed, providing the capacity for mobilizing instantaneous and reflexive survival responses when the hominid was confronted with immediate mortal threat. It is worth considering whether phenomena now regarded as intrinsic to PTSD may be derived from these early physiologic survival reactions. First, in the face of mortal threat, high levels of arousal (rapid heartbeat, muscle tension, hyperalertness) would be useful, providing instantaneous readiness for flight (and if necessary, fight) responses. Second, rapid withdrawal from the threat and a period of avoidance of the vicinity would have been adaptive to ensure distance and protection from the danger. Finally, rehearsal of the memory of the trauma associated with high levels of emotion, although unpleasant, would lay down strong memory traces of novel threats, ensuring durable learning and hence a rapid response to further warning signs indicating return of the danger.

If this somewhat speculative evolutionary-learning model of PTSD has any validity, then core PTSD symptoms (rehearsal of memories, avoidance, and arousal) may have had adaptive survival functions in the early post-trauma phase, at least before humans had developed higher-level cognitive, or thinking, capacities to solve problems, predict future events, and communicate with others. It follows, therefore, that we need to be cautious in assuming that PTSD symptoms always are abnormal, maladaptive, or dysfunctional, especially in the early phase after trauma exposure. In that context, it is important in judging the salience of PTSD symptoms to consider carefully their timing and course, the factors that encourage or obstruct their resolution, and whether or not they lead to functional disability.

Elsewhere, I have expanded the evolutionary survival model to include wider social factors that assist individuals and communities to adapt following exposure to mass violence (Silove, 1999b). The evolving model of Adaptation and Development after Persecution and Trauma (ADAPT) is based on the observation that communities make active efforts to survive and adapt even in the most testing circumstances (Silove, 2004). I postulate that five social pillars support a platform of adaptation:

1. Establishment of security
2. Maintenance and repair of family and social bonds
3. Creation of effective systems of justice
4. Reestablishment of social roles and identities
5. Building of institutions that create communal coherence and meaning whether religious, spiritual, existential, political, or cultural

In the broad sense, I have argued that the psychosocial recovery of communities depends on how effectively reconstruction programs attend to these broad social domains. In relation to PTSD, the establishment of peace and security is most salient. The following case studies derived from work with the Vietnamese and East Timorese illustrate some of these points.

Vietnamese Refugees

Vietnamese refugees represented the largest group of forcibly displaced persons arriving in Australia from the mid-1970s until the mass displacements associated with the wars in the former Yugoslavia (Steel, Silove, Phan, & Bauman, 2002). Of the 100,000 Vietnamese who arrived in Australia over an extended period of time, a large number resettled in the southwest of Sydney, a newly developed area of the city where the torture and trauma service, STARTTS, is located. Since their arrival, concerns have been raised repeatedly that the Vietnamese underutilize mental health services (Steel et al., 2002). Their apparent failure to use services seemed to be at odds with the community's extensive exposure to trauma including war, forced displacement, hazardous journeys of escape by boat, and detention in refugee camps in Southeast Asia. Reasons considered for the underutilization of services (Steel et al., 2002) included:

- Communal stigma associated with mental illness
- The tendency for Vietnamese to keep personal problems within the family
- The claim that Vietnamese tend to "somatize" symptoms (that is, complain of physical symptoms such as headaches rather than psychological symptoms)
- The possibility that indigenous beliefs about illness led them preferentially to use traditional healers such as Chinese doctors
- The belief that they felt alienated from mainstream mental health services

Some of these observations may account to a limited degree for their service utilization patterns. For example, our earlier studies (Phan & Silove, 1997) suggested that the Vietnamese did adhere to a complex array of traditional beliefs about mental illness and, in addition, that they were somewhat dissatisfied with the level of communication and explanation provided by mainstream services. It is important to note, however, that they were happy with their interactions with the STARTTS torture and trauma service (Silove et al., 1997). Nevertheless, none of these factors seemed to account fully for the fact that relatively few Vietnamese attended services for trauma-related psychiatric problems.

Rates of Mental Disorder among Vietnamese Refugees

One issue that was not sufficiently considered was the possibility that, in spite of their refugee backgrounds, resettled Vietnamese suffered low or only moderate rates of common mental symptoms such as anxiety, depression, and PTSD. We undertook an epidemiological study using census data to identify a representative sample of 1,100 adult Vietnamese living in the community in Sydney (Steel et al., 2002). The group reported substantial rates of exposure to the traumas associated with war and displacement. Nevertheless, rates of common mental disorders (depression, anxiety) were substantially lower than among the Australian-born population, whereas the rates for PTSD were approximately the same. It did appear that those Vietnamese who acknowledged having a disorder were more disabled from a psychosocial perspective, suggesting a cultural tendency to report symptoms only when the person is seriously affected, but that effect did not explain in full the differences in prevalence rates between the two communities. Importantly, Vietnamese who had clinical disorders were as likely to consult their family physicians for these problems as the Australian-born, but the lower prevalence rate of disorder meant that their overall utilization was diminished.

Trauma Severity and Time

How do we reconcile high levels of trauma exposure and relatively low rates of mental disorder among resettled Vietnamese? A further analysis of the trauma data showed some very interesting results (Steel et al., 2002). A graduated effect was evident with Vietnamese exposed to high levels of trauma reporting higher rates of mental disturbance than those with moderate levels who, in turn, had more substantial rates than the nontraumatized. Importantly, however, the time lapsed since the trauma exerted a powerful effect: The longer the time since the trauma, the less likely were survivors to have ongoing mental health problems. So, at 10 years after exposure, those with moderate trauma did not differ from their nontraumatized counterparts in their rates of mental disorder. The group that had been exposed to severe forms of trauma also showed decreasing levels of mental problems over time, but a small subgroup of these (about 4% of the Vietnamese population) still had higher rates of trauma-related mental disorder at 10 years, a subgroup that therefore clearly warrants further mental health attention.

Our study was based on a retrospective design, but the findings broadly accord with those of two longitudinal studies (Beiser & Hou, 2001; Westermeyer, Neider, & Callies, 1989), each undertaken over a 10-year period in North America, with both showing a steady decline in psychological symptoms in Southeast Asian refugees over time. One of those studies (Beiser & Hou, 2001) included predominantly Vietnamese participants and also showed that at final follow-up, levels of mental disorder were lower among Southeast Asians compared to native-born Canadians.

The Recovery Environment

Clearly, several explanations might account for these findings. As indicated, a higher threshold for reporting symptoms (possibly because of stigma or other cultural inhibitions) may account for some of these trends. Another possibility is that the Vietnamese as an ethnic group simply are less vulnerable or that the most resilient fled as refugees. A closer examination of our data shows, however, that for those Vietnamese where the trauma was recent, the rates of mental disturbances were very high (Steel et al., 2002), challenging any claim that Vietnamese have an inherently lower symptom response to stress. Other studies support the observation that subgroups of Vietnamese are as susceptible as any other population to high levels of mental disturbance such as PTSD and depression when exposed to severe stress (Mollica et al., 1998).

Our own explanation, albeit speculative, is that there is a sensitive dynamic between trauma-related symptoms and the social environment, mediated through higher brain centers that are known to inhibit limbic fear responses. The Vietnamese arrived during a golden age of refugee policy in Australia. Although there was some public resistance to their arrival by boat, the government of the time effectively allayed societal fears and welcomed the newcomers by providing them with permanent residency, eligibility for citizenship, potential for family reunion, and unrestricted access to a wide array of resettlement and general services including cost-free health care and education. In that sense, the government attended to all five of the aforementioned adaptive systems: The Vietnamese were offered conditions of safety and a secure future; they were encouraged to re-unite with their families; they lived in a just society that at the time celebrated multiculturalism; they had unfettered opportunities to pursue new roles and bicultural identities; and they were given every opportunity to pursue their religious and traditional practices.

Anyone who knows the community living in the southwest of Sydney will attest to their success in public life, in the professions, and in maintaining their traditions. Indeed, the capacity to live a bicultural life may itself be protective, with members of the Vietnamese community competing effectively in the wider society in work environments but still enjoying strong communal support in the form of traditional family networks in which bonds remain strong.

That is not to argue that the Vietnamese community is free of all vulnerabilities related to the traumas of the past. Two important indicators of latent community vulnerability emerged in recent times. On one occasion, a Vietnamese-government-sponsored entertainment troupe visited Australia, provoking a storm of protest from the community. At a clinical level, several ex-patients made contact complaining that this event had triggered troubling memories and associated PTSD symptoms that had been in remission for some time. An almost identical community response occurred when a local radio station began broadcasting programs obtained directly from the Vietnamese government radio service, an unintended provocation that offended the many refugees who had fled that regime.

The lesson appears to be, therefore, that past persecution does lead to individual and communal vulnerabilities but that supportive recovery environments can play a strong role in facilitating adaptation for the majority of affected persons. Vulnerabilities remain, however, with environmental triggers, if salient enough, provoking symptoms. That latent vulnerability is consistent with a psychobiological survival response that is dampened by conditions of social safety but is never fully extinguished. Also, in a minority of the severely traumatized, symptoms do not resolve and may persist for long periods of time, making it imperative that those persons receive clinical interventions. Although the percentage of these chronic cases seems small (in our Vietnamese sample, 4%), the absolute numbers are substantial. For example, in a Vietnamese population of approximately 60,000 adults in Australia, this percentage would translate into 2,400 persons who remain disabled by trauma-related symptoms even 10 years after exposure.

The East Timorese

The experiences of our team in attempting to assist the East Timorese community provides further lessons regarding issues of timing and context in assessing mental health needs and priorities for populations exposed to mass psychological trauma.

History

East Timor (now the independent country of Timor Leste) is a half-island territory lying between northern Australia and the eastern islands of the Indonesian archipelago. The territory was a Portuguese colony for 400 years. During World War II, the Japanese invaded the colony, perpetrating mass human rights violations against the local community. After reverting to Portuguese rule, an independence movement gained ground leading to the expulsion of the Portuguese governor and a subsequent short-lived civil war in 1974. After a period of bloodshed, the dominant party, Fretilin, restored order. Soon thereafter, Indonesia invaded the territory with the tacit support of the Great Powers. During the invasion and the ensuing 24-year period of low-grade armed resistance, over 200,000 persons (25% of the population) died as a consequence of warfare, famine, and illness. The history of this period records episodes of indiscriminate bombing, large-scale military campaigns that forcibly displaced communities, extrajudicial "disappearances," torture, and other reprisals against the civilian population (Silove, 1999a, 2002).

In 1999, after the fall of the Suharto regime, the interim administration of Indonesia succumbed to international pressure and allowed a referendum to be held in East Timor on the question of independence. Atrocities and intimidation by pro-Indonesian militia escalated into widespread violence after the plebiscite, resulting in the displacement of 80 percent of the population and the destruction of 70 percent of the existing infrastructure. Over the following year, the United Nations restored stability and in 2002, East Timor became a sovereign nation. Although the country remains one of the poorest in the world, East Timor is unusual as a contemporary postconflict country in that the transition has been accomplished with minimal ongoing violence and insecurity.

East Timorese Refugees Arriving in Australia

After the Indonesian invasion of East Timor, several thousand refugees from that territory fled to Australia. Refugees from this first wave were offered permanent residency and access to all services. During the 1990s, the resistance struggle in East Timor increased in intensity, leading to an escalation of violence, torture, and widespread human rights abuses. As a consequence, a second wave of refugees began arriving in Australia, but in this instance, the host government challenged their right to seek asylum. A protracted legal struggle has been fought for many years, and East Timorese asylum seekers continue to live in a state of insecurity, fearing that they might be forcibly returned to their home country (Silove et al., 2002).

Mental Health Services for East Timorese in Australia

Australian torture and trauma rehabilitation services have worked with East Timorese refugees and asylum seekers for many years. In Sydney, however, we observed that relatively few East Timorese were accessing STARTTS in spite of the service appointing an East Timorese bicultural counsellor and the fact that the majority of the community lived within the precinct of the service (Silove et al., 2002). Anecdotal evidence from community groups suggested that the asylum seeker group in particular was suffering a high degree of psychosocial duress.

We thus initiated a researcher-advocacy program (Silove et al., 2002) for asylum seekers aimed at engaging the community, establishing a referral base for general health, legal, and welfare services, documenting the difficulties the community faced, and providing immediate assistance to those in psychological need. The program made gradual progress with a growing sense of mutual trust developing with asylum seekers as we offered a range of interventions, particularly medicolegal reports supporting visa applications and referral for health services.

The data we gathered lent support to impressions that the asylum-seeking group had suffered wide-ranging traumas including torture, other forms of political violence, and related human rights violations. In addition, asylum seekers faced ongoing postmigration stresses such as fears of being repatriated, lengthy separations from family, feelings of alienation in the host country, and administrative obstacles to finding work and achieving financial independence. As a consequence, levels of distress were high, as indicated by rates of PTSD and depression that exceeded 50 percent (Silove et al., 2002).

The Cascade of History: Crisis Intervention in Australia

In 1998–1999, just as the researcher-advocacy program was gaining full momentum, East Timor was overcome with the humanitarian crisis triggered by the referendum. After the referendum, several thousand East Timorese were airlifted to Australia, where they were housed in temporary safe havens around the country. Our team provided a crisis mental health and psychosocial service in the safe haven established in Sydney while simultaneously initiating a community-run drop-in center to assist the resident East Timorese population, since many were anxious about the safety of family in the home country. Although the impact of trauma was clearly pervasive, the model we adopted was one of crisis intervention and the promotion of adaptive responses. We attended to individuals and families in extreme distress, and we created a framework that encouraged cultural activities and community cohesiveness that drew in isolated community members to the drop-in center.

In the safe haven, a range of activities were initiated, including sport, recreation, and outings for the children, linking the camp population with the Australia-based East Timorese community, the church, and NGOs, holding immigration-related information sessions for the adults, providing short-term counseling for families, facilitating training opportunities, and mediating in cultural and other misunderstandings that arose with government officials and camp authorities.

In essence, our crisis approach was consistent with the ADAPT model for short-term interventions in that we contributed to:

- Making persons feel as safe as possible
- Strengthening family and community bonds
- Promoting issues of social justice in the way survivors were dealt with
- Providing meaningful activities and roles by preparing displaced persons for future work through training
- Linking the community to institutions that provided a sense of meaning, particularly the church and the local East Timorese community

Mental Health Interventions in East Timor

In the midst of our work with the local and displaced East Timorese population in Sydney, we were approached by exiled community leaders to plan a mental health and psychosocial intervention in East Timor itself once it became feasible to enter the territory. Our deliberations about how to approach the challenge were influenced by several factors (Zwi & Silove, 2002). Those of us who had exposure to refugee camps and other war-affected populations in low-income countries (Silove, Ekblad, & Mollica, 2000) were aware that traumatic stress accounted for only one aspect of the mental health problems facing those communities. In those settings, community mental health services generally were poorly developed, family and community supports were undermined, and traditional healers might not be accessible. As a consequence, patients with severe mental disorders such as psychotic conditions (schizophrenia, bipolar disorder) and neuro-organic conditions (in particular, epilepsy) were at substantial risk of neglect, abandonment, and in some cases, of abuse. A minority of these persons might manifest bizarre or frankly dangerous behaviors, posing a threat to themselves and others and thereby creating a multiplier effect of social instability affecting the family and the wider community. Families that were struggling to survive in conflict-affected settings faced the additional burden of caring for highly disabled or disorganized members with mental illnesses without recourse to skilled assistance.

Mental Health Services in East Timor

We were aware from our contacts within East Timor that there were no specialist mental health personnel in the territory and no facilities for the mentally ill (Silove, 1999a). In addition, in the crisis of 1999, virtually all community health centers had been burnt down and most of the health personnel had fled. Hence, although the team that we formed—Psychosocial Recovery and Development in East Timor (PRADET)—was strongly oriented toward trauma, we were aware that of necessity our focus would have to broaden to include the severely mentally ill (Zwi & Silove, 2002).

With funding from AusAID, the Australian government overseas aid agency, and the Department of Health in New South Wales, we established a psychosocial resource center in burned-out buildings above Dili, the capital of East Timor. Fifteen nurses and one East Timorese doctor were recruited to participate in intensive preliminary mental health training in Sydney. They then returned to East Timor with the support of expatriate mental health staff and visiting psychiatrists from Australia. Clinics were established in and around Dili, and these were gradually extended to the districts of the country with the assistance of the United Nations High Commissioner for Refugees. Further training and supervision were provided to the core staff as well as to general health staff, personnel working in NGOs, and members of church and volunteer groups. An interagency was established with other NGOs in order to create a network of services that coordinated mental health and psychosocial work.

Our prediction that we would need to give attention to the severely mentally ill was borne out by early experiences (Silove et al., 2004). The largest diagnostic group referred to PRADET included persons with psychotic illnesses who were in dire situations because of their severe mental disturbances. An example was Jose, a 35-year-old man who, in retrospect, had been psychotic for 18 years and who had been manacled to a tree by his family to prevent him from wandering and engaging in altercations with the neighbors. During the emergency in 1999, the family's house was burnt down and threats from the invading militia forced members of the household to flee, leaving Jose behind. The militia were alerted by Jose's erratic behavior and aggression, torturing him and leaving him in a ditch to die. Fortunately, a neighbor discovered him and helped him to reach his family, who had returned from the hills. They were obliged to chain him to a tree while they attempted to rebuild their house. He escaped, causing his family a great deal of difficulty in apprehending him at a time when they were struggling to survive. When PRADET was called, medication was prescribed, the assistance of other NGOs was solicited to provide the family with food and temporary accommodation, relatives were educated about the nature of the illness, and discussions were held with the village *chefe* (chief) about how the community could support the family. Within three months, Jose was well enough to be released from his chains and, after a period of time, was able to assist the family in planting the rice crop, the first time in 18 years that he could cooperate with his relatives.

Cases such as these indicate the complex interaction between mass conflict and mental illness. The combination of repression and warfare over decades had left East Timor underdeveloped so that basic services for the mentally ill were absent. The crisis of 1999 placed the severely mentally ill at increased risk since their caregivers were forced to flee, leaving patients vulnerable to abuse and neglect.

After nine months, we audited the work of PRADET, reviewing a random subset of case notes (Silove et al., 2004). It was clear that psychosis was the most common diagnosis treated in this early phase, but epilepsy, depression, anxiety, and PTSD were also represented. An analysis of the reasons for referral indicated that all cases seen were in dire social circumstances: They were incapacitated, extremely distressed, suicidal, or acting dangerously; and their families or other support networks were incapable of caring for them or containing their disruptive behaviors. As such, these patients posed an extreme risk to their own and their family's survival in a context in which attention to basic needs (food, shelter, security) was pressing.

The Trauma Dilemma

Clearly, the number of cases who consulted our service with a diagnosis of PTSD was small relative to the expected prevalence of that disorder in the community at large. An epidemiological survey undertaken in 2000 (Modvig et al., 2000) found the rate of PTSD to be 34 percent in East Timor. The dilemma created by figures such as these is obvious: How does a poor and devastated country such as East Timor provide interventions for PTSD to such a large percentage of the population? It is inconceivable that individual or group therapies could be provided to all cases in such a context— indeed, it would not be feasible or economically viable to offer treatments to such a large percentage of the population in even the richest and best-organized countries.

Fortunately, evidence suggests that such interventions are not needed. There is no evidence that mass debriefing of trauma-exposed populations is warranted or effective (Raphael & Wooding, 2004). Also, as indicated by our Vietnamese study (Steel et al., 2002), most members of a trauma-affected community can be expected to recover naturally given secure environmental conditions. The ADAPT model outlined above predicts that individuals and collectives will make active efforts to recreate their lives and that their efforts will achieve maximal psychosocial impact under conditions of security and social stability.

East Timor has been remarkable as a postconflict country in that, with a few exceptional outbreaks of violence, the social environment has been peaceful and stable even though the community continues to struggle with problems of poverty, displacement, and underdevelopment. In most instances, communities have returned to their villages and traditional life has resumed. Truth and reconciliation processes have been instituted, children have returned to schools, and the health system is operating reasonably effectively. When one wanders about villages in the countryside, a common response of villagers to inquiries is that they are no longer scared and that although life is a constant financial struggle, the suffering of the past seems vindicated in that the cherished goal of national independence has been achieved.

Our preliminary impressions from an ongoing epidemiologic study being undertaken in East Timor is that the rates of PTSD are many times lower than those recorded in 2000 (Modvig et al., 2000) in spite of the fact that very few persons have received trauma counseling. If confirmed, such a finding suggests, albeit tentatively, that peace and security may provide the best "therapist" for most members of a postconflict population suffering from early traumatic stress reactions.

Conclusions

The present chapter attempts to trace a personal odyssey of discovery aimed at understanding more fully the complex issue of psychological trauma in the context of mass conflict. Although that journey is by no means complete, some pointers have emerged over time. Initially, I joined in the spirit of enthusiasm about describing and identifying PTSD and then searching for the optimal clinical treatment for that disorder. Although such an endeavor continues to be justified, it has become pressing that we distinguish more clearly between self-limiting trauma reactions and longer-lasting, disabling psychopathology. Epidemiologic studies in postconflict countries undertaken in the 1990s appeared to show high rates of PTSD in diverse contexts affected by mass trauma and displacement. If these findings were accepted at face value, the practical implications were daunting. Our experience suggested that patients seen in clinics with severe and long-standing traumatic stress reactions posed challenges to treatment, requiring patience, skills, and a multidisciplinary approach to achieving incremental gains over time. Hence, it was inconceivable that the resources needed for such interventions could be mobilized for large subgroups of the population identified by most epidemiological studies in low-income, postconflict countries.

The dynamic model of PTSD postulated herein provides a tentative solution to the dilemma in that it allows for consideration of normative as well as morbid outcomes following exposure to trauma. If the PTSD constellation is regarded as a psychobiological survival reaction that interacts dynamically with the social environment, there is the potential that recovery can be driven by appropriate humanitarian and reconstruction programs, especially if they effectively repair the key psychosocial systems identified by the ADAPT model. Our research among the Vietnamese and our recent preliminary findings among the East Timorese suggest that safe and stable post-traumatic environments may exert a powerful impact in dampening communal post-traumatic fear responses in the majority of survivors.

As a consequence, under optimal recovery environments, the numbers experiencing severe, disabling, and protracted traumatic stress reactions may be smaller than previously estimated among refugee populations. Nevertheless, as indicated, even a conservative prevalence rate of 4 percent of the population with chronic PTSD represents a major challenge to treatment services especially in devastated and resource-poor postconflict countries. The additional issue in most postconflict countries is that persons with other mental disorders also require attention. Hence, in such settings, a strong argument can be made for developing community mental health services with a capacity to deal with a wide range of presentations including the minority with persisting and severe traumatic stress reactions.

The important qualification is that mental health services should be designed to encourage access for the minority who do not recover from traumatic stress reactions, since it is well known that persons exposed to gross human rights violations can be reluctant to attend services. Yet, when they have a chance to do so, within a safe and supportive context, many find the rehabilitation process to be productive and comforting. An East Timorese combat veteran who had fought in the hills for 20 years said, "At first I thought this place (the mental health service) was for mad people only. Now that I have come here, I realize that I was a bit *bulak* [mad] from the fighting . . . I felt that I was losing control. Actually, I am not mad, I am just *hanoin barak* [thinking too much]. The service has helped me see that these feelings are normal and that many of my countrymen have the same problems . . . that has been very helpful. Also, for the first time in 25 years, I am not scared all the time when I am in my village—that helps a lot!"

References

American Psychiatric Association. (1980). *Diagnostic and statistical manual of mental disorders* (3rd ed.). Washington, DC: Author.

———. (1994). *Diagnostic and statistical manual of mental disorders* (4th ed.). Washington, DC: Author.

Beiser, M., & Hou, F. (2001). Language acquisition, unemployment, and depressive disorder among Southeast Asia refugees: A 10 year study. *Social Science & Medicine, 53*, 1321–1334.

Goldfield, A. E., Mollica, R. F., Pesavemto, B. H., & Faraone, S. V. (1988). The physical and psychological sequelae of torture, symptomatology, and diagnosis. *Journal of the American Medical Association, 259*, 2725–2729.

Modvig, J., Padaduan-Lopez, J., Rodenburg, J., Salud, C. M., Cabigon, R. V., & Panelo, C. I. (2000). Torture and trauma in post-conflict East Timor. *Lancet, 356*, 1763.

Mollica, R. F., McInnes, K., Pham, T., Smith Fawzi, M. C., Murphy, E., & Lin, L. (1998). The dose-effect relationships between torture and psychiatric symptoms in Vietnamese ex-political detainees and a comparison group. *Journal of Nervous & Mental Disease, 186*, 543–553.

Mollica, R. F., McInnes, K., Sarajlic, N., Lavelle, J., Sarajlic, I., & Massagli, M. P. (1999). Disability associated with psychiatric comorbidity and health status in Bosnian refugees living in Croatia. *Journal of the American Medical Association, 282*, 433–439.

Phan, P., & Silove, D. (1997). The influence of culture on psychiatric assessment: The Vietnamese refugee. *Psychiatric Services, 48*, 86–90.

Raphael, B., & Wooding, S. (2004). Debriefing: Its evolution and current status. *Psychiatric Clinics of North America, 27*, 407–423.

Reid, J., Silove, D., & Tarn, R. (1990). The development of the New South Wales Service for the Treatment and Rehabilitation of Torture and Trauma Survivors (STARTTS)—the first year. *Australia and New Zealand Journal of Psychiatry, 24*, 486–495.

Shrestha, N. M., Sharma, B., van Ommeren, M., Regmi, S., Makaju, R., Komproe, I., et al. (1998). Impact of torture of refugees displaced within the developing world: Symptomatology among Bhutanese refugees in Nepal. *Journal of the American Medical Association, 280*, 443–448.

Silove, D. (1998). Is posttraumatic stress disorder an overlearned survival response? An evolutionary-learning hypothesis. *Psychiatry: Interpersonal and Biological Processes, 61*, 181–190.

———. (1999a). Health and human rights of the East Timorese. *Lancet, 353*, 2067.

———. 1999b). The psychosocial effects of torture, mass human rights violations and refugee trauma: Towards an integrated conceptual framework. *Journal of Nervous & Mental Disease, 187*, 200–207.

———. (2002). Conflict in East Timor: Genocide or expansionist occupation. *Human Rights Review, 1*, 62–79.

———. (2004). The global challenge of asylum seekers. In J. Wilson & B. Drozdek (Eds.), *Broken spirits: The treatment of traumatized asylum seekers, refugees, war and torture victims* (pp. 13–31). New York: Brunner-Routledge.

———, Coello, M., Tang, K., Aroche, J., Soares, M., Lingam, R., Chaussivert, M., Manicavasagar, V., & Steel, Z. (2002). Towards a researcher-advocacy model for asylum seekers: A pilot study amongst East Timorese living in Australia. *Transcultural Psychiatry, 39*, 452–468.

———, Ekblad, S., & Mollica, R. (2000). The rights of the severely mentally ill in post-conflict societies. *Lancet, 355*, 1548–1549.

———, Manicavasagar, V., Baker, K., Mausiri, M., Soares, M., de Carvalho, F., et al. (2004). Indices of social risk among first attenders of an emergency mental health service in post-conflict East Timor: An exploratory investigation. *Australian and New Zealand Journal of Psychiatry, 38*, 929–932.

———, Manicavasagar, V., Beltran, R., Le, G., Nguyen, H., Phan, T., et al. (1997). Satisfaction of Vietnamese patients and their families and refugee and mainstream mental health services. *Psychiatric Services, 48*, 1064–1069.

Somnier, F. E., & Genefke, I. K. (1986). Psychotherapy for victims of torture. *British Journal of Psychiatry, 149*, 323–329.

Steel, Z., Silove, D., Phan, T., & Bauman, A. (2002). The long-term impact of trauma on the mental health of Vietnamese refugees resettled in Australia. *Lancet, 360*, 156–162.

Summerfield, D. (1999). A critique of seven assumptions behind psychological trauma programmes in war-affected areas. *Social Science & Medicine, 48*, 1449–1462.

Westermeyer, J., Neider, J., & Callies, A. (1989). Psychosocial adjustment of Hmong refugees during their first decade in the United States: A longitudinal study. *Journal of Nervous & Mental Disease, 177*, 132–139.

Zwi, A., & Silove, D. (2002). Hearing the voices—mental health services in East Timor. *Lancet, 360*, 45–46.

CHAPTER 2

Serving the Mental Health Needs of Postmigratory Adult Refugees in Sweden: A Transitional Augmentation Approach

Solvig Ekblad

Introduction: Adequacy and Appropriateness

This chapter is applicable to psychologists working in the resettlement of postmigratory refugees. One of the outstanding challenges a refugee faces is in receiving permission to live in a safe country. Once there, refugees with trauma-related problems may seek help from psychologists and other mental health professionals. However, they may not. How can we as psychologists work with psychological distress within the refugee's community if a refugee may be reluctant to utilize formal psychological and other mental health services? A psychologist must consider the adequacy and appropriateness of clinical-based services as the basis of our response to the mental health needs of refugees. The following questions are among those that are relevant to a psychologist's concerns:

- What causes the illness?
- Why is the illness happening now?
- How has the cause triggered the illness?
- What is the prognosis?
- What kind of intervention is needed?

These questions are discussed in this chapter. The case is from Sweden but the knowledge may be relevant to Western and Western-oriented societies in general. I believe that it is important "to be knowledgeable about a broad range of assessment techniques, data generating procedures, and standardized instruments whose validity, reliability, and measurement equivalence have been investigated across culturally diverse sample groups" (American Psychological Association [APA], 2002, p. 41). This knowledge is important because "clients unfamiliar with mental health services and who hold world-views that value relationship over task may experience disrespect if proce-dures are not fully explained . . . and the client may not adhere to the suggestions of the therapies" (APA, 2002, p. 48).

In addressing issues around postmigratory refugee and mental health care, the discussion examines ideas around the attitude, skill, and knowledge of the psychologist and poses the following goals. In regard to attitude, the final goal is to understand the other person and learn to adapt oneself to that person's beliefs. In order to develop this essential insight, it is necessary to challenge assumptions based on one's own culture. Before these assump-tions can be challenged, they must be identified; thus, knowledge of one's own self and culture is the starting point.

In regard to skill, the psychologist must (1) recognize family structure, communication patterns and styles, and approaches to the refugee, (2) be sensitive to and aware of beliefs and practices of the refugee (especially ones that influence health care), and (3) learn to fit the care with those beliefs and practices. Note that in reference to (2), the emphasis is not necessarily com-plete knowledge but awareness and sensitivity.

Finally, in regard to knowledge, the psychologist must use the knowledge of one's own cultural norms to learn to recognize the characteristics com-mon to each culture in caring for clients and families.

In order to facilitate the reading, understanding, and application of this chapter, please note that concepts as applied herein mean the following:

Health is a state of complete physical, mental, and social well-being, not merely the absence of disease or infirmity (World Health Organization [WHO]; 1948).

A *refugee* is a person who, "owing to a well-founded fear of being perse-cuted for reasons of race, religion, nationality, membership in a particular social group, or political opinion is outside the country of his nationality and is unable to or owing to such fear, is unwilling to avail himself of the protec-tion of that country" (United Nations High Commissioner for Refugees [UNHCR], 1951).

Mental health resources include "individual, family, community, psycho-logical, social, and economic strengths, which can help individuals and groups of people cope with stress, trauma, and suffering. This also includes human, financial, and institutional resources (including policies and action plans) which can be mobilised to support the establishment of mental health programmes" (WHO, 2001, p. vii).

Postmigration stresses are secondary trauma. Examples include administra-tive barriers in resettlement, such as limited or denied access to housing, health care, or jobs; or difficulties in family reunion.

Sense of coherence means the psychological dimensions affecting health and includes (1) *comprehensibility*, or the extent to which a person can make sense of internal or external stimuli; (2) *manageability*, or the extent to which one perceives that resources are available; and (3) *meaningfulness*, or the perception that life is meaningful and worth living despite its hardships (Antonovsky, 1993).

Sweden as a Refugee Reception Country

According to official Swedish statistics (Statistics Sweden, 2003), of the total 9 million inhabitants in Sweden today, more than1 million individuals are foreign born (11.5%). During the past 10 years, the number of people seeking asylum has been between 5,000 and 33,200 each year. Our country was a relatively homogenous population until recently, so it has just started to confront the effects of multiculturalism. If the second generation of immigrants is included, the number grows to about 20 percent. Sweden faced a major increase in asylum seekers in 1992, when many came from the former Yugoslavia (84,018).

In 2003, 33,160 persons applied for asylum in Sweden. The largest groups were from Serbia and Montenegro (5,305), Somalia (3,069 persons), and Iraq (2,700 persons). A total of 46,857 persons were granted residence permits in Sweden in 2003, 6,460 of them as refugees or on other protective grounds (Migrationsverket, 2004). Nine hundred and forty-two persons were brought to Sweden within the so-called refugee quota. Residence permits were granted to 24,553 persons because of family ties, 5,509 to visiting students, and 782 on grounds of adoption. In accordance with an agreement between the European Union and the European Economic Area (EU/EEA), residence permits were issued to 9,234 persons. As the newcomers are moving to urban areas, the health issues are more complex in some county governments than in others.

In order to get asylum, a clear, consistent, and believable story (e.g., being tortured and detained due to political beliefs) is requested. However, this process of seeking asylum spans many months (at present, 404 days on average in Sweden). During that time, new statements and appeals are made. When the asylum seekers meet a psychologist, the psychologist can piece together a more comprehensive narrative of the refugee's experience; however, this story may be inconsistent with the original statement. Trauma experts know that it is often difficult and sometimes impossible to give a coherent narrative story. These traumatic memories are emotional and perceptual rather than declarative. Still, the possibility for an asylum seeker to get asylum (legal recognition) depends on the ways that person expresses autobiographical memories.

Integrating Health and Community Services in the Resettlement

In 1990 Sweden met with other European Union member states at the Dublin Convention. There, the member states agreed to streamline policy regarding asylum seekers by clarifying responsibility for refugees and adhering to a "principle of first-asylum-country." This principle means that refugees are not allowed to seek asylum in multiple countries and that they must apply for asylum in the first country entered. This principle prevents multiple states from examining a refugee and shuttling them from country to country in the interim, and requires that one, and only one, member state handles the refugee's case. The Dublin Convention was signed in 1990 and went into effect in most of Europe, including Sweden, in 1997.

Also in 1997, the Integration Office published guidelines on how municipalities may assist the integration of refugees by using individualized introduction plans. Such plans have the purpose of providing the individual with the prerequisites needed to become economically independent and part of Swedish society. This and later documents declare that any health problems experienced by newly arrived adults or children should be identified and attended to through health care and social provisions (Integrationsverket, 2004).

When an asylum seeker is granted a residence permit in Sweden, that person is entered in the civic registry and given a national registration number. Once registration is complete, it follows that the same rights and obligations as all other inhabitants living in Sweden become available. A national Swedish policy regarding health care during the first period of time for newly arrived, foreign-born people who have permission to stay in Sweden was signed by several national authorities in spring 2004 (Integrationsverket, 2004). This agreement was greatly and urgently needed to focus on a coordinated operation between society and its agencies and initiatives and the individual and that person's responsibilities and rights. The goals of this policy include:

- To increase health information about access, rights, and responsibilities
- To increase professional cooperation between the various agencies and those newly arrived
- To identify somatic, mental, and social risk factors for illness and offer suitable interventions when needed
- To work for the best of the child according to the Convention on the Rights of the Child
- To increase access to health examinations for newcomers, including asylum seekers
- To increase the management of absence from planned activities during the introduction program for newcomers
- To improve the reception of newcomers with disabilities
- To promote basic training and competence development among staff in health promotion

In unifying European resettlement programs, this national view would also be spread to other European countries.

Morbidity and Illness versus Coping

In general, the rates of mental health problems among refugees are uncertain and vary among different groups (patients or inhabitants in the community). So far, the evidence does show that in relation to several welfare indicators (e.g., employment, housing, poverty, and contact with neighbors), the situation is a negative one for refugees in Sweden. Refugees incur significant morbidity in mental disorders when compared with Swedish-born inhabitants. On the other hand, positive factors that enable high-risk individuals to be psychologically resilient include having an effective support environment, positive personality characteristics with a sense of coherence, or access to reliable resettlement organizations. The response and functioning of parents during resettlement may also have a profound effect on their children.

Asylum Health Care versus Universal Health Services in Sweden

Sweden's health care policy states that subpopulations such as ethnic groups should have equitable access to health care (except some trauma services). It concludes that access mostly depends on being an official resident, that mainstream services seldom understand and respond to cultural differences among "outsiders," and that more special interventions are required (for more details, see Ekblad, 2004, p. 159). Ekblad (2004) gave a summary of Sweden's health care and refugee status:

> Under the Health and Medical Services Act, immediate health and medical care must be offered to a person currently staying within the county, even if that person is a nonresident. The same applies regarding immediate dental care, since asylum seekers and other foreign citizens who have app9lied for residence permits in Sweden are not registered as residents. Thus, county councils (or the equivalent) are under a limited obligation to provide heath and medical care for these groups of people, similar to the policies for temporary aliens. As permission is obtained for residence permits and settlement as a registered resident in a municipality, the county council (or the equivalent) requires similar obligations of this person as is required of Swedish citizens.

Under the Communicable Diseases Act, all examination, treatment, and care (medication included) necessary for the control of disease in connection with an epidemic is free of charge for the patient within the scope of county council (or the equivalent) health and medical care, as long as the patient is health-insured under the National Insurance Act. Under the State Compensation (refugee reception, etc.). Ordinance, county councils and municipalities receive economic compensation from the state in accordance with certain principles.

If the adult person is taken ill during the waiting period, he or she is entitled to emergency medical care and emergency dental care. The person is
required to pay a personal charge for every visit to a doctor at a health center or to a nurse, while asylum-seeking children are entitled to medical and
dental care on the same terms as other children in Sweden. Even so, there is
no charge for maternity care, preventive child and mother care, and care
under the Swedish Communicable Diseases Act. Dental care is free of
charge for children under 18 (Migrationsverket, 2000). If personal expenses
are high, the person may apply for medical care through a special grant
(Ekblad, 2004, p. 181).

A Reflection through a Case Study of Almira

Critical Incidents

Almira arrived by herself in Sweden as an asylum seeker in 1995 at
the age of 18. In March 1997 she received permission to stay two years.
She came from a wealthy Bosnian family in a village outside Belgrade.
The family had prospered in trade and had been leaders of their community. As the political tension had increased in the former Yugoslavia, the
family had been detained several times, and their savings had been lost
by the end of 1992. In 1994, Almira had become engaged to a medical
student who was at the military hospital, and in the autumn of that year,
she had started university studies to become an engineer. Three months
later, the university had been closed and Almira had returned to her parents' home.

She was forced to flee in the beginning of January 1995 because she
was accused of spreading Islam, although she and her family were not
practicing Muslims. She reported a history of persecution, arrest, detention, imprisonment, and torture in her village. She had been ill treated
on 10 separate occasions between 1985 and 1995. She had been subjected to various forms of torture, including exposure to cold showers or
prevention of personal hygiene; deprivation of water, food, and sleep;
beating; being stripped naked and subjected to sexual torture (ethnic
cleansing) by police and military officers in groups; deprivation of medical care; isolation; threats against her family; and threats against her own
life while a gun was held to her head. On one occasion, she was imprisoned for six months when she was nearly 17 years old. The family members' status in the village was debased, and the neighbors gave insulting
nicknames to them. Almira had been hurt, had felt hopeless, and was full
of despair and anger when she decided to flee to her brother in Sweden.
She left the country after the last detention and in agreement with her
fiancé and her parents. She had hopes that her fiancé could follow her to
Sweden.

Social and Economic Conditions during the Asylum Process and Asylum

The Swedish Migration Board processes the applications: Officers at the Migration Board investigate the reasons and justification for each refugee applicant to determine allowance to stay in Sweden, and the process is confidential to maintain privacy. Like other asylum seekers, Almira received a SIV card, which demonstrates that the person is seeking asylum in Sweden, while signing up for daily or housing benefits; visiting a doctor, nurse, or dentist; or obtaining prescriptions at a pharmacy. Almira was informed of the following provisions and rights:

- Family-based activity: The adults together with the staff are responsible for planning and conducting activities.
- Education: School is compulsory for children.
- Language: Swedish language instruction for is available for adults, including general instruction about life in Sweden.
- Work: If the asylum case takes more than four months to decide, the applicant can work in Sweden.
- Health checks and medical care: The applicant is offered a free health examination. In this examination, medical samples will be taken and the person will have the opportunity to talk to medical staff.

Step 1. Psychological Assessment

Key Clinical Questions

A combination of quantitative and qualitative methods based on revised valid and reliable instruments in cross-cultural research is valuable.

A newcomer such as Almira may discuss postmigration stress in relation to:

- Her personal and social characteristics (e.g., personality; gender; age; family status; education; ethnic, cultural, or religious background)
- Her past events in her home country (e.g., life in Bosnia with her family when life was normal, what happened, what changed, her feelings about life once it was no longer normal, and events that led up to her flight)
- Her resettlement (e.g., the journey, experiences of initial resettlement, waiting time for asylum)
- Her preoccupation and conditions at the time of the interview (e.g., feelings about changes she is facing, in career goals and family roles)
- Her perceived health, including her use of tobacco, alcohol, and drugs

At the end of the assessment, the asylum seeker is asked if the questions have been (1) difficult to answer, (2) relevant, and (3) not insulting. The asylum seeker is also asked to return for follow-up treatment in one, three, and six months.

Bringing in the Psychologist: Role and Goals

Sometimes, the physician or another clinical health professional may assess that the refugee has memory problems, intellectual capacity reduction, motor anxiety, and personality disorder, prompting an examination by a psychologist. When the psychologist meets with the refugee, the psychologist is expected to attempt to perform three fundamental tasks: (1) to establish rapport and trustworthiness, (2) to understand the refugee's challenges (both problems and resources), and (3) to have the ambition to make a difference. Just as the psychologist has such an agenda for the meeting, the refugee has agendas and is expected to assume responsibilities. However, these tasks are challenged when the psychologist and the refugee do not share the same language. The psychologist is also encouraged to respect the refugee's boundaries when choosing an interpreter, who should not be a family member, an authority in the community, or unskilled in refugee mental health. The first example—an interpreter who is not a family member—is especially important in regard to parents and children. Children often learn the host country's language sooner than their parents; however, according to the Convention of the Right of the Child, children should not interpret for their parents, because (1) the issues that parents would want to discuss may be too abstract for children to explain, (2) parents may be unwilling to tell children what kind of traumatic events they have gone through, (3) allowing children to interpret will affect their status in the family.

The Value of Interpreters

When the psychologist is able to recognize that postmigration stress and acculturation have resulted in physical and psychological symptoms, the psychologist has the opportunity to validate the refugee's distress. The psychologist may also provide support and resources for the refugee's acculturation and describe values and manners in the host (i.e., Swedish) society. To be able to offer such validation and advice, the psychologist and the refugee must be able to communicate with one another.

Unfamiliar words are among the most salient instances of cultural distance between refugee and psychologist. Any newcomer who needs an interpreter when meeting social and health care staff or other officials in the asylum and/or resettlement process—like Almira—has the right to one. Relations between interpreters and refugees of the same language may be complicated by gender, social class, religion, region of origin (especially dialects), and other social, political, and historical factors; nevertheless, interpreters are an important tool and they should be welcomed into the process. Interpreters should always introduce themselves and explain that they interpret for all in the room and practice professional secrecy. During the interview, the psychologist talks directly to the refugee while the interpreter sits in a triangle with the other two.

Providing an Assessment

Preparation and Conduct

Before the meeting with the refugee:

- Review the policy with the interpretation service.
- Inform the interpretation service that the meeting may be difficult (i.e., traumatic life events may be discussed). If the interpreter was also a refugee and is lacking psychological distance from personal traumatic memories, the interpreter may be unable to provide an objective interpretation on hearing the trauma story.
- Determine the required abilities of the interpreter: which language and which dialect? Also determine whether or not the interpreter needs to know any special vocabulary to communicate with the refugee. Finally decide which gender interpreter would be more appropriate.
- Select a neutral room in the office and put "Please do not disturb" on the door.
- Welcome the interpreter into the staff room; don't leave the interpreter in the waiting room.
- Invite the interpreter to stay for a follow-up talk about the process after the refugee has departed from the room.

During the assessment and follow-ups:

- Ask everyone to shut off mobiles, pagers, and similar devices in order to be fully present at the talk.
- Inform everyone of the aim of the interview and the role of the interpreter. Let the refugee know that after the refugee's departure, the psychologist and the interpreter will stay to discuss interpretation issues (not to discuss the refugee).
- Maintain a respectful, humane, and polite manner during the dialogue.
- Give short and clear questions, avoiding technical terms.
- Listen to the expressive characteristics of patient's voice (pitch, speed, emotions, silence, pause).
- Use the time during interpretation to reflect on the content.
- Dare to interrupt, as you are responsible if the information does not come to the patient in a proper way.
- Do not interrupt the interpreter during interpretation.
- Explain assessment and treatment. Also, explain why that particular treatment is recommended.
- Make sure that the patient understands the symptoms.
- Let the patient give a summary of the interview. Discuss rehabilitation, follow-up meetings, schedule, and the experience of the interpretation.

After the meeting:

- Review the session with the interpreter after the refugee has left. The aim of such a debriefing is to go over the interpretation process and discuss interpretation challenges—not to discuss the refugee.

Purpose

- To verify whether the symptom depends on trauma or other factors.
- To recognize and identify psychological distress, perceptual and developmental disabilities, and brain damage in asylum seekers.
- To determine what personal and social resources the refugee has, including a strong identity, a sense of coherence, or a sense of humor: Does the refugee have an ability to relate and to act? Does the refugee have a good self-image?

Tools: Definitions and Organization

Available assessment tools include a personality test, an intelligence test, a neurological test, a language test, a rehabilitation test, and different kinds of validated trauma and postmigration screening instruments, together with a narrative approach to let the refugee tell the story of personal trauma. All of these psychological assessments are not sensitive to language and culture differences in norms and should not be used in every such case.

Preparing a Psychological Assessment

- Recognize that the refugee and the psychologist usually have different needs, expectations, and motives in psychological assessment.
- Consider that the motivation for the refugee to participate in a psychological assessment may be influenced by the person who referred the refugee.
- Remember that there are differences in definitions of concepts and norms (i.e., personality, intelligence, quality of life, adaptation, integration, normality, etc.). Also, remember that there are differences in perception of the body and view on development, child-rearing, roles in the family, time, space, causes, or situations that may influence the result of the psychological assessment.
- Select the proper tools in view of the refugee's cognitive, intellectual, mental, and social capabilities, school years, culture, and so forth, in order to perform a realistic assessment.
- Consider that questionnaires, registration, and so forth can contribute to the refugee's anxiety, because the assessment situation can cause flashbacks to earlier traumatic events.
- Evaluate the results of the psychological testing in view of both the general refugee crisis and the specific postmigration stress the refugee is undergoing.

- Consider how the refugee is handling paper and pen (to write or to draw). Also, note if the refugee is able to see parts and wholeness, to think abstractly and linearly, and to think and understand arrangements of picture sequences.

Almira's Case

The first time I met Almira for a psychological health screening was in the winter of 1997, just when she had received asylum from the Swedish immigration office. She was absentminded and had difficulties sleeping and concentrating. It was difficult to communicate with her during the screening interview, even through an interpreter. Almira had very high scores for depression and trauma. She had left her fiancé and her parents in the former Yugoslavia. In a session in the beginning, she stated, "I remember how my family and Bosnian group in the village, our collective gave me protection and security, a feeling of belonging and identity, as well as emotional and practical support when I was young, but during the increased crises they failed." The loss of meaning that her stable family used to provide left her in a state of bewilderment and uncertainty, with feelings of helplessness, hopelessness, and vulnerability to suicidal thoughts and post-traumatic stress disorder (PTSD) during the two years of waiting time; these negative feelings caused her to either not discuss trauma at all or to tell stories inconsistently, which influenced her credibility as an asylum seeker.

In Sweden, Almira was not without social resources: Instead of living at a reception center, she chose to live with her brother and his family, who gave her a lot of emotional and practical support. She also received support from her cultural organization group as well as from the neighbors and staff in the reception program. However, Almira had such an extreme nightmare that her screaming woke up everybody at home. This incident made it obvious that Almira needed professional support to manage her problems. The medical care unit responsible for asylum seekers and refugees told me that they had too much to do and could not take care of Almira. She was offered treatment by me and a psychiatrist on our clinical team at the outpatient psychiatric clinic.

Step 2. Ecological Model of Intervention

The newcomer requires support and access to gender-, culture-, and age-sensitive interventions to promote health care and mental health.

Level 1: Health Information and Education in Group

Like every asylum seeker, Almira was invited for a health screening, including a dental examination, blood tests for communicable diseases (e.g., malaria, tuberculosis, HIV/AIDS, dysentery, and respiratory infections), an eye exam, a hearing exam, and a motor skills exam. Soon after arrival in

Sweden in the beginning of 1995, the nurse in primary care referred her to a public health group because her problems were mostly related to mental illness but not considered to be in a state of emergency during her waiting time for asylum. She received medication to aid sleep but because biological diversity across ethnic groups played a role in her differential sensitivity to that group of psychotropic medication, she stopped using these pills.

Almira was put in a group of other asylum seekers in a public health program that aimed to give information and general instruction on health matters and medical services in Sweden. Information also included contraception, the availability of gynecological health checks, and Swedish abortion law. During the course of four months, she met with the group twice a week and took a course given by a nurse regarding stress management, knowledge about public health, and promotion of mental health. As a group, they walked for exercise twice a week for an hour.

In her home country, Almira and her family had never experienced mental health services. Therefore, sensitive explanation was needed when informing her about the mental health services, including that they would be confidential and voluntary, and that receiving care would not change her status as refugee.

Throughout Sweden, several refugee psychiatric clinics for adults and children make treatment available for asylum seekers, and in Stockholm, the Red Cross Center and a refugee medical center offer care to refugees who have suffered torture or been wounded in war. Because Almira settled in a suburb of Stockholm, she received treatment at the closest psychiatrist outpatient clinic.

I met Almira over the course of one year after she was granted asylum. The treatment strategies that I used were designed to promote "normalization." This normalization technique emphasizes sources of strength and coherence in the new environment, but may in some circumstances become a source of distress, re-traumatization, and sense of marginalization if used to excess and exclusion. A new kind of social resource was access to the Internet and a mobile phone, with which she had contact with her fiancé in the home country. I supported Almira in reestablishing the five adaptive systems and will give some examples.

To increase her feelings of safety, I used an intervention at the individual level by teaching Almira different strategies to manage her anxiety and traumatic memories. She also received medications from our psychiatrist.

I tried to influence the attachment system by supporting her management of the separation from her family and relatives in the home country. At the community level, her identity/role system was supported by giving her psychosocial support to introduce her to a practice and studies center where she secured a coach.

My intervention at the policy level was to try to speed up her reunion with her family by writing to the Swedish Migration Board and asking them to give priority to her case because of her health and social conditions. At last, the authority gave priority to her case. When I tried to speed up the reunion process, I paid attention to a Swedish foreign affair policy problem that put her family in danger: Because the Swedish Embassy was closed in Belgrade, her fiancé had to go to the Swedish Embassy in a nearby country several times to get the visa documents. During this period of separation, Almira's PTSD and depressive symptoms worsened, which prompted an invitation to start Cognitive Behavioral Therapy.

Level 2: Individual Therapy, Cognitive Behavioral Therapy (CBT)

CBT began by outlining Almira's symptoms of post-traumatic stress disorder, depression, and disability, including her suicidal thoughts after torture and beatings. Issues of roles and responsibilities within a traditional Bosnian family—postmigration and now in Sweden—were explored. She was asked her long-term goals and future ambitions regarding her acculturation as a family and as an individual? What were the obstacles? Were the relatives supportive of her? If yes, how could they support her in her acculturation process? If no, what were the main alternatives?

Level 3: Cultural Treatment

Linguistic and cultural issues may become barriers to treatment. Psychological tests to assess cognition may be irrelevant due to challenges in equivalence and illiteracy. A newcomer's idioms of distress may rely on a complex system of proverbs and metaphors that may cause miscommunication, early termination of treatment, or nonuse of mental health services. The level of stigmatization associated with mental illness and suffering varies from culture to culture, and motivates the level of desire to hide such complaints. In some cultures, there is reluctance to express emotions or to reveal traumatic experiences, such as sexual torture, until trust has been established. Beliefs that suffering is inevitable or that one's life is predetermined may deter some refugees (e.g., those with a Muslim background) from seeking health care. Cultures may use more or less effective traditional medicine or religious/traditional ceremonies for treatment and be less familiar with the Western mental health interventions. In more traditional cultures, disturbances of mood are not viewed as mental health problems but as social or moral problems and are handled within the culture. Cultural communication of manifest mental illness and social problems may in different cultural context be communicated as "thinking too much," a cognitive dysfunction.

Hence, pressuring refugees to tell their story may be counterproductive and may influence an underlying mental disorder such as psychotic illness. Indirect methods may be sufficient in such circumstances. Mental illness, including suicidal thoughts and paranoia symptoms, may subject the individual to discrimination. In Almira's case, it was valuable to ask the name of her symptom and the attitude and expected treatment in her home context. It is also valuable to note her tendency to disassociate and her view of authorities, which included being passive in a doctor–patient relationship. By contrast, Western social science is practiced in a context of less hierarchy than she would have experienced in Bosnia. If the expectations of the power balance between staff and patients are much more relaxed than in the refugee's home country, the disparity may have a negative impact on the refugee's trust in officials.

Cultural difficulties extend beyond the mental sphere as well. Physical examination and body assessment is of special importance when dealing with torture. In Almira's case, it was important to ask if it would be acceptable in her culture for a male physician to examine her. In sum, our view of autonomy must respect the individual's cultural values in order for any decision-making process to succeed. In sum, culturally rooted traditions of religious beliefs and practices may determine a refugee's willingness to seek mental health services.

How to Show Respect during an Assessment

- Introduce yourself. Give information about your profession, the aim of assessment, resources available for rehabilitation, and professional secrecy.
- Give time for listening and reflection. Establish trust by showing you are ready to listen to the story and to hear the expectation and the hopes, at the refugee's own pace and in respect to the refugee's needs.
- Develop competence in assessment of suicidal thoughts, the understanding communication of somatization, and reading a patient who is silent. Unlike patients with psychosis, torture survivors may suffer quietly, despite our knowledge that torture increases risk of disability and co-morbidity.
- Develop competence in working with interpreters.
- Focus on the determination of needs and disabilities, the development of a plan for normalization, and the identification of resources.
- End the talk by discussing the "here and now" and/or the future, regarding such items as rehabilitation, collaboration with reception agencies, and so forth.
- As a psychologist working with asylum seekers and refugees, ask for supervision and a "coach" in order to reduce your irrational reactions to refugee encounters (avoidance, curiosity, overprotection, lack of professional distance); seek a helper when the professional demands increase.

Flight into exile and the process of seeking asylum include additional post-migration stressors that may complicate the effects of a torture experience and therefore make treatment more difficult. A psychiatrist at the outpatient clinic who had met Almira because of her sleep problems referred her to our local team of psychologists for assessment of her psychological problems. The purpose of CBT was to investigate whether CBT was effective in a refugee who had fled into exile.

In the psychiatric examination, she reported recurrent flashbacks and nightmares when faced with reminders of the torture (e.g., particular smells), problems with sleep and nightmares, problems with concentration, sensitivity to irritation, fatigue, cognitive problems ("thinking too much" of the torture events), pains in the neck, and feelings that she was still under threat from home country authorities (i.e., police and military officers who had raped her), although she knew that she was safe in Sweden. She was longing for her family and also for her fiancé, who tried to come to Sweden as a relative, (relatives must arrive within two years after her permission to stay to get into the resettlement program in the community). She tried to reduce her anxiety, anger, and sensitivity to irritation by drinking wine and walking outside in the morning for one hour while smoking.

At the psychiatric outpatient clinic, she was offered a course of CBT, started by me as a psychologist, and supervised and evaluated by a senior clinician in CBT. The written informed consent was translated by an authorized translator and orally back-translated by another authorized translator. The two versions were compared, a few revisions made, and Almira accepted it. She was reassured of professional secrecy: We emphasized that information would not be made available to a third person without her permission. Treatment started in October 1997. (For assessment and more details about CBT see Basoglu, Ekblad, Bäärnhielm & Livanou, 2004.)

The inclusion criteria were a history of torture, the absence of severe depression with serious suicidal intent, and the willingness to receive CBT. To control for possible effects of time and clinician contact, two baseline assessments were conducted in four weeks by me because there were no independent assessors available at the clinic at the time of Almira's CBT. Treatment started after the second baseline and spanned four months total, and assessments continued posttreatment at one, three, and six months.

At the first baseline, Almira received information about her symptoms and their relationship to her torture experience. After that, she was given information about the rationale of CBT. Almira was informed that prolonged exposure to trauma cues would reduce distress and increase a sense of control over traumatic stress challenges. After the second baseline, she was given actual exposure instructions in 12 sessions, about once a week and with the help of a female interpreter that Almira could trust.

Almira's CBT started by asking her to list in a hierarchical fashion (from least to most distressing) the activities that she avoided as a result of the trauma. She avoided traveling on buses because that triggered flashbacks of several incidents when the police caught her on a bus. She postponed several meetings with her immigration officer because she did not want to talk about the torture experience. She did not want to watch TV or other media because news depicting violence reminded her of being tortured. She avoided social contacts as she had difficulties trusting other people. Furthermore, she avoided sleeping because of her fear of nightmares about the torture.

After writing the list, Almira, in consensus with me, her psychologist, was instructed to perform treatment targets, that is, daily self-exposure for about an hour to situations that were distressing for her until she did not feel anxious. The first exposure was to ride buses and was performed with me. The next exposures were to meet the immigration officer, to read a newspaper, and to talk with people in the street. She kept a diary, recording her homework assignments, her anxiety, and her self-control ratings before, during, and after each session. She started with these treatment targets of least anxiety-evoking situations and continued during treatment to the more distressing situations. Anxiety was rated on a 0–8 scale before, during, and after each exposure task. When she had a rating of 2 (she said that she was unable to come down to 0 because her experience of torture had changed her personality), she continued with the targets.

During each weekly session, any cue and environmental circumstance that increased her distress at the time of each exposure task was discussed with the patient. She received verbal praise for each task and was encouraged to perform subsequent exposure tasks. Her CBT focused less on cognitive than behavioral interventions. At the end of the four months' treatment and during the three follow-ups afterward at one month, three months, and six months, the improvement was stable. Her fiancé came to Sweden during the second month of the treatment, which may have also influenced her well-being. After six months, she has become a medical student and has married her fiancé who has continued with his medical studies here as well. They have their own flat, and have positive hopes for the future.

Do Psychological Assessment and Mental and Psychosocial Services Have Any Effect?

By working in partnership with different health and adaptive systems, and including and respecting the refugee during the process to detect and understand mental and psychosocial needs, psychologists can find and implement the proper arrangement. By emphasizing mental health promotion of the basic needs at first and indirectly working with disorder, improved well-being can be achieved.

My interpretation of Almira's case is that without this treatment approach, she would have been hospitalized, which would have made normalization of her life difficult and would have been very expensive for society.

Ethics

In postmigration stress and resettlement mental health services, the psychologist may get intimate information on the refugee's life before flight and after resettlement. Screening and other assessment information concerning personal experiences may be intrusive and invasive. The psychologist or the interpreter may also have refugee backgrounds and may be sensitized to trauma experiences. All these circumstances may generate ethical dilemmas, as explained in relation to the case described above. On some occasions, the psychologist as interviewer has the dual identity of mental health professional on the one hand and researcher using the framework of the medical system and studying a vulnerable patient, a refugee with postmigration stress, on the other.

Therefore, I recommend following the guidelines for biomedical research ethics in qualitative mental health research and clinical work set out in the World Medical Association Declaration of Helsinki (2000). This declaration noted that two of the basic principles are (1) the right of the research subjects to safeguard their integrity must always be respected (Principal No 21) and (2) that each potential subject must be adequately informed of the aims, methods, anticipated benefits, potential hazards, and the discomfort the study may entail (Principal No 22). Furthermore, four ethical concepts are used in general: autonomy, non-malfeasance, beneficence, and justice (for a review, see Bäärnhielm & Ekblad, 2002).

Recommendations and Conclusions of Statements

Statement #1. Many refugees are influenced by loss and separation from close attachment figures, and a high level of affective social support reduces the vulnerability for psychiatric disorders, especially depression and social dysfunction.

Statement #2. An early mental health prevention reception program for asylum seekers and new refugees is essential for recovery. Regular clinical-based service needs to be complemented with a smörgåsbord of culturally grounded, community-based strategies that are usually not included in mental health care.

Statement #3. Human rights violations precipitate PTSD and suicidal thoughts.

Statement #4. A strong sense of coherence is correlated with low feeling of pain, low PTSD, and low depressive symptoms.

Statement #5. Psychological barriers to the use of health and social services among refugees may be heightened by mistrust, stigma, cost, and clinician bias.

References

American Psychological Association. (2002). Guidelines on multicultural education, training, research, practice, and organizational change for psychologists. Retrieved March 9, 2005, from http://www.apa.org/pi/multiculturalguidelines/guideline4.html

Antonovsky, A. (1993). The structure and properties of the Sense of Coherence Scale. *Social Science and Medicine, 36,* 725–733.

Bäärnhielm, S., & Ekblad, S. (2002). Qualitative research, culture and ethics: A case discussion. *Transcultural Psychiatry, 39*, 469–484.

Basoglu, M., Ekblad, S., Bäärnhielm, S., & Livanou, M. (2004). Cognitive-behavioral treatment of tortured asylum-seekers: A case study. *Journal of Anxiety Disorders, 18*, 357–369.

Ekblad, S. (2004). Migrants: Universal health services in Sweden. In J. Healy & M. McKee (Eds.), *Health care: Responding to diversity* (pp. 159–181). Oxford, England: Oxford University Press.

————, & Jaranson, J. (2004). Psychosocial rehabilitation. In J. P. Wilson & B. Drozdek (Eds.), *Broken spirits: The treatment of traumatized asylum seekers, refugees, war and torture victims.* New York: Brunner-Routledge Press.

Integrationsverket. (2004). Retrieved March 9, 2005, from http://www.integrationsverket .se

Migrationsverket (2000). Retrieved March 9, 2005, from http://www.migrationsverket .se

————. (2004). Retrieved September 29, 2005, from http://www.migrationsverket .se/info-material/om_verket/ek_redovisningar/ar2004_sammandrag_en.pdf

Mollica, R. (2003, October). *New definitions of health. Lecture on health promotion, mental health and mutual assistance associations.* Cambridge, MA: Harvard Program in Refugee Trauma.

Statistics Sweden (2003). Statistical yearbook of Sweden, volume 89. Stockholm: Author.

United Nations High Commissioner for Refugees. (1951, July). Convention Relating to the Status of Refugees. Geneva, Switzerland: Author.

World Health Organization. (1948). *Constitution of the World Health Organization.* Geneva: Basic Documents. Retrieved March 10, 2005, from http://w3.whosea .org/aboutsearo/const.htm

————. (2001). Rapid assessment of mental health needs of refugees, displaced and other populations affected by conflict and post-conflict situations [Document no. MNH/MHP/99.4. Rev.1]. Geneva, Switzerland. Retrieved March 10, 2005, from www.acdi-cida.gc.ca/cida_ind.nsf/0/60d4aa717ccfeb7d85256ae7004de477/$FILE/Hu8.pdf

World Medical Association (2000). World Medical Association Declaration of Helsinki: Ethical Principles for Medical Research Involving Human Subjects. Adopted by the 18th World Medical Association General Assembly, Helsinki, Finland, June 1964, and amended in October, 2000, Edinburgh, Scotland. Retrieved October 1, 2005, from http://www.wma.net/e/policy/pdf/17c.pdf

A Framework for Developing and Implementing Multiple-Family Groups for Refugee Families

Dheeraj Raina, Stevan Weine, Yasmina Kulauzovic,
Suzanne Feetham, Merita Zhubi, Dzana Huseni, and Ivan Pavkovic

Introduction

Refugee Mental Health Services and Family Interventions

The first wave of clinical mental health responses to refugees in resettlement countries took the form of trauma clinics in the United States (Kinzie & Tran, 1980) and torture rehabilitation centers in Europe (Garcia-Peltoniemi & Jaranson, 1989). Generally, their focus was on treating individuals for post-traumatic stress disorder, using psychotherapy and medications. More recently, increasing numbers of affected populations, the growing sensitivity to cross-cultural approaches, and the heightened recognition of the public health risk posed by mental health problems (De Girolamo & McFarlane, 1996) have led to increased interest in family interventions for refugees (de Jong, 1999).

Following refugee trauma, the family is often the only remaining social structure in an unfamiliar and difficult environment. Families must mediate individual family members' connectedness to the world—a burden that is complicated because the family itself may be traumatized (Weine et al., 2004). Among refugee families, the family plays a major role in shaping individual survivors' response to distress, coping ability, and choices. An individual survivor's adaptation to life after trauma is influenced by the family's adaptation, which in turn is affected by the stage of the family life cycle and the individual development of family members.

How can mental health, health care, and social service professionals best address the actual needs of refugee families in ways that build upon the strengths that reside in those families? Serious attempts to face this question with family interventions are scarce. Perhaps this scarcity results from the difficulty of developing and implementing new interventions that are empirically based, theoretically justified, and scientifically evaluated, all in a family frame (Campbell & Patterson, 1995; Gilliss & Davis, 1992). Creating family interventions requires actual engagement and collaboration with families, communities, and service organizations under circumstances that are often far less than ideal. Refugee communities and related service organizations are often both in transition and resource poor themselves. Another difficulty is that there is no way to adequately approach family interventions with refugees without adopting a broad intellectual view, taking into account such concerns as ethnic nationalism, colonization, traumatization, immigration, cultural transition, poverty, ethnicity, gender, and development.

Responding to the Case of Kosovar Resettlement in Chicago

When Kosovar refugees started arriving in Chicago in 1999, our university/community collaborative group (currently named the International Center on Responses to Catastrophes at the University of Illinois at Chicago) had five years of experience providing mental health services to Bosnians and conducting services-based studies concerning refugees. We were already conducting the first systematic study of a family-focused intervention with a refugee population: the CAFES (Coffee and Family Education and Support) intervention for Bosnian refugees in Chicago (Weine, 1998). CAFES is an intervention that uses time-limited multiple-family groups. It is rooted in the literature on innovative community and family-focused interventions with other marginalized populations (Elliot & Tolan, 1999; McKay, Gonzalez, Stone, Ryland, & Kohner, 1995; Szapocznik et al., 1988). As its name indicates, CAFES takes a different approach from the family therapy literature on refugee mental health, which has often emphasized problematic interpersonal aspects of the survivor experience (Weine, 1998). CAFES is based upon family strengths (Rolland, 1994; Walsh, 1998) and family ecological approaches (Bubolz & Sontag, 1993; Klein & White, 1996).

In spring 1999, officials from the State of Illinois Department of Human Services expressed concern that the newly arriving Kosovars might not readily access existing refugee mental health services and asked if we thought they could benefit from a CAFES-like approach. The CAFES team shared that concern and thought that a CAFES intervention for newly resettled Kosovars could fit this population's needs.

We formed an exploratory team that included academic professionals, persons from the Kosovar and Bosnian refugee communities, and persons from refugee service organizations in Chicago. The team consisted of the following persons.

- Project Director: Stevan Weine, MD, a psychiatrist with clinical, teaching, and research experience who had led the development and implementation of CAFES for Bosnian refugees and is the Director of the International Center on Responses to Catastrophes
- Project Manager: Yasmina Kulauzovic, OT, an occupational therapist who was also the project manager for CAFES
- Family Outreach Workers: Merita Zhubi and Mejreme Delisi, Kosovar immigrants (not refugees) from the erstwhile Yugoslavia who had no professional training or experience but were actively involved in the Albanian-speaking community in Chicago
- Mental Health Outreach Worker: Dzana Huseni, RN, a nurse by training and a Bosnian refugee with Kosovar heritage who spoke Albanian fluently and had experience doing casework and therapy at a refugee mental health clinic
- Psychiatrist: Dheeraj Raina, MD, a psychiatrist doing a fellowship in refugee mental health who had experience providing clinical treatment at a refugee mental health clinic
- Consultants: Ivan Pavkovic, MD, a senior psychiatrist from Croatia practicing in U.S. public sector mental health; and Suzanne Feetham, PhD, RN, a family nursing researcher

We looked to the existing literature but could find no direction there about developing a family intervention with newly arriving refugees. However, some reports did address related concerns. Williams (1996) called for the development of preventive interventions to address mental health problems among refugees and torture survivors. There were also a few reports on preventive interventions with refugee youth (Lum, 1985; Owan, 1985), and on mutual assistance associations (Barger & Truong, 1978; Vinh, 1981). In addition, there was a literature on multicultural approaches and practices that explored the opportunities and difficulties involved when interventions cross cultural boundaries (Clifford, 1997; Marsella, Friedman, Gerrity, & Scurfield, 1996; McGoldrick, Giordana, & Pearce, 1996; Sue & Sue, 1999). However, none of these addressed Kosovars or Albanian culture. We read available texts concerning Kosovars in journalism, history, politics, and literature that focused primarily on the Serbian colonization of Kosovo and its consequences (Judah, 2000; Malcolm, 1998; Marx & Karp, 2000; Mertus, 2000).

Based on our experiences with CAFES and preliminary knowledge of the needs and strengths of Kosovar families, the exploratory team committed to developing a response called Tea and Family Education and Support (TAFES, so named because Kosovars prefer tea). The overall aim was to make TAFES a contextually appropriate modification of CAFES (Weine, 1999) and to begin providing its services for the newly arrived Kosovar refugees.

To learn from the experience of building a multiple-family group intervention for refugees, the team also committed to documenting and analyzing the process of developing and implementing TAFES. The sections that follow present a framework for developing and implementing multiple-family groups with refugee populations, illustrated with some examples from the experience with TAFES in Chicago.

Development

Developing a multiple-family group intervention for refugee families is a process that involves seven steps (see Table 3.1): (1) identifying a family conceptual framework; (2) understanding family meanings, needs, and strengths; (3) understanding community contextual realities; (4) identifying organizations' service capabilities; (5) selecting or adapting an intervention; (6) integrating with existing services; and (7) articulating specific aims and expected outcomes. The following sections describe each element, with examples of how they were applied in the development of TAFES.

Table 3.1
Elements of Development

---

1. Identifying a Family Conceptual Framework

2. Understanding Family Meanings, Needs, and Strengths

3. Understanding Community Contextual Realities

4. Identifying Organizations' Service Capabilities

5. Selecting or Adapting an Intervention

6. Integrating with Existing Services

7. Articulating Specific Aims and Expected Outcomes

Identifying a Family Conceptual Framework

A multiple-family group intervention must be informed by a theoretical framework that adequately explains the mental health issues concerning refugee families. The conceptual framework must be readily understandable by team members because it will be used to guide all subsequent steps of development and implementation, all the way through to evaluation. An existing family conceptual framework may be applied or modified as appropriate to best fit the current intervention context.

In the case of TAFES, we had previously developed the Prevention and Access Intervention for Families (PAIF) model for work with Bosnian families. It was based upon several years of clinical, research, and advocacy work. The PAIF model draws from family ecological theory, help-seeking theory, the social network approach, and the Family Systems–Illness Model (Bubolz & Sontag, 1993; Pescolido, 1986; Rogler & Cortes, 1993; Rolland, 1994). We will briefly summarize these theories.

Family ecological theory depicts the uniqueness of the family as a social organization and its absolute certainty in shaping human life. It explains how families adapt to changes in the environment. Help-seeking theory provides a framework for understanding the process by which family members seek mental health services. It explains the critical phases of problem recognition, the decision to seek help, and the decision to select specific services. The social network approach to mental health services looks at the role of community social networks in accessing or implementing effective services.

Rolland's Family Systems–Illness Model is a model for assessment, psychoeducation, and intervention with families facing psychosocial demands associated with illness and disability. This model focuses on "normal" families struggling to master difficult life experiences, especially chronic illness. It claims that in order to meet the challenges of a disorder, the family needs to (1) understand the expected pattern of practical and emotional demands of a disorder over its course; (2) understand itself as a functional unit in systems terms; (3) gain an appreciation of individual and family life cycles, in order to stay attuned to the changing fit between demands of the disorder and developmental issues for the family and its individual members; and (4) understand the values, beliefs, and multigenerational legacies that underlie health problems and the types of caregiving systems they establish.

This model suggests that a "normal" family can cope affirmatively with an overwhelming life experience if its members understand the long-term demands of this experience, appreciate how the members function as a system, are sensitive to life-cycle demands of other family members and of the family as a whole, and attend to values and beliefs that influence caregiving approaches in their family.

The PAIF model, which draws from the above approaches, makes the following four central assumptions:

1. The family is the primary social unit for individual refugees. It mediates refugees' connections to other families and to community groups and organizations, to the resettlement service system, and to mental health and health service systems.

2. The family as a system is critically important for guiding and supporting its members' approaches to a wide range of choices that have major influence on their adjustment and recovery as refugees.

3. Traumatization and displacement in refugee families can overwhelm and undo the inherent strengths that reside in families, because their existing values and behaviors may not fit so well the demands of their present and future lives. They also may not fit the resources external to the family, including those of other families and community and service organizations.

4. Through support and education aimed at helping refugee families to adapt their family beliefs and behaviors to better fit the demands of the new situations, family interventions can influence how families will take the appropriate steps toward adjustment, acculturation, and recovery.

An intervention based on the PAIF model does not necessarily aim to treat a symptom or a disorder. The prevention component of such intervention aims to help families draw upon their own strengths and resources to cope together with survival and displacement, thus minimizing or preventing the secondary and tertiary consequences of their trauma. The access component seeks to improve families' ability to obtain appropriate care, from sources outside of the family, for possible mental health consequences of trauma and displacement. This model tries, through the modality of multiple-family groups, to help families help themselves, or to get additional help for themselves.

It is important to note that this conceptual framework is very different from that which typically guides existing refugee mental health services. These tend to be clinic-based services, driven by traumatic stress theory that emphasizes the individual and psychopathology. These approaches are also associated with an attitude of waiting for patients to present (Winett, King, & Altman, 1989). These services can be helpful to those willing to present, but they do not primarily attend to the myriad of challenges facing those refugee families who would never present for mental health services, such as the challenges the Kosovar families described.

Understanding Family Meanings, Needs, and Strengths

To identify family meanings, needs, and strengths within a given refugee community, it is necessary to have sufficient immersion among multiple families in multiple settings. This immersion may involve such approaches as open-ended interviewing, participant observation, and focus groups. Team members should enter into this process with certain questions and assumptions about important aspects of family life already formulated. It is essential that they be prepared to make revisions to the intervention plan based upon the needs, meanings, and strengths of the families themselves. Important realms to investigate include definitions of families; family roles and obligations; gender roles; family beliefs; family communication; family attitudes toward suffering and injustice; family attitudes regarding youth and education; family attitudes regarding work and finances; distress in family members; available information among family members; social contacts or networks of family members; and attitudes toward the migration or return of family members.

Prior to initiating TAFES, we conducted qualitative interviews and participant observation with Kosovar families and other key informants in multiple settings. In April 1999, Weine went to Germany in order to meet with families who had arrived in the prior two weeks from Kosovo via Macedonia (with Sabina Luebben and other German colleagues of the Frankfurter Arbeitskreis Trauma und Exil organization). From March to August 1999, team members met with the first Kosovar arrivals in the United States. In August 1999, Weine and Zhubi visited Kosovo in order to conduct further ethnographic inquiry on Kosovar families and on the psychosocial services of both international and Kosovar organizations.

All the Kosovars we met were highly oriented around family. Their families tended to be large, and in the cases of the more rural families they were organized as extended families comprising several nuclear families (of the brothers). Kosovars explained that they depended first and foremost on their families for support and guidance: "Our families are everything to us." Their primary obligation was to protect and support their family members, which includes protection against other Kosovar families. Kosovar families tend to be highly patriarchal, with the eldest man making the important decisions and serving as the gatekeeper for all family members' relationships with outsiders. It is also necessary to note that Kosovar culture has a tradition of family blood feuds that remains a part of the culture (Kekezi & Hida, 1991). For example, if a man's wife or daughter is insulted by a man from another family, then the insulted family is obligated to protect the family's honor.

One central concern of Kosovar families was the question of whether to return to Kosovo. In Germany, all the refugees said they wanted to return to Kosovo as soon as possible. One man said, "Yes, of course I want to return. We did not run away. We were forced." None admitted to being interested in the possibility of life in Germany or the United States. Even though the fate of Kosovo was not known at that early point (April 1999), Kosovars still reported that most refugee families would far prefer to be in Kosovo than to resettle in the United States.

Yet many did stay in the United States. In Chicago, it was estimated that approximately one-fourth of Kosovar refugees returned to Kosovo within months of liberation, approximately one-half resolved to stay, and about one-fourth of the families reported that they were still in a dilemma. One woman said, "We want to stay for the kids." Another said, "Everybody who went back now wants to come back to America." We learned about some of the factors involved in this dilemma. Most Kosovar families had a tradition of sending members abroad to work, and they also valued greatly the opportunity to get their children educated. Many appeared to be seeing their refugee experience through those lenses.

Families expressed serious concerns regarding work and finances. One man said, "I would like to work, but I see what kind of jobs people are getting, and I do not know what I am going to do." This concern was especially great for refugees who were educated and had skilled and professional occupations. Many said that because they were refugees, they expected better treatment than other immigrants. They wanted to work and make money, but were unfamiliar with work life in America (i.e., how to keep a job, how to get promoted, how to handle conflicts in the workplace, how to find a new job). Parents expressed concerns about the impact of events upon their children and about how the children would get the best education. Children and parents were unfamiliar with American schools and were having a lot of difficulties adjusting to school life. One worker said, "They are afraid their kids will become so Americanized here that they will lose control over them."

In both Germany and the United States, Kosovars were reluctant to ask for help from outside of their family for emotional and social problems. Each family supported not only their own members, but to some degree those in other families. This support reflected in part a Kosovar cultural value of family cohesiveness and solidarity, but it also reflected the fact that little or no social or mental health services had been available to them in Kosovo. Mental health services in Kosovo were primarily oriented to serving those with serious, chronic mental illness. Gender was also a factor here. Women did not speak to helping professionals without the permission of men in their families. Men, even helping professionals, could not visit women in their homes if the husband or father was not there, and if the husband or father had not met them first.

All the families visited in Germany and Chicago had had family members separated, missing, or killed. They had had very recent trauma exposure and loss-induced changes in their families. These factors implied that high rates of trauma-related mental health problems were to be expected, especially post-traumatic stress disorder (PTSD) and depression. They also had a history of oppression and violence that had made their lives especially difficult over the past 10 years. If large numbers of refugees were to arrive in Chicago (as they soon did), then it was likely that they were going to be seen at a very early juncture in the displacement and resettlement process (even earlier than had been the case with Bosnians).

In Chicago, individuals and families from Kosovo were highly alienated from the American health care and mental health systems, and especially from the approaches of mental health services. Nobody spoke openly about wanting mental health services, and families expressed tremendous fear and reservations about getting such help, even when suffering was present. It was clear that if the family (which usually meant the family's patriarch) didn't want it to happen, then it would not happen. Families tried their best to take care of their own. They also recognized that they needed help, but were confused or conflicted about where to turn. One said, "We will never be the same." After getting services, another said, "I wouldn't have known if I needed help." They relied on the older generation of Kosovar and Albanian immigrants, with more experiences in the United States, to guide them.

Based on these interviews and observations, the exploratory team provisionally concluded that refugee families had the following central concerns: (1) whether to stay or go; (2) how to adjust to work life in America; (3) how to help children; and (4) how to help vulnerable family members. We presumed that all Kosovar refugee families could potentially benefit from family support and education intervention that was focused on these concerns. In addition, we presumed that some Kosovar family members were at risk for PTSD and depression, and that those persons could benefit from clinical mental health services, if they so desired. But because these families were largely unfamiliar with mental health services, they were likely to need family education concerning trauma-related mental health issues as part of a family-focused prevention intervention.

Understanding Community Contextual Realities

In addition to learning about the families, it is necessary to learn about their community context, including such issues as cultural and social processes, tensions, crises, and obligations. The approach to learning about community context is similar to the previous one for understanding family. It depends upon multiple sources, qualitative approaches to data collection and analysis, and openness to revising. Specific issues of concern include defining the preexisting migrant community; identifying leaders, groups, and institutions; identifying attitudes of existing communities toward refugees; identifying communication channels in the community; and identifying the prevailing historical narratives by which the community defines the refugee experience.

Between March and May 1999, the TAFES exploratory team engaged in discussions with key informants in the Chicago Albanian community regarding how best to address the mental health needs of an anticipated large number of Kosovar arrivals. Interviews were also conducted with the small numbers of recent Kosovar arrivals and with older immigrants from Kosovo. We learned that in Chicago, the Kosovars were associated with a larger ethnic Albanian community. This Albanian community was highly dispersed throughout the huge metropolitan area, without any central organizations. There were no community, cultural, or social clubs. The organizations that were committed to working with Albanians were a travel agency, several restaurants, and several mosques. However, most Kosovars did not identify themselves as very involved in Islam, so it appeared unlikely that most families would take the initiative to seek help from the mosques. There was also a weekly radio show that was a reliable way of communicating with persons in the community. An Albanian newspaper published in New York was distributed throughout the ethnic Albanian community.

Kosovar life and culture primarily centers on the family. Families tended to gather themselves or get together with other families in their homes. It was common to hear the Kosovar immigrants who had been in the United States for years express concerns about how to keep their children connected with Kosovar values and language in America. They also had these concerns for the newer refugees.

Almost all Kosovars and Albanians that we spoke with were taking an active role in helping or rescuing family members in Kosovo, including sponsoring them to come to the United States as refugees. There was a tremendous sense of obligation to help, and there were many examples of altruism, such as older immigrant families hosting newer refugee families in their homes, or nearby. Because many of the immigrant families lived in the outer suburbs, it appeared that many of the refugees would also resettle there. It also appeared that the refugee resettlement organizations would probably not be assuming as large a role here as was the case in the resettlement of

Bosnian refugees. The combination of geographical disbursement and fewer ties to organizations was part of the reason that the exploratory team thought a family-focused, community-based outreach intervention was necessary and appropriate.

The team recognized the Kosovars' strong attachment to their homeland at this incredible historical moment. Kosovar refugees spoke of Kosovo as their homeland, which has been marked by colonization and oppression by the Serbian government, and a recent vicious campaign of depopulation. Kosovars are attached to Kosovo as a place where they knew suffering throughout their lifetimes. Treating them kindly as refugees does not change what many of them wanted. One said, "I am thankful for all this but my sadness has no price"—sadness because they were apart from their homeland. Another said: "I hope as soon as possible we can go back and free Kosovo."

Identifying Organizations' Service Capabilities

Multiple-family group interventions aim in part to help refugee families increase their access to other existing services, organizations, and resources outside the family. This expansion of access requires identifying the range of capabilities and resources that exist among multiple organizations that provide various services to refugees. Such organizations may include those that provide resettlement services, mental health services, and general medical services to refugees. They also include schools and religious and cultural organizations. Knowledge can be gathered through visits and dialogue with persons in these various organizations, and with refugees who have utilized their services. These contacts allow the multiple-family group team to identify areas of potential collaboration and coordination of services with these organizations. The multiple-family group project must organize itself, and simultaneously it must also develop productive collaborative relationships with other community and service organizations.

Regarding TAFES, refugees in Chicago were fortunate in the sense that the city has extensive and highly developed networks of organizations for refugee services, including resettlement social services, primary care health, and refugee mental health. One possible drawback was that several of the service organizations tended to be concentrated primarily in one part of the city, the Uptown neighborhood, although there have been more recent efforts to extend services out into the suburban areas where many refugees were resettling. In addition, other community-based organizations, such as mosques and schools, also became involved in providing some social services, although they may not have been especially focused on working with refugees.

There were no preexisting health or mental health services specifically for Albanians or Kosovars in Chicago, although there were several refugee service organizations that were prepared to offer health and mental health services to the Kosovars. Refugee mental health services in Chicago were well known to us through both direct clinical work (team members had worked at both agencies for years) and services-based research, including studies of refugee mental health providers. These services were organized with a clinic-based approach, typical of the field of refugee mental health as a whole.

The refugee mental health service network has tended to operate in the following way. Referrals to refugee mental health services are made from resettlement agencies or from the primary care workers. Thus, community social service providers and primary medical care providers play crucial roles in referring possible patients. However, these referrers tend to have understandable difficulties in confronting refugees' fears and discomfort with mental health services. Neither they nor the mental health provider organizations, nor anyone else, had conducted any systematic public health education in Chicago's refugee communities regarding trauma-related mental health. The refugee family was not a particular focus for any of the providers, including the mental health providers. These were some of the reasons for the concerns expressed by many observers and participants about how Kosovars would fare in this referral network.

Our university/community project already had multiyear, multidimensional collaborative relationships with the two refugee mental health clinics that involved provision of clinical services, teaching, and research. We asked the appropriate persons in these organizations if they would be willing to incorporate a family outreach approach into their service system. They reported that they perceived it as having not enough emphasis on mental health, and being too much like resettlement work. Conversely, when we approached the persons in resettlement organizations they also said no, reporting that they saw it as having too much emphasis on mental health. We conveyed our concerns that there was likely to be a gap between the agencies' approaches and the families' realities that could translate into access problems. Our argument did not prevail.

The state's director of refugee services proposed that instead we think of developing a university-based project that would work cooperatively with the refugee service organizations. We were willing to do so, and the state was willing to support it. However, we were aware that this path was not without difficulties. First, we still faced the challenge of how, as a family-focused intervention team, to work cooperatively with service providers and organizations that did not put the family in first place. Second, we were aware that our solution was essentially a short-term one that could provide services to Kosovars during the earliest phase of resettlement (no more than the first year), but was essentially not designed to result in lasting changes in service organizations. Besides, at that very early juncture, it was not clear how many Kosovars would arrive, whether they would stay or return, and to what extent service organizations would commit to working with them.

Selecting or Adapting an Intervention

The conceptual framework that is the foundation of a team's approach to understanding refugee families and communities, and to recognizing the capabilities and limitations of other service organizations, should also guide the selection or adaptation of the multiple-family group intervention. The intervention itself may have to be designed from the ground up, or it may be adapted from a similar intervention that was used for another group of refugee families in another time and another place. In designing or modifying multiple-family group interventions, it is important to take into consideration all the aforementioned factors concerning families, communities, and organizations.

Given that our team had already developed and implemented the multiple-family group intervention called CAFES (Coffee and Family Education and Support) for Bosnian refugee families in Chicago, we could draw upon that experience. However, simply using CAFES as it was would have been inappropriate and likely ineffective for Kosovar families, if not harmful. The Kosovar families presented important differences in family structure, language, culture, refugee experiences, and historical experiences that had to be taken into account. We made several structural and content changes for the TAFES intervention and prepared a modified group intervention manual, as well as a new intervention manual for outreach to families.

The structural changes were as follows.

- Knowing that these families preferred to be together, whole families were invited to attend the groups (a play group was provided for young children).
- In response to the sense of urgency that Kosovar families felt, the group was designed with fewer sessions over less time (six sessions over eight weeks for TAFES, instead of nine sessions over sixteen weeks for CAFES). Meetings were held once weekly for the first four weeks, then every other week.
- Fewer families were invited per group (four to six per group), because families were generally larger and high rates of participation were anticipated.
- Rather than being based in one community center, TAFES meetings were held in several different locations proximate to where the newly resettled Kosovar families were residing in the Chicago metropolitan area. Meetings lasted two hours and were held on weekday evenings or on weekends, to best accommodate families with working members.
- The entire manual had to be prepared in the Albanian language.

Content modifications were also made. First, given the concerns about stigma and access for families, it was decided to make engagement a higher priority for TAFES than it had initially been with the CAFES project. Recruitment methods were refined and an additional manual was prepared to guide the telephone and home contacts with families. Second, the multiple-family groups focused less on bicultural questions of family identity, as in the CAFES sessions (where it was necessary for Bosnians who were then several years into their displacement), and more on family cohesiveness, adjustment, and choices in the face of recent calamitous life events.

The central questions that were addressed with families in the groups represented a reframing of the highest-priority concerns that had emerged from the exploratory investigation of Kosovar families: (1) where is our family now? (2) should we stay or should we return? (3) how do we adjust to work life in America? (4) how do we speak with our children about all that has happened? (5) how do we get help for sadness, fear, and sleep problems? The TAFES intervention consisted of four phases:

1. Joining (family home visits and TAFES 1/week one)
2. Defining the Family and its Needs and Obligations (TAFES 2/week two, TAFES 3/week three)
3. Using Resources Outside of the Family (TAFES 4/week four)
4. Working Together in the Family (TAFES 5/week six, TAFES 6/week eight)

Integrating with Existing Services

Given that an overall aim of the multiple-family group intervention for refugee families is to help families to get help from other services, especially mental health services, it is necessary to make integrating with existing services a focus of the intervention development. The multiple-family group program must take responsibility for collaboration and coordination of services for participating families. Special concerns include accurate, respectful, and efficient communication and referrals, and avoiding unnecessary duplication of services or destructive tensions and competition between service agencies.

For example, the first priority in TAFES was to see that appropriate mental health services were available to Kosovar refugees who wanted these services as a consequence of being in the TAFES groups. As noted earlier, mental health services for refugees in Chicago were provided by several voluntary agencies. Our university group had been involved in providing mental health services to Bosnians in collaboration with the largest of those agencies, Heartland Alliance's Chicago Health Outreach (CHO), and had collaborated with the other service organizations in other ways. We wanted TAFES to work collaboratively with this mental health program, which was also going to be involved in the delivery of mental health services. Discussions with the leadership of CHO enabled us to articulate a common ground for working together. It was agreed that we would be the provider of family outreach and multiple-family groups and that they would be our preferred provider for mental health services. We also agreed to involve the new Kosovar mental health worker (DH) from the CHO in our project. As a nurse, she was to dedicate a proportion of her time to community outreach.

This outreach would include family home visits and mental health contacts in the community. She would assist in referring clients to TAFES and in working to see that mental health clients identified by TAFES were seen rapidly and appropriately. We agreed to provide the CHO with a psychiatrist (DR) doing a fellowship in refugee mental health who would work together with this nurse in providing clinical psychiatric services for Kosovars, either at the CHO clinic or in the community.

Integrating with existing services also involved non–mental health services, including social service agencies, resettlement agencies, primary care providers, hospitals, dentists, immigration lawyers, mosques, and schools. TAFES engaged in ongoing communication and collaboration with all of the above, especially the schools. During the first few multiple-family groups, the TAFES team realized that we had not anticipated one particular central concern of the Kosovar families—their apprehension about American schools. Although most of the parents were highly motivated to make use of the educational opportunities offered to their kids, they expressed concern about their own inability to properly negotiate complexities of the school system. For example, they had difficulty understanding why some of their children were placed in a grade level lower than their grade back in Kosovo. Some of them did not comprehend the meaning or significance of notes from teachers requesting a parent–teacher meeting. Others complained about the inadequacy of certain school-related services, such as transportation, and expressed frustration with their own inability to communicate these concerns to the schools.

Our team responded to these concerns by meeting directly with a school that had a concentration of Kosovar students. We communicated the families' concerns to teachers and school administration, and we elicited their impressions of challenges facing the refugee students. We described our project and its aims, and explained how we could help improve communication between the families and the school. This dialogue led to the school allowing us to host some multiple-family groups in its building. Having the sessions there allowed the families to feel greater comfort about the school environment. In addition, we modified the content of the presentations during the TAFES groups to specifically address the families' concerns about school and education.

Articulating Specific Aims and Expected Outcomes

It is essential for a multiple-family group intervention with refugee families to be organized around clearly stated specific aims and expected outcomes. Even if there is no research dimension to the intervention, having clear primary aims and outcomes facilitates the multiple-family group work. This is especially important given that multiple-family groups necessarily introduce a large amount of variability that can at times be distracting and overwhelming.

The primary aims of a multiple-family group informed by the PAIF model include both prevention and access. In short, prevention means helping family members to help themselves, and access means helping them to get help from other sources outside of the family. Prevention aims include increasing social support, social network, and family communication. Access aims include increasing knowledge, enhancing attitudes, and increasing service utilization. Other aims that address the community and organizational imperatives of the multiple-family group program should also be specified.

The TAFES aims were as follows. Regarding strengthening families, the aim of TAFES was to enhance access and to enhance prevention. A second aim of this project was to develop relationships with key mediators within the Kosovar community and the organizations that serve them. The team aimed to educate them about critical Kosovar family issues and to provide channels for ongoing communication and collaboration. A third aim was to provide specialized family-focused training to a group of Kosovar providers. A fourth aim was to facilitate or to provide mental health services to those Kosovars interested in receiving services. Finally, the fifth aim was to conduct quantitative and qualitative evaluations of these service activities that would contribute to a knowledge base on family-focused services interventions with refugees.

To evaluate the effectiveness of the TAFES intervention in strengthening families, it was necessary to specify study hypotheses that corresponded to measurable outcomes. We used the same primary hypotheses as in the CAFES study, where it was hypothesized that participation in the TAFES intervention would lead to improvements in four realms: (1) increased social support; (2) enhanced family processes (i.e., family hardiness); (3) improved knowledge and attitudes concerning mental health services for families; and (4) increased mental health service utilization. All instruments were translated into Albanian, using appropriate cross-cultural procedures (Keane, Kaloupek, & Weathers, 1996). To evaluate the effectiveness of TAFES regarding other aims, we developed a structured format to record qualitative notes of each session with every multiple-family group. Whereas the instruments selected to test the primary hypotheses were administered at designated time intervals, the qualitative data were reviewed by our team on a weekly basis to assess the extent to which TAFES was addressing the families' main concerns, and to identify issues we had not prepared for but were important to the families. These data were then used to modify the content of the group presentations to keep them relevant for the families. For example, this review led to the identification of concerns regarding schools and the inclusion of these concerns in the group sessions.

Implementation

Implementing a multiple-family group involves seven steps (see Table 3.2): (1) hiring staff; (2) training and supervising staff; (3) engaging refugee families;

(4) conducting multiple-family groups; (5) facilitating mental health contacts; (6) relating with other service providers; and (7) evaluating and disseminating project results. What follows is a description of these seven steps, based on how we addressed them in the TAFES intervention with the Kosovar community in Chicago.

Table 3.2
Elements of Implementation

---

1. Hiring Staff

2. Training and Supervising Staff

3. Engaging Refugee Families

4. Conducting Multiple-Family Groups

5. Facilitating Mental Health Contacts

6. Relating with Other Service Providers

7. Evaluating and Disseminating Project Results

Hiring Staff

Multiple-family groups for refugee families should be run by persons who have characteristics that best prepare them to serve as key mediators between the refugee families and the life in refuge. These mediators should be from the same ethnonational group as the refugees, but should also have at least several years of experience adjusting to life in the new country. They should be educated, but not necessarily in health sciences and not at a professional level. (In our experience, health professionals tend to approach the multiple-family group through a professional lens that is not family-focused, an approach that refugee families then perceive as being "health services as usual.") It is important that TAFES staff have had experiences doing group work of some kind (i.e., soccer coach, teacher, organizer). They have to be bilingual and able to combine the experience of being former immigrants or refugees with their experience of familiarity with American life. From the beginning—even during the hiring process—it is essential to emphasize with all staff the importance of being open and flexible, positive and energetic, committed and engaged. These qualities are recognized as being essential for successful multicultural practice (Sue & Sue, 1999).

In the case of TAFES, we were able to hire two Kosovar women to serve as TAFES family workers and group facilitators and one Bosnian/Kosovar woman nurse to serve as the mental health outreach worker for TAFES. Both women hired as family workers had immigrated several years ago and did not have any mental health background, but they were connected with the larger Kosovar immigrant community in Chicago to varying degrees. One of them had experience in co-managing a family business. Both had reached out to the Kosovar refugee families even before they were approached by TAFES, and the refugees found it easy to accept them as caring, respectful, and respected equals. The refugees confided in the family workers and sought their advice regularly. Consequently, both women were extremely effective in their roles as both family workers and group facilitators.

Our mental health outreach worker was herself a refugee from Bosnia-Herzegovina. The families had a natural level of comfort with her as a result of having shared similar traumatic experiences. All three women spoke Albanian fluently and were proficient in English. We were not set on hiring only women, but we soon discovered that one advantage of having them in this role was that it was more acceptable to Kosovar families for women, rather than men, to conduct home visits. In addition, one psychiatrist working as a fellow in refugee mental health at the University of Illinois at Chicago (UIC) was the psychiatrist for TAFES.

Training and Supervising Staff

Staff working with multiple-family groups require specific training in family issues and in multiple-family group modality. Staff should receive didactic training in the following areas: (1) principles of prevention and access interventions; (2) roles of the family in prevention and access; (3) family ecological theory; (4) the Family Systems–Illness Model; (5) multiple-family groups; (6) psychoeducation; and (7) ethnocultural issues. Didactic lectures should be supported by directed readings and viewing of videotaped examples of intervention sessions and practice exercises. In addition, it is important that staff receive practical and concrete tips on addressing common, potentially disruptive group processes (e.g., conflict resolution or dealing with monopolizers). Training must also include strategies to improve engagement of the families, because if families do not engage, then there will be no multiple-family groups. Training must be ongoing and responsive to any unexpected situations that arise and pose difficulties for the staff.

For TAFES, we drew upon a training program for CAFES that had included a manual and a videotape. We modified the CAFES curriculum in order to provide the facilitators with approximately 20 hours of seminars conducted by the project manager (YK), the project director (SW), and other team members over the first three months of the project. In addition, our experience with CAFES taught us that it was essential to have ongoing supervision throughout the duration of the intervention. The TAFES psychiatrist met weekly with TAFES staff for supervision, and the TAFES director also met with the entire TAFES staff on a weekly basis. The purposes of these meetings were to discuss the TAFES intervention and to develop strategies to address new situations or difficulties as they arose. All meetings involved a continual intercultural dialogue that required a careful balancing of American and Kosovar values, priorities, and behaviors.

The family workers experienced the different phases of training as useful in different ways. During the didactic training, they learned strategies to manage groups. In addition to meeting them for weekly supervision, the

TAFES psychiatrist often traveled to multiple-family groups with them and attended most group sessions as a participant–observer. Frequently, the time traveling was used to discuss preparation for that day's group, and the journey back was spent reviewing dynamic processes from that group. The staff valued this experience of almost immediate feedback that helped them to improve their group facilitation skills. The weekly meeting of the entire staff was the idea workshop of the project, where the progress of the project was discussed, qualitative data were reviewed, and difficulties faced by the staff were addressed using a problem-solving approach.

The staff managed the family outreach visits quite well, but had particular difficulties during group sessions that required both repeated education and practice to master. Their migrant experience had made them comfortable with the relative equality of gender that they had begun to experience in their own families. Yet in the public space, they had a difficult time setting appropriate limits on men who threatened to disrupt the group process. Furthermore, although they understood the importance of being available to the refugee families, in the early phases of TAFES they often felt exasperated by their inexperience at balancing the demands of those families and their own lives. They briefly experienced conflict in their own families due to this inexperience, but addressing these issues directly in supervision had a positive impact on staff's sense of competence.

Engaging Refugee Families

Engaging refugee families refers to the process by which families are contacted, informed about the group, and invited to attend the group; the process also includes the families' attendance and choice to continue attending the group. Because refugee families are considered a difficult-to-reach population, the work of engaging families is not only challenging, but can make or break a multiple-family group intervention program. Therefore engagement is an essential focus of multiple-family group work.

Refugee families may be identified by networking throughout the refugee community and among service organizations. Phone contact must be followed in a timely manner by family visits. Ideally, the initial family visit must be conducted by staff who will be leading the multiple-family groups. During the initial contact with the family, staff should greet families appropriately, learn about their current situations, and provide a detailed introduction to the group. They should help families to consider any obstacles that might interfere with their attendance, such as work and other time constraints. The attitudes of all members of the family toward participation must be explored. The overall approach is to identify family needs and concerns and to encourage families to attend the groups. The initial visit must be followed by regular phone contact and, if necessary, by additional home visits for the duration of the intervention.

Some of the most important strategies for keeping families engaged in multiple-family groups are being available, establishing a positive affective bond with family members, conveying an attitude of respect for the family's values and concerns, maintaining regular contact, addressing barriers to participation directly, being open to any negative feedback about the program or staff, and giving specific feedback to families about problems that occur.

All Kosovar refugee families in the Chicago area were eligible to participate in TAFES. Home visits were conducted with 62 Kosovar refugee families over the course of one year, with most families visited at least twice. These visits were used as a means to meet the family, to discuss issues of central concern to the family, and to invite them to attend the TAFES meetings. The engagement manual assisted the TAFES workers in talking with the families in a positive and proactive way about the issues of staying or returning, adjusting to work life, talking with children, and getting help for sadness or fear. Engaging the family in TAFES entailed listening to the families' major concerns, clearly articulating the focus of the groups, and then identifying the links between the two. Overall, the team felt that the ability to engage families was enhanced as a consequence of the increased emphasis on engagement, as embodied in the TAFES outreach manual.

In most TAFES families, the parents were either searching for work or working, and the children were in school during regular business hours. Most families explained that they could not commit to attend all sessions if the groups were conducted during the day. Therefore, we held most group sessions in the evening. Families felt it extremely important not to leave young children at home during the groups. We addressed this concern by providing babysitters from within the refugee community who watched the children in the same building where the groups were conducted. The training of the family workers to talk with the families about post-traumatic stress disorder and depression, and our team's decision to provide mental health services through outreach, helped overcome logistical barriers (e.g., transportation and taking time off from work) and the stigma that usually limit access to these services.

Conducting Multiple-Family Groups

The multiple-family group itself is the centerpiece of the family intervention activities that we have thus far been discussing for refugee families. These are time-limited family support and education groups. It is important to distinguish these groups from clinical mental health or family therapy interventions, because if refugee families get the sense that the multiple-family group is a mental health service or family therapy by another name, then they will tend to avoid it for the same reasons that they avoid mental health services. The group context offers opportunities for families to learn from other families and try out new adaptive patterns of relating. Family members can relate to the experiences of their counterparts in other families, gain a cognitive frame for perspective on their own crisis situation, reduce guilt and blame, and feel less stigma and isolation as a result of their problems. The group facilitators should strive to help families overcome isolation and build supportive networks. They should sensitize family members to potential problems in a nonthreatening manner, provide families with the information necessary for solving problems, and create an atmosphere where family members can examine their own ways of relating to other family members and motivating them to change by normalizing their concerns.

Eight TAFES groups were conducted with a total of 39 families (averaging five families per group). In putting groups together, it was decided to have groups that were homogeneous with respect to being from either rural or urban areas. The TAFES meetings were led and coordinated by two trained Kosovar facilitators. TAFES group meetings began with tea and 15 minutes of social conversation. This introduction underscored the friendly, collegial relationship among family members and facilitators. The facilitators would check in with each family, catching up on the events of the past week or two. This time also allowed families to socialize with one another in a relaxed context. Then one of the facilitators asked participants to form a circle, began by summarizing the last group, and then introduced the theme of that day's group.

Generally, a brief didactic presentation would be followed by a group discussion. Some discussions involved dividing the group (older members and younger members) to address a topic, then bringing them back together. Both female and male family members participated in the groups. Women wanted to participate in the group discussion, but they often deferred to the men. One of the TAFES facilitators' goals was to help women's voices to be heard, requiring the facilitators to work hard toward that end with both men and women. The facilitators wrapped up the discussions by identifying key points concerning that day's topic for the families to remember and use. The groups then ended on a social note, with 15 minutes spent conversing and relaxing before saying good-bye.

Facilitating Mental Health Contacts

When multiple-family groups are effective in educating families about the mental health consequences of trauma and in reducing the stigma of seeking psychiatric services, then greater numbers of family members will be referred for those services. The staff providing those services must work in close coordination with group facilitators and family outreach workers, yet they must respect appropriate boundaries and maintain confidentiality. Efforts must be made to provide mental health services through community outreach, rather than expecting the family members to come to a designated clinic that they may not be able to access easily due to transportation issues, time constraints, or residual stigmas.

In collaboration with our partner organizations, the TAFES program facilitated new mental health contacts with 33 families and new refugee mental health program visits with 17 families. When Kosovars were identified as needing clinical psychiatric services, then the TAFES team either provided appropriate services or assisted the person in being seen by an appropriate service provider. We found that through their participation in the group, many persons did express interest in receiving mental health services through CHO. Few were willing to go to another provider at another organization. Once they had established a trusting relationship with a member of the TAFES/CHO team, they wanted to stick with them. This preference meant that the TAFES/CHO collaboration became involved in providing more home mental health visits (including supportive psychotherapy and medication treatment) than were anticipated. However, this program allowed many persons to receive mental health services that they would not have had otherwise. The majority of persons receiving mental health services were diagnosed with PTSD and depression, and received appropriate treatments.

Relating with Other Service Providers

The aim of a multiple-family group intervention with refugees is to complement the services provided by other mental health and non–mental health organizations. It is expected that many of those organizations will have concerns regarding patient/client diversion. These concerns must be addressed through regular interaction with these agencies, and by educating them that increased family utilization of appropriate services provided by outside agencies is a measure of the success of a multiple-family group intervention. The program staff should consider it part of their obligation to serve as a broker of information about existing services (immigration, resettlement, health, mental health, schools, employment, English language instruction) for the families and to assist them in making contact with other providers and provider organizations.

The TAFES workers actively sought information from providers and their organizations, and they shared that information with the families. Given that Kosovars were largely unfamiliar with these types of helping agencies, we sought to orient families to the best way of utilizing what the various service organizations had to offer. Still, we often had to explain the aim and activities of our project. We found, however, that we were able to establish positive and mutually beneficial relationships with the other service organizations, especially with schools, health care providers, and mental health care providers.

When one of the family members engaged with TAFES was distraught about a traffic ticket, the group facilitators' knowledge of services available enabled them to guide him to free legal help through a caseworker at a refugee resettlement agency. "The lawyer helped me get rid of the ticket," the man explained. "I wouldn't have known what to do if I hadn't been here (in TAFES)." In such instances the TAFES staff made follow-up contacts with the refugees, as well as with the particular service organization involved, in order to facilitate access and feedback about access. Educating key local members of a community where Kosovars were resettled led to charitable assistance to some of the neediest refugee families. When the families expressed a desire for mental health services but were reluctant to take the first step to access those services, the staff would often make the appropriate calls for them and set up appointments for mental health visits.

In the early stages of Kosovar refugees' resettlement, TAFES staff even educated some refugees about negotiating with their apartment rental office and educated staff from that office about culturally determined behaviors of the refugees. For example, we educated the office staff about the discomfort that Kosovar women felt if a male staff member came knocking at their door for any reason when the men of the family were not around. These efforts were crucial in accomplishing the access aims of TAFES.

Evaluating and Disseminating Project Results

Even intervention programs without a research component should be evaluated for their potential effectiveness. The evaluation of a multiple-family group intervention should incorporate several different perspectives. First, the participation of families in all the activities of the program may be monitored. Second, an ongoing evaluation of the processes of the multiple-family groups may be conducted through ethnographic methodology. This approach helps to constantly evaluate the families' central concerns and allows the project to modify the intervention on an ongoing basis, in response to unanticipated concerns expressed by families. Third, the outcome indicators of the group may be evaluated through quantitative and statistical methods (perhaps involving longitudinal follow-up and a control group). At a minimum, dissemination activities should include sharing the results of the data with the community and with service and professional audiences, and making the manuals available to willing collaborators.

TAFES was evaluated from different perspectives. The effectiveness of multiple-family groups was assessed using standard, valid questionnaires to measure families' social support network, knowledge, and attitudes about trauma-related mental health, family processes, and service utilization. Assessments were made at the beginning of engagement and at six months after the multiple-family groups ended. The mental health aspect of TAFES was evaluated using standard questionnaires for PTSD and depression that were administered pretreatment and at three- and six-month intervals. Families and individuals demonstrated significant improvements in knowledge and attitudes, their social support network, service utilization, PTSD, and depression.

The TAFES psychiatrist recorded field notes of TAFES group meetings and other family contacts, and the TAFES director took notes from supervision meetings. This material was regularly reviewed and analyzed, with the following questions in mind: What are families' biggest concerns? How are families experiencing TAFES? What do families think about mental health services? What services would be most useful from their point of view? What does making services more family-oriented mean to families? What contextual factors influence these meanings for families? This ethnographic approach helps to identify the nuances of families' experiences that are often not captured in standard questionnaires.

Different families experienced TAFES in quite different ways, some of which were less predictable than others. One family member explained, "Even though we don't remember everything, it was useful. Even if we leave (this town) we know we will stay in touch with each other. We are like one big family in this group." Most families were more comfortable with women as outreach workers and group facilitators. Some men's difficulties with that arrangement were represented by a male family member's comment as he withdrew from the multiple-family groups: "I don't want to come here any more to hear what these two women have to say." Some families described how TAFES helped them connect to other families. They said, "This way we get to meet each other. Otherwise, we were scattered all over the place. Before coming to this group, we didn't know where the others lived."

The families' response to information presented to them by TAFES staff was diverse. Some responded to information about mental illness by immediately framing their family members' difficulties in the depression and PTSD paradigms. "Our children are not the same," said one mother, as she realized that irritability can be associated with depression. "They are more aggressive. We are more aggressive." Another woman in the same group, referring to the TAFES psychiatrist, added, "That's why we have you and the doctor." In one group, the open acknowledgement by a member that she was receiving mental health services prompted a prolonged discussion about mental illness that led to several additional members of that group seeking those services. In another group, despite acknowledging that psychiatric symptoms are not their fault, family members stated, "We are not going to talk about our feelings in front of everyone. We can help each other to find jobs, but we can talk about feelings only between husband and wife. That is our tradition." Nevertheless, as noted earlier, TAFES led to increased utilization of mental health services among those engaged in the groups.

The systematic evaluation of the outcome of the TAFES groups was presented at community and professional meetings and has been published. As our final activity, we engaged with service organizations involved with the Kosovar community to teach them the TAFES approach and to assist them in possibly developing other family interventions for Kosovar families.

Overview

With examples from the making of TAFES in Chicago, this chapter has articulated a framework to guide the development and implementation of multiple-family group interventions for refugee communities. It represents the first known guide for helping professionals to build multiple-family group interventions that are more meaningful to refugee families, and better suited to their needs and strengths than are the standard individually and pathologically focused clinical interventions. Other publications by our collaborative group focus specifically on the multiple-family group itself and on engagement, access, and specific family issues (Weine et al., 2003; Weine et al., 2004; Weine, Knafl et al., in press; Weine, Kulauzovic et al., in press).

The overall purpose of developmental work is to better understand the realities of the refugees; to recognize the needs and strengths of individuals, families, and communities; and to see what conceptual framework and what types of services offer the best chance of being helpful. One should never think that they have "the answer." It is absolutely essential to approach each new experience with openness and flexibility. The developmental work is a matter of identifying the specific ways that a multiple-family group approach could be modified to best fit the situation of a particular refugee community.

Developing a multiple-family group for a refugee population requires committing to a learning process that must be initiated well before the beginning of actual service delivery. This learning process depends upon having some knowledge base of existing theory and practice concerning refugee mental health and family interventions, but it also involves gaining new knowledge concerning the refugee community, the refugee families, and the local service organizations. It also involves identifying a family conceptual framework, modifying interventions, and establishing community relations. Most importantly, this learning process involves establishing relationships with the refugee community that will build trust and familiarity and lead to positive collaborations.

It is helpful to view development as an iterative process, whereby greater immersion exposes one to new voices that utter new concerns and provide new information, which necessitates a response that leads to further immersion through dialogue and the refinement of service initiatives. For example, a critical issue to be clear about is how a refugee group defines family, and how to make the intervention best fit their definition (Litman, 1974). This issue had implications for nearly all aspects of TAFES and was especially important in determining the group composition of multiple-family groups.

The overall aim of implementation is to offer an intervention that is conceptually grounded, empirically supported, and ethnoculturally relevant, and to use it to serve a high proportion of the target population. Doing so requires working collaboratively with resettlement, health, mental health, and educational service organizations. It requires training and supervising non–health professionals to deliver services. Clients must be identified, recruited, and engaged into the multiple-family groups. Some will need to be appropriately referred for other types of services, including mental health services as well as health, education, employment, housing, and legal services. Finally, an evaluation of the process of adaptation and of the outcome of the services must be conducted, and the results of the work must be disseminated. That we were able to achieve these steps of implementation with Kosovars in Chicago testifies to the feasibility of this model in a population of newly resettled refugees.

The process of implementation is not without difficulties. Engaging with families through a multiple-family group intervention means needing to accept, or at the very least accommodate the ways the families think and live. For example, the greatest single source of difficulties in our experiences with Kosovars concerned gender. Kosovar families tend to be highly gender-rigid, especially in relation to the gender attitudes of United States providers (Fox & Murry, 2000). Differences in ideology and philosophy must be negotiated in order to find ways to collaborate with families that work. We found ourselves having to make necessary adjustments (i.e., not visiting Kosovar women and children without permission from the men) and choosing to push gender issues in other ways (i.e., encouraging women to speak in groups).

Another problem area concerns conflicts within or between families. When families do not get along, it can be highly difficult to bring them into a multiple-family group. In some cases, multiple-family groups may have to be reconfigured. In the case of TAFES, we were able to manage both of these potential obstacles so that they did not provide a significant impediment to the overall project. Implementation of projects of this nature requires tremendous flexibility and willingness to compromise, especially when core cultural values are at stake for both families and providers. Refugee families who have suffered from oppression, traumatization, discrimination, and deprivation are likely to react unfavorably toward perceived insults or slights.

It is important to acknowledge the limitations of this framework for development and implementation. Because it was based upon work with two refugee groups (Kosovars and Bosnians) in the United States, this framework is not necessarily applicable to all refugee groups in all places. Moreover, this chapter is one narrative account of select parts of a process that involved many individuals, families, and organizations. It is necessarily limited by the exclusion of a number of other voices. Finally, this process of development and implementation took place across cultural boundaries, which always introduces the possibility of misunderstandings.

Conclusions

1. Multiple-family groups have an important role to play in psychosocial initiatives with refugees. They address important meanings, needs,

and strengths of refugee families and communities that are not otherwise being addressed by existing clinical services.

2. To build multiple-family group interventions for refugees necessitates a collaborative approach that involves service providers, family and community members, and multiple disciplines.

3. Field reports and scientific evaluations concerning family interventions with refugees and immigrants are also necessary. Future investigations concerning multiple-family group interventions should draw upon mixed methodologies to investigate both the outcomes (with standardized measures) and the families' points of view (with ethnography and other qualitative methods).

References

Barger, W. K., & Truong, T. V. (1978). Community action work among the Vietnamese. *Human Organization, 37*, 95–100.

Bubolz, M. M., & Sontag, M. S. (1993). Human ecology theory. In P. G. Boss, W. M. Doherty, R. Larossa, W. R. Schumm, & S. K. Steinmetz (Eds.), *Sourcebook of family theories and methods: A contextual approach* (pp. 419–448). New York: Plenum.

Campbell, T. L., & Patterson, J. M. (1995). The effectiveness of family interventions in the treatment of physical illness. *Journal of Marital and Family Therapy, 21*(4), 545–583.

Clifford, J. (1997) *Routes: Travel and translation in the late twentieth century.* Cambridge, MA: Harvard University Press.

De Girolamo, G., & McFarlane, A. C. (1996). The epidemiology of PTSD: A comprehensive review of the international literature. In A. Marsella, M. J. Friedman, E. T. Gerrity, & R. M. Scurfield (Eds.), *Ethnocultural aspects of posttraumatic stress disorder* (pp. 33–85). Washington, DC: American Psychological Association.

de Jong, J. T. V. M. (1999). TPO Program for the identification, management and prevention of psychosocial and mental health problems of refugees and victims of organized violence. A collaborative program of the Transcultural Psychosocial Organization and the World Health Organization.

Elliott, D., & Tolan, P. H. (1999). Youth violence, prevention, intervention and social policy: An overview. In D. Flannery, & R. Hoff (Eds.), *Youth violence: A volume in the psychiatric clinics of North America* (pp. 3–46). Washington, DC: American Psychiatric Association.

Fox, G. L., & Murry, V. M. (2000). Feminist perspectives and family research: A decade review. *Journal of Marriage and Family, 62*, 1160–1172.

Garcia–Peltoniemi, R., & Jaranson, J. (1989, December). *A multidisciplinary approach to the treatment of torture victims.* Paper presented at the Second International Conference of Centres, Institutions and Individuals Concerned with the Care of Victims of Organized Violence, San Jose, Costa Rica.

Gilliss, C. L. & Davis, L. L. (1992). Does family intervention make a difference? An integrative review and meta-analysis. In S. Feetham, S. Meister, C. Gilliss, & J. Bell (Eds.), *Nursing of families: Theory/research/education/practice* (pp. 259–265). Newport, CA: Sage.

Judah, T. (2000). *Kosovo: War and revenge.* New Haven, CT: Yale University Press.

Keane, T. M., Kaloupek, D. G., & Weathers, F. W. (1996). Ethnocultural consider-
ations in the assessment of PTSD. In A. Marsella, M. J. Friedman, E. T. Gerrity, &
R. M. Scurfield, (Eds.), *Ethnocultural aspects of posttraumatic stress disorder* (pp. 183–208).
Washington, DC: American Psychological Association.

Kekezi, H., & Hida, R. (Eds.). (1991). *What the Kosovars say and demand.* Tirana, Albania:
8 Nentori.

Kinzie, J. D., & Tran, K. A. (1980). An Indochinese refugee psychiatric clinic: Culturally accepted treatment approaches. *American Journal of Psychiatry, 137*, 1429–1432.

Klein, D. M., & White, J. M. (1996). *Family theories: An introduction.* Thousand Oaks,
CA: Sage.

Litman, T. J. (1974). The family as a basic unit in health and medical care: A social-
behavioral overview. *Social Science & Medicine, 8*, 495–519.

Lum, R. G. (1985). A community-based mental health service to Southeast Asian
refugees. In T. C. Owan (Ed.), *Southeast East mental health: Treatment, prevention,
services, training, and research* (pp. 283–306). Washington, DC: U.S. Government
Printing Office.

Malcolm, N. (1998) *Kosovo: A short history.* New York: New York University Press.

Marsella, A., Friedman, M. J., Gerrity, E. T., & Scurfield, R. M. (Eds.). (1996).
Ethnocultural aspects of posttraumatic stress disorder. Washington, DC: American
Psychological Association.

Marx, T., & Karp, C. (2000). *One boy from Kosovo.* New York: Harper Collins Juvenile
Books.

McGoldrick, M., Giordana J., & Pearce, J. (Eds.). (1996). *Ethnicity and family therapy*
(2nd ed.). New York: Guilford Press.

McKay, M., Gonzalez, J., Stone S., Ryland, D., & Kohner, K. (1995). Multiple family
therapy groups: A responsive intervention model for inner-city families. *Social
Work with Groups, 18*, 41–56.

Mertus, J. (2000). *War's offensive on women: The humanitarian challenge in Bosnia, Kosovo
and Afghanistan.* Bloomfield, CT: Kumarian Press.

Owan, T. C. (1985). Southeast Asian mental health: Transition from treatment services
to prevention—A new direction. In T.C. Owan (Ed.), *Southeast Asian mental health:
Treatment, prevention, services, training, and research* (pp. 141–167). Washington, DC:
U.S. Government Printing Office.

Pescosolido, B. A. (1986). Migration, medical care preferences and the lay referral
system: A network theory of role assimilation. *American Sociological Review, 51*,
523–540.

Rogler, L. H., & Cortes, D. E. (1993). Help-seeking pathways: A unifying concept in
mental health care. *American Journal of Psychiatry, 150*, 554–561. New York: Guilford
Press.

Rolland, J. S. (1994). *Families, illness, and disability: An integrative treatment model.* New
York: Basic Books.

Sue, D. W., & Sue, D. (1999). *Counseling the culturally different: Theory and practice*
(3rd ed.). New York: John Wiley & Sons.

Szapocznik, J., Perez-Vidal, A., Brickman, A. L., Foote, F. H., Santisteban, D., Hervis,
O., & Kurtines, W. (1988). Engaging adolescent drug abuses and their families in
treatment: A strategic structural systems approach. *Journal of Consulting and Clinical
Psychology, 56*, 552–557.

Vinh, H. T. (1981). Indochinese mutual assistance associations. *Journal of Refugee
Resettlement, 1*, 49–52.

Walsh, F. (1998). *Strengthening family resilience.* New York: Guilford Press.

Weine, S. M. (1998). A prevention and access intervention for survivor families. [Grant proposal to the National Institute of Mental Health RO1 MH59573–01].

———. (1999). *When history is a nightmare: Lives and memories of ethnic cleansing in Bosnia-Herzegovina.* New Brunswick, NJ: Rutgers University Press.

———, Feetham S., Kulauzovic Y., Besic S., Lezic A., Mujagic A., et al. (2003). Family interventions in a services research framework with refugee communities. In K. Miller and L. Rasco (Eds.), *From clinic to community: Ecological approaches to refugee mental health* (pp. 263–293). Mahwah, NJ: Lawrence Erlbaum Associates.

———, Muzurovic, N., Kulauzovic, Y., Besic, S., Lezic, A., Mujagic, A., et al. (2004). Family consequences of political violence in refugee families. *Family Process, 43,* 147–160.

———, Knafl, K., Feetham, S., Kulauzovic, Y., Klebic, A., Sclove, S., Besic, S., Mujagic, A., Muzurovic, J., & Spahovic, D. (2005). A mixed-methods study of refugee families engaging in multi-family groups. *Family Relations, 54,* 558–570.

———, Kulauzovic, Y., Besic, S., Lezic, A., Mujagic, A., Muzurovic, J., et al. (in press). A family beliefs framework for developing socially and culturally specific preventive interventions for refugee families and youth. *American Journal of Orthopsychiatry.*

Williams, C. L. (1996). Toward the development of preventive interventions for youth traumatized by war and refugee flight. In R. J. Apfel & B. Simon (Eds.), *Minefield in their hearts: The mental health of children in war and communal violence* (pp. 201–217). New Haven, CT: Yale University Press.

Winett, R. A., King, A. C., & Altman D. G. (1989). *Health psychology and public health: An integrative approach.* New York: Pergamon Press.

CHAPTER 4

MENTAL HEALTH REFORM AND ASSISTING PSYCHIATRIC LEADERS IN POSTWAR COUNTRIES

Stevan Weine, Ivan Pavkovic, Ferid Agani, Ismet Ceric, and Vlado Jukic

Introduction: Postwar Mental Health Reform

The movement to reform existing mental health service systems is predicated on the principle that societies can and should offer more humane care for persons with mental illness. In the United States and Europe in the 1960s, mental health reform was part of a broad political and social movement that was concerned with increasing the civil liberties of marginalized persons. Reform has entailed protecting the legal rights and civil liberties of persons with mental illness, providing mental health care in the least restrictive settings, and supportively engaging the families of the mentally ill.

In Western countries, reform efforts have changed the shape of mental health services over the past several decades. Their promises have often not been fully realized, due in part to long-standing financial, political, and cultural constraints. For example, in the state of Illinois (as in other states in the United States), reform efforts are presently concerned with helping those persons with mental illness who are not engaged in the public mental health system, but who may be in other systems (e.g., prisons or nursing homes)—or in none at all.

Mental health reform in postwar countries entails many of the same difficulties, as well as tremendous complexities that are not seen during peacetime in Western countries. In postwar countries there is usually no broad, in-country emancipatory movement pushing institutions and leaders to change their attitudes or practices toward socially marginalized persons. Instead, there is often a national struggle concerning state formation or human rights, which is usually the society's highest priority. That means that mental health reform must compete with many other pressing public and private priorities even more aggressively than in peacetime.

In recent years, much attention has been given in psychiatry to the mental health consequences of war upon individuals. War may lead to diagnosable mental disorders in individuals such as post-traumatic stress disorder (PTSD) and depression, or to substance abuse and behavioral problems. It is important to acknowledge that war's consequences may also include tremendous destruction at societal, organizational, and community levels. In particular, the destruction of service institutions, the confusion of professionals and their organizations, and the destruction of infrastructures and economies may seriously complicate efforts to provide any care at all for the mentally ill. This destruction may provoke an urgency that may in turn facilitate the impetus to reform. However, these destabilizing processes also generate tremendous needs and insecurities amongst institutions, professional practitioners, policymakers, and leaders. Thus, war's destruction may also complicate any desires or efforts to engage in reform of mental health and health systems. In postwar circumstances, those with some power or position may seek not to reform, but to hold their ground.

Humanitarian Interventions

In the past several decades, there has been an increase in humanitarian interventions from the West in postwar countries throughout the world. These interventions have come from national governments, from inter- and intragovernmental organizations (United States Agency for International Development, the UK Department for International Development, the European Agency for Reconstruction, United Nations Development Programme, United Nations Children's Fund, the United Nations, the World Bank, and the World Health Organization), and especially from nongovernmental organizations (NGOs), such as the Nobel Prize–winning Doctors without Borders. These interveners have increasingly included more of a focus on mental health and psychosocial care, especially related to the traumas of war and other forms of political violence. In Western countries, a growing legion of professional experts in trauma-related mental health, refugee mental health, torture rehabilitation, conflict resolution, and disaster psychology have become engaged in postwar countries.

International humanitarian interveners have also included those who come to postwar countries as agents of reform in all dimensions of society, including mental health. Coming from outside a given country, these organizations have themselves introduced the provocation and the rationale for reforms. For example, it is not uncommon that in responding to a humanitarian emergency related to a war or natural disaster, outside interveners quickly perceive that the existing infrastructure for public mental health services is inadequate (e.g., regarding the need for intensive care and forensic psychiatric services, or the need for community-based services for the chronically mentally ill). Oftentimes, the most striking contradiction in postwar mental health is between the relatively large amounts of financial and human resources that have been directed toward treating war-related mental health problems (such as post-traumatic stress disorder) and the far smaller amounts of resources that have been directed toward addressing long-standing, severe mental illness (such as acute psychotic illnesses or schizophrenia).

Unfortunately, the capacities of most of the humanitarian organizations to do the work of mental health reform have been limited. Most have tended to operate on a short-term rather than a long-term basis. They have tended not to engage in political processes at the local state level, as would be necessary to build institutions that will outlast the emergency phase. Most have not had the capacity to change the economic basis of the problems, and they often unintentionally exacerbate problems because the money they spend changes the situation. Humanitarian organizations have also presented their solutions accompanied by cultural attitudes that are biased in favor of introducing the "modern" to replace "local backwardness." Thus, they are unlikely to effectively meld with local structures and processes that show more promise for sustainability after the emergency-phase money runs out.

In recent years, an intense public debate has ensued over the status of international humanitarian interventions. It has even led to the characterization of "humanitarianism in crisis" (Rieff, 2002). The question being asked is: Do humanitarian interventions work? In *A Bed for the Night*, David Rieff argues that the more basic humanitarian interventions work better than the more ambitious ones. Neither Rieff nor anybody else has extended this critical reflection on humanitarian interventions to the area of mental health, let alone mental health reform.

Mental Health and Humanitarian Interventions

Given that mental health interventions are a significant part of humanitarian interventions, it is important to ask: Do mental health interventions actually work as humanitarian interventions? Some mental health humanitarian interventions in the Balkans may have been of short-term benefit, but which ones, for whom, and at what cost? Although there is little evidence documenting either the effectiveness or lack of effectiveness of these interventions, many people have voiced their concerns. Medical anthropologists have raised concerns specifically regarding the appropriateness of the PTSD model for persons in non-Western sociocultural contexts (Das, Kleinman, Lock, Ramphele, & Reynolds, 2001). The Dutch psychiatrist Joop de Jong (2002) has questioned the emergency and clinical focus of humanitarian interveners. As an alternative, de Jong has proposed a public mental health framework for postwar mental health that has been implemented through the Transcultural Psychosocial Organization (and is perhaps reflected in those few other humanitarian organizations that share this longer-term and broader vision of humanitarian interventions).

No known studies have investigated the relationship between short-term successes or failures among humanitarian interveners and the longer-term process of mental health reform. Success may breed success, or it may breed more complications. Thus, it is important to ask whether international humanitarian interventions have helped in the process of mental health reform. How has exposure to the humanitarian ideologies and practices of international interveners influenced local psychiatric leaders? Has the internationals' humanitarianism helped to equip the local leaders to work more effectively for reform?

Chapter Aims

This chapter explores these issues from the vantage point of a multiyear international collaboration between mental health reformers from Kosovo, Bosnia-Herzegovina, and Croatia and university-based U.S. psychiatrists. It describes a process of collaborative conversations on mental health reform and leadership. It also describes the construct of a humanitarian obligation as one important factor involved in psychiatric leaders' efforts at mental health reform in postwar societies. The overall aim of this chapter is to illustrate how internationals may go about facilitating mental health reform in postwar countries through assisting local psychiatric leaders. Consistent with the vision of the entire volume, this chapter presents a ground-level view of the approaches that were helpful in facilitating mental health reform in three distinct postwar countries. First, we briefly introduce the players: three psychiatric reformers from postwar countries and U.S.-based psychiatrists from the International Center on Responses to Catastrophes.

Psychiatric Reformers in Postwar Countries

With their societies emerging from war's destruction, psychiatric leaders in three Balkan countries have been working to change the organization of mental health services and the provision of care to the mentally ill. The three countries—Croatia, Bosnia-Herzegovina, and Kosovo—all belonged to the former Yugoslavia prior to its destruction. Each country had a war, although their circumstances were quite different before, during, and after their wars (Malcolm, 1998; Silber & Little, 1995). In general terms, Kosovo was the poorest and most undeveloped, Bosnia-Herzegovina suffered the most human and physical destruction, and Croatia was the least destroyed and most well-off. These differences would have important implications for the work of mental health reform.

Each of the three psychiatric reformers had been acting independently from the others, although each acted in collaboration with existing local, regional, and international mental health and health organizations. This illustrates the important point that neither international nor local interveners interested in reform go it alone, but stand on the shoulders of at least a few other interveners who share their interests in reform. For example, all of them regarded their reform activities as generally consistent with World Health Organization (WHO) policies and programs in postwar countries (World Health Organization, 2001). The WHO is primarily focused on the development of community-based mental health services to meet overall mental health needs, much more so than on the trauma-related mental health consequences of war that are often the focus of international NGO activity.

The International Center on Responses to Catastrophes

The International Center on Responses to Catastrophes (ICORC, formerly known as the Project on Genocide, Psychiatry, and Witnessing) at the University of Illinois at Chicago entered the field in 1995 as an academic organization looking to work collaboratively on behalf of mental health reform, primarily with other university-based professionals in postwar countries. ICORC's overall mission is to promote multidisciplinary research and scholarship that contribute to improved efforts to help those affected by catastrophes including war, epidemics, and poverty.

To date, ICORC has been working in these Balkan countries for 10 years, seeking to guide and support their national mental health leaders in their efforts to rebuild and reshape services. ICORC's Dr. Ivan Pavkovic and Dr. Stevan Weine made initial contact with Dr. Vlado Jukic from Croatia, Dr. Ismet Ceric from Bosnia-Herzegovina, and Dr. Ferid Agani from Kosovo during wartime in their respective countries. Ever since, ICORC has remained continually engaged with them in their reform work.

All of ICORC's work with them was based upon the assumption that local psychiatric leaders were the principal actors and that the U.S. role was to be supportive, educative, and facilitative. Thus, ICORC believed that although the local psychiatric leaders might need certain specific kinds of assistance from the Americans, their professional status required ICORC to engage them in a collaborative and two-way process of exchange and learning.

Mental Health Law and Reform

One initial emphasis of ICORC's collaborative activities in the Balkans was to work with the psychiatric leaders around the issue of legislation in each of the three countries. The psychiatric leaders wanted to know whether they should work toward introducing mental health law. The making of mental health reform law is regarded as a basic and necessary step in mental health reform internationally. In Illinois, for example, as in much of the rest of the United States, mental health laws guide the delivery of care for persons with mental illness in both public and private institutions, especially in hospital-based care (e.g., laws regarding restraints and seclusion, and involuntary treatment).

ICORC consulted with the psychiatric leaders, and together they discussed how the roles of mental health law in these three countries couldn't be more different. In Croatia, introducing mental health law was appropriate because there were hospitals and professional staff that had the capability to implement those laws. In Bosnia-Herzegovina, the majority of the hospitals had been destroyed, but there were still adequate professional staff and plans for rebuilding hospitals and other clinical structures that could likely implement mental health law. Kosovo had neither the hospitals nor the staff to adequately implement mental health law.

ICORC worked with the psychiatric leaders in Croatia to write and secure passage of mental health law as a first step in the reform process. In Bosnia-Herzegovina, ICORC also worked with the psychiatric leaders to write mental health law, but this step was not regarded as the first or most important one in reform work. In Kosovo, ICORC strongly advocated that the psychiatric leaders oppose writing and passing mental health law at that point in time, and instead advocated the training of a sufficient number of professional staff and the building of service organizations.

All recognized the important limitations regarding mental health reform in postwar countries. In mental health and in other realms, international interveners have sometimes rushed too quickly to pass laws that local organizations have not had the capacity to uphold. This haste can be counterproductive, in that it may undermine confidence in laws and structures and may even serve to exacerbate the problems that reform was meant to alleviate.

The psychiatric leaders and ICORC recognized that mental health reform was much more than simply passing a law. Reform was a vision of where the reformers wanted mental health services to go, as well as an understanding of the longer-term processes and the journey that it would take to get there. Together, Balkan and U.S. psychiatric leaders agreed that it would be valuable for the psychiatric reformers to have an opportunity to more deeply and specifically understand a vision of reform, *both as a distant goal and as a process which they are embarked upon.*[1]

An Experiential Curriculum

In February 2001, the three Balkan psychiatric leaders came to Chicago for an experiential curriculum on mental health reform organized by ICORC at the University of Illinois at Chicago. They spent several weeks talking with persons at many levels of mental health services in Illinois, from the state commissioner of mental health to community-based case managers. It provided them with knowledge of reform based on a detailed experience within one specific, regional sociopolitical context. They saw what decades of reform work had achieved, and what it had not. They came to admire the mental health system of care, but they were also concerned about all those persons who were not helped by the system because they were not a part of it.

In addition to meetings with key players in Illinois reform, ICORC held an ongoing seminar with the three Balkan reformers and the U.S. psychiatrists to reflect upon the experiential meetings and to consider the implications for reform in each of their three countries. For the three reformers, this seminar was their first opportunity to talk to one another about their reform work. Each was encouraged to articulate lessons learned from reform in Illinois and to refine their strategies for designing and implementing mental health reform in their counties.

Problems in Implementing Reform

Over the subsequent year, the work of reform moved forward. The Croatian government passed mental health laws and accepted a reform plan. Bosnia-Herzegovina funded the building of community mental health centers and was moving toward acceptance of a reform plan. Kosovo completed a Strategic Plan for Mental Health Services that was accepted by the United Nations Mission in Kosovo and the World Health Organization, and was training more mental health professionals and looking for funding to build community mental health centers.

But problems in implementing the reform plans were evident in all three countries. There were problems in how to draw upon the financial and professional resources being introduced into local countries by the international humanitarian interveners without being thrown off the path of reform. There were also problems in how to "sell" the cause of reform to local professionals, to local government, to local communities, to the mentally ill and their families, and to the general public. These problems presented serious obstacles to mental health reform.

Progress in mental health reform would be dependent upon not only laws and policies, but also their linkages with changes in public attitudes and with government and community support for a system of mental health care (Weisstub & Arboleda-Florez, 2000). Together, it was decided that a follow-up meeting of the reformers group was needed to focus on the question: How do we move from where we are now?

Collaborative Conversations

The situation presented by psychiatric leaders in postwar countries can be considered an example of what the French sociologist Pierre Bourdieu (1993) called a "difficult spot . . . difficult to describe and think about" (p. 3). Bourdieu was referring to difficult spots such as immigrant housing projects, urban slums, and inner city schools. Based on his conversations with individuals and families, managers, helping professionals, activists, and leaders, Bourdieu was concerned that the dominant professional discourses often failed to accurately represent the objective social and economic conditions—for example, by condemning people for their cultural differences rather than focusing on poverty or discrimination as causal factors. Also of concern was that professional discourses often managed to "objectify" people, for example, by offering incomplete ungrounded portrayals of them. Bourdieu's approach is in accord with our efforts to devise a new way of conversing with reformers about postwar mental health reform in their countries.

No doubt psychiatric leaders are amongst the elite of their societies. But the mental health systems that they were trying to rebuild or build presented conditions that were truly difficult spots. These leaders faced serious problems of resources, legitimacy, identity, and power that had an impact on their roles as mental health reformers. More than that, their effectiveness as leaders of reform was bound to their abilities to effectively analyze the field and communicate their vision of reform to all those persons, constituencies, and organizations that they sought to influence. For example, at times they were overly bound by professional discourses that failed (analogous to Bourdieu's claims) to describe the socioeconomic and human conditions that made reform necessary. How could they do better?

Bourdieu's approach to inquiry brought together the multiple perspectives of interviewers and interviewees, who practiced what he called nonviolent communication. Interviewees selected interview subjects through personal contact, so that the parties were better known to one another. That familiarity permitted a greater exchange of ideas and a mutual understanding of the purposes of the research, as well as greater symmetry in the exchanges. The aim was to "reduce as much as possible the symbolic violence exerted through the relationship" (Bourdieu, 1993, p. 609). Bourdieu's approach to interviewing and inquiry provided a helpful guide for the collaborative conversations that had begun with the mental health reformers over the prior year, but which everyone then wanted to refine.

This chapter describes in some detail the collaborative conversations that occurred in August 2001. Drs. Jukic, Ceric, and Agani returned to Chicago to participate in a collaborative conversation that included the three reformers in ICORC's ongoing Faculty Workshop on Leadership and Ethics, comprising state and university psychiatric leaders. The reformers already knew some of these Americans from the experiential seminar, which made it easier to establish a comfortable rapport. These Americans (who themselves had been involved in mental health reform work in the United States) joined the conversations and served as interviewers of the reformers, along the lines suggested by Bourdieu, for segments of the conversation. One additional reason for introducing these Americans to the collaborative conversations was because they contributed a discourse, described in the next section, for talking about psychiatric leadership that had evolved beyond the limitations of mainstream mental health.

A Discourse on the Nature of Obligations

The work started on Wednesday with Kosovo. Thursday was for Bosnia-Herzegovina, and the group finished on Friday with Croatia. The mornings were devoted to reviewing the state of mental health reform in each country by describing "the field" and "the future." Halfway through each day, the focus shifted from the reform work itself to the leaders of reform and the quality of their leadership. Each afternoon this conversation was approached from the perspective of a discourse on the nature of obligations, which the American group had found to be a helpful tool for understanding the dilemmas, choices, actions, and conflicts inherent in psychiatric leadership. It was hoped that this tool would allow the conversations to better avoid the potential problems of objectification that Bourdieu described. The discourse describes a leader's obligations in four dimensions: personal; professional; institutional; and humanitarian.

The American group had been examining these issues through group conversations on their situations as administrators, advocates, clinicians, educators, and researchers in Illinois. The visit of the three Balkan psychiatric leaders presented an opportunity for adapting the conversation on obligations to three other contexts. They were asking for support and guidance on how to move the process of reform ahead. ICORC wished to facilitate reform in those countries through collaborative work with them and also wanted to advance their understandings of the nature of obligations and the usefulness of engaging in such conversations with people from postwar societies. All agreed that *conversation cannot be separated from course of action*, which in this case was their work on mental health reform. One American explained, *We have some ideas how to begin and to try in an open and friendly way to be as direct as possible without being insulting.*

Every attempt was made not to reify the situation in those three countries, as Bourdieu would have feared possible. Specifically, everyone wanted to avoid some of the common rhetorical pitfalls that obstruct the conversation on trauma-related mental health of the international helping hand. Commonly, international interveners or experts have often claimed that "they" (local persons) are awash in "ancient ethnic hatreds" and need Western scientific-based understandings (of post-traumatic stress disorder, for example) in order to move ahead. The problem with this approach is that the international interveners often do not really get to know the Kosovars, or the Bosnians, or the Croatians. What was different about these collaborative conversations on reform and obligations is that they tried to get to know how these leaders perceived the issues confronting them, and they paid close attention to how locals (and internationals) constructed their worlds through language.

All participants in the conversations were dedicated to working closely with words, in several respects. It was assumed that the conversations could help both the reformers and the Americans to become more cognizant of the language that binds them; the dogmas that create obstacles on the path to reform; and the new words, sayings, and stories that can encourage the move down the path of reform in an effective direction. The conversations were a tool for better discerning and modifying the speech acts that shape the Balkan leaders' professional and public roles as leaders of reform. However, everyone considered it essential that they remain convincingly themselves and not simply imitators of American vocabulary. Too often, the result of consultation from international professional experts is precisely that—imitation.

The Field and the Future

The three reformers gave the basic facts that revealed the vastly different, though comparably difficult, circumstances for mental health reform in their countries. Kosovo emerged from the war with 19 psychiatrists and 140 hospital beds, and no community mental health services. Kosovo was far below minimal standards for a developing nation with more than 2 million people. Between 1989 and 1999, Serbian authorities had denied Kosovar professionals education and training, access to health care institutions, and contact with international professional and scientific organizations and colleagues. Kosovar professionals referred to this time as "ten years lost." As awful as the war was, recovering from war was in many ways less difficult than recovering from those lost years. In 1999, the World Health Organization reported, "The people are severely traumatized and a mental health system is almost non-existent. . . . There is little hope for the future of mental health" (Urbina, 1999, p. 1).

In Bosnia-Herzegovina, the 1992–1996 war against a civilian population meant that *more than half the population suffered from war-related disorders,* Ceric said. But the psychiatric profession and government mental health policy had long placed the greatest emphasis upon institutional care for the severely mentally ill. There was no national plan for addressing this perceived public mental health catastrophe of war-related disorders. On top of that, most of the mental institutions were destroyed or badly damaged, and there were no community mental health facilities to take their place. The professionals themselves were not prepared to make the shift to community mental health.

In Croatia, the majority of mental health institutions and the bureaucracies that supported them were not destroyed by the war, and in some respects they were strengthened, given the overall insecurity in society. Most of the chronically mentally ill were housed in mental hospitals, where 77 percent of psychiatrists worked. This situation had been diverting human and fiscal resources that would have to be reallocated elsewhere if persons were to be cared for in less restrictive settings nearer their families and homes, and if other pressing needs (such as those of war veterans or youth substance abusers) were to be appropriately addressed. Neither the structures nor the mentalities for moving psychiatric professionals and mental health services into the community really existed.

In all three countries, reform involved an evolution from institutional to community-based care. In Bosnia-Herzegovina, the challenge was to consolidate some of the postwar gains, such as the funding of community mental health centers, and to build psychiatric leadership that could advance reform in the years to come. What greatly complicated these goals in Bosnia-Herzegovina, Ceric reported, was that *Bosnia is a Frankenstein state. It is made of many different parts.* Statewide political structures were limited, and national planning was highly difficult to accomplish. Thus, national reform was nearly impossible.

In Croatia, there was actually the possibility of making major institutional changes, although these transformations would have to involve bold political steps by the Croatian government that would radically change the methods of financing mental health services. Jukic said, *Now our hospital has a very big position in Croatia. It was built 120 years ago. It is the synonym for psychiatric service in Croatia. To transform it into some other institution is impossible.*

In Kosovo, where mental health services were far less developed than in either Bosnia-Herzegovina or Croatia, the challenge was to get to a place from which one could even begin to hope for meaningful changes. Agani's account emphasized the importance of developing systems of care that would be family-based and culturally acceptable. His narrative enthusiastically expressed all that he and his colleagues hoped to do, provoking Ceric to comment, *Ferid is an optimist, but I think he will have many problems in his job. He is a little naïve, but that is good in his situation. To be very realistic is not good.* Ceric then shared his own experience of having begun with high expectations that reform would move far more quickly and successfully than it actually had. The situation in Illinois certainly confirmed the view that the results of reform would likely fall short of the expectations of reformers.

The Role of International Humanitarian Interventions in Mental Health Reform

One theme that emerged from the collaborative conversations was that these reformers did not regard the majority of the international community's nongovernmental organizations (NGOs) as having a commitment to mental health reform. They came as outside organizations that for the most part were "not serious" and "the humanitarian mafia" was "corrupting." These organizations did not engage in the long-term processes of transforming local institutions. Instead, they created new entities that employed local people, under the management of international experts, to accomplish short-term missions. *All of these organizations are emergency organizations. They can disappear in the moment,* reported Ceric. More than that, their very presence and methods of conducting business changed the field in a way that could potentially hamper the progress toward reform.

The psychiatric leaders discussed how NGOs entered into postwar countries in the wake of complex emergencies without sufficient coordination, and they created an incongruous patchwork of psychosocial services. Most efforts were short term and lacked a clear sense of the public mental health and health needs that underlay the current crisis. But the NGOs often had a lot of money that they had to spend fast, and one thing that they often did was pay local professionals to work in their programs, rather than in local organizations. This situation was found more often in Bosnia-Herzegovina and Kosovo, which had experienced greater destruction of mental health infrastructure than had Croatia. Ceric saw dangers in the NGOs' approach: *They try to corrupt you. To give you some money. If you accept that then you lose everything in one moment.*

Not only were most of these efforts not sustainable in the long term, but they were also a major drain on the legitimacy and capacities of local professionals and service organizations that otherwise could be engaged in reforming local structures. In the Balkans, many international mental health professionals working through international organizations simply bypassed or ignored local mental health institutions and the professionals engaged in them. Ferid Agani spoke of the role of the international community: *Many people tried to help us, but sometimes it was very counterproductive. Some of them thought that we know very little and that we don't have any insights.*

The reformers recognized the important role played by intergovernmental organizations, especially the World Health Organization, in all three countries. The role that the WHO played was to oversee responses to the public mental health crisis with an eye toward building sustainable mental health systems. The WHO did not directly fund initiatives, but tried to influence and shape the initiatives of governments, nongovernmental organizations, and local psychiatric leaders. Still, some of local leaders expressed concerns that what little part of the internationals' efforts (including those of the WHO) was allocated to reform tended to rely too much on proclamations. Ceric said, *Everything is declaration.* Internationals attempted to bind local psychiatric leaders and mental health systems to international standards, including some standards that were not achievable even in the far better economic circumstances of the rich world. Hearing about examples in Kosovo from Ferid Agani, one American workshop participant reflected, *I am reminded of the 1960s in this country. You have individuals trying to export their ideology. They want you to die trying to accomplish what they believe in, and are setting you up to fail.*

The role of international standards in mental health reform efforts received considerable reflection in the collaborative conversations. Applying international standards does not in and of itself advance the cause of reform. In many cases the standards may not be appropriate, and they may need to be modified to fit a particular context. In other cases, the standards may be helpful as an ultimate goal, or even as a guide or milepost. But if they are too far out of reach, then they can also distract or demoralize those doing reform work.

Leadership and Obligations

Each afternoon for four hours, one American member was chosen to take the lead in interviewing one reformer and facilitating the entire group conversation on leadership and reform, in part by utilizing the discourse on the nature of obligations.

Ferid Agani was interviewed first. *I come from a family that has a feeling of dedication to the nation, to the people, not only to the individual,* he said. *I am known as somebody who has chosen to do something and who will give something.* Ferid's uncle, Fehmi Agani, was a political philosopher, a member of the Kosovar Academy of Arts and Sciences, an author, a political leader, and a writer of the Kosovar constitution (Kekezi & Hida, 1991). He was murdered by Serbian forces in May 1999 during their accelerated campaign of ethnic cleansing. Ferid is the heir to that family political legacy, and it is this obligation originating from the family Agani, in essence both a personal and a humanitarian one, that drives all his other obligations.

The group came to understand that one of Agani's troubles as a reformer was that he was often overwhelmed while trying to satisfy the many desires of many international organizations (and especially donors) that espoused humanitarian goals, but few of which matched his professional or institutional concerns regarding reform. It also did not help that (at the time) the local professional and institutional entities that he was bound to often did not share his vision for reform, and were themselves bound to ideas or practices that offered short-term security for some but no viable long-term plan for public mental health.

The group advised Agani to stick to his humanitarian vision while making the difficult choices that keep him, his professional colleagues, and the emerging system of mental health care afloat. He must continually serve as a *translator to his compatriots, to explain to them what is happening to them, how they have to change.* In a word, it was the classical definition of intelligentsia that he must fulfill. But the group agreed with Agani that the effort should be to build those changes upon a traditional family-based system of providing care that protects Kosovar cultural values while drawing upon the resources of the international community.

Ismet Ceric of Bosnia-Herzegovina was driven by a personal quest to find ways to help the survivors of trauma. For him, Bosnia-Herzegovina was a *post-traumatic society.* As a leading psychiatrist, he had been involved in many of the efforts to address war damages and to implement reform. But the nature of the political situation in Bosnia-Herzegovina was such that there was no one structure that was in a position to move reform ahead nationally: *Psychiatric services are Balkanized.* Under these conditions, he adapted a personal leadership style. Through committees, coffees, media, diplomacy, and arm-twisting, he labored to keep things moving in the direction necessary to heal the postwar society. Ceric was widely regarded as an extraordinary spinner and negotiator.

The group learned how his commitment to this personal vision was played out against a highly complex field of personal, institutional, humanitarian, and professional obligations. His conflict of obligations became most apparent to the group when considering that Ceric was central to the processes of reform but had little infrastructure to support him. He functioned exceedingly well on the boundary, but he was then 65 years old and he could at most continue for a relatively limited time. The group believed that *the question is the future. What is your obligation to build continuity? You have an obligation not only to today, but to think of it going beyond you*. Ceric helped to facilitate many organizational changes that were integral to reform but did not necessarily have anything to do with trauma. However, it was urgent that Ceric prepare for tomorrow and help to develop a leadership cadre that could replace him to continue the work of reform. If he continued as the central and only mover in an otherwise decentralized system, the work of reform would end when he could no longer continue.

Vlado Jukic has been the director of the biggest psychiatric hospital in Croatia. It has 1,000 beds and 750 employees, and is one of the country's five large mental institutions. Reform in Croatia requires that *the need is to go into the community. There is no going into the community if 77 percent of psychiatrists are in hospitals*. But, for Jukic, the dilemma was that *to do something in the reform of psychiatry in Croatia is to destroy our hospital*. Jukic did not want to be, "the last director." He was caught between an obligation to this institution and a humanitarian obligation; the first told him to resist change, and the second told him that tremendous organizational changes must occur in Croatia. At the same time, he wanted and needed the respect of others. He was reluctant to act, in part because he feared that his actions would marginalize him.

Jukic presented his situation as a professional dilemma. *Every day in Chicago we see people on the streets who are schizophrenic patients*, he said, and seeing them convinced him that the correct professional choice was to keep the big mental hospitals as they were. *They are in the street because people in Chicago, and psychiatrists, think that they want to live like that.* The group believed that his real dilemma was not actually professional, but involved balancing the personal and the institutional.

Reform required that Jukic prioritize the personal and humanitarian over the institutional and take steps to change his institution. He must also endeavor to support the redeployment of hospital staff into community-based systems of care and to see to their retraining and continuing supervision. He must risk falling out of favor with his employees, and even risk the loss of some of their jobs. He must develop a more convincing way of articulating—to himself, to his colleagues, and to policy makers—why this shift is necessary. Thus, resolving the matter of his one big hospital is necessarily part of even larger changes in Croatia. In order to convince the necessary parties, the group believed that Jukic's reform message must be firmly grounded in humanitarian obligations before professional, personal, and institutional obligations. Otherwise nobody would listen, let alone engage in making major and difficult changes.

After this meeting in August 2001, all participants parted encouraged, but they knew that there was no guarantee for the reformers or the reform. The collaborative dialogues and work would have to continue. There would be subsequent collaborative conversations, but each of those would be another story.

Mental Health Reform and the Humanitarian Obligation

The process of collaborative conversations with psychiatric leaders from three postwar countries confirmed some preexisting assumptions about mental health reform in postwar countries. Local psychiatric leaders play a necessary role in mental health reform. As leaders of mental health institutions and as policy makers, they are the most likely to be in a position to make the institutional changes that would advance reform. Consequently, one advantage for internationals who want to work in reform is that their efforts can be focused on that relatively small number of psychiatric leaders who are in a position to make system-level changes.

The collaborative conversations demonstrated that it was local psychiatric leaders' humanitarian obligations that really drove their leadership on reform. The humanitarian obligation was their sense of being bound to help those members of the public who suffered as a consequence of serious mental illness. Humanitarian obligations were necessary, but slippery and difficult to translate into institutional and professional structures of understanding, especially in societies engaged in profound social and cultural transitions. Each reformer had the most trouble using humanitarian arguments to overcome obstacles presented by the institutional and professional realms. It was also observed that the leader's work of bridging the humanitarian, the institutional, and the professional could also be very taxing on the leader personally, requiring courage, patience, perseverance, and sacrifice.

Also important was the leader's handling of the humanitarian obligation in relation to the humanitarian ideals and practices promoted by international interveners. Local psychiatric leaders' humanitarian obligations were often not equivalent to the humanitarian ideals and practices advocated by internationals. The local psychiatric leader's humanitarian obligation needed more tailoring to fit the local realities, whereas the humanitarianism represented by international interveners was more reflective of globalizing agendas that tended to favor the priorities and interests of strong states.

International psychiatric interveners should better understand the possibilities and pitfalls of globalizing processes in a specific context. They should search for innovative ways for local psychiatric leaders to advance a reform process that draws upon the humanitarianism of strong states, but is consonant with local processes of state formation and development.

The Case of Reform in Kosovo

As a specific example of how a reformer learned to reformulate the humanitarian obligation, consider Ferid Agani, leader of mental health reform in Kosovo. The situation for mental health reform in Kosovo was so desperate that it was necessary just to get to a point from which one could even legitimately have hope for something better. Agani estimated that it would take several years before there were trained professionals or basic service organizations in place to allow proper reform to begin. In the meantime, it was essential for him to mount a convincing vision for himself, his colleagues, young trainees, policymakers, and funders that would enlist their enthusiasm and support. Agani did not believe in the vision of trauma-related mental health that was being sold to him by many international humanitarian interveners. He did not believe that their paths were the way to the future of mental health reform in Kosovo. He saw that those efforts were not consistent with Kosovar values and way of life, and that they offered little to build Kosovar institutions.

Agani believed that the key organizing principle was that of the Kosovar family, and thus he proposed to organize a family-centered mental health system, recognizing (in the beginning intuitively, and after collaborative conversations rationally and emotionally) the need to draw upon international experience and expertise in this field. He partnered with American mental health professionals with family expertise and built the Kosovar Family Professional Education Collaborative.

By linking his vision of the future of mental health with the Kosovar family, he succeeded in getting people on board and keeping them together for several years while he brought the system to a point of hope. In a span of three years, the Kosovars made remarkable strides forward. After four years, they had built and opened seven community mental health centers and three homes (sheltered houses) for integrating up to 10 chronically mentally ill people into the community; established seven regional psychiatric inpatient units; opened the Faculty of Psychology; and trained 30 new psychiatrists and a number of other mental health professionals. More importantly, the future development of their mental health capacities is ensured by relatively small, but sustainable, allocations from the Kosovo budget. The Kosovars were finally at the point where they could begin to have hope.

Collaborative Conversations and Implications for Interveners

At the time, and in follow-up meetings, the reformers each acknowledged that the collaborative conversations were very useful to them. Never had they had an opportunity to focus so intently and deeply upon the issues of mental health reform. Never had they been encouraged to frame their mental health leadership status in terms of the process of reform—where they are now, where they must go, and how they get there from here. They also liked the group process, which gave them opportunities to learn from one another and to compare reform efforts in different contexts (including not only postwar countries, but also the state of Illinois). Importantly, the process allowed them to laugh with one another and at us, too (especially the Americans disagreeing with one another), and to recognize themselves in one another. The collaborative conversations provided them with an intensive experience of group mentorship on a dimension of their work that they knew needed mentorship, which was rarely, if ever, available elsewhere. They brought all of these insights and experiences back to their work as leaders of reform in their countries, and it appeared to make a difference.

Although the workshop provided a comfortable setting for talking about reform, it is important to note that the conversations were neither straightforward nor easy. Often, neither the listeners nor the speakers were able to distinguish between a pressing need, an actual response, or a hope. One person described a dilemma of the reformers: *You have to play the game of the day and you start believing your narrative.*

Reformers can become so bound to certain ways of articulating the case for reform to those they are trying to convince that they become less attentive to actual realities, including the distinctions between needs, responses, and hopes. Reform cannot proceed unless the reformer has the ability to communicate these matters effectively, often in extreme circumstances and amid competing agendas. Progress in reform depends on being able to accurately read the situation, and on not being overly constrained by one's own explanations. That is why much of the collaborative work together has focused precisely on *finding the language to go in a direction that reform has to go.*

The further development of collaborative conversations on mental health reform and assisting psychiatric leaders would be enhanced by its application elsewhere. Both the U.S. and Balkan psychiatrists who participated in the conversation on the obligations of leadership strongly believed that other reform leaders could benefit from that type of collaborative intervention—if it were appropriately translated into the new contexts. Since reform in any locality depends on more than a few psychiatric leaders, future collaborative conversations should include further conversations with these leaders as well as with representatives from younger generations and other sectors in their countries.

Since many countries face the challenge of mental health reform amid persistent social crises, these conversations could also be conducted with psychiatric leaders from other postwar countries engaged in mental health reform. The landmark 2001 *World Health Report on Mental Health* describes the global agenda for improving mental health for people worldwide, and it requires that psychiatric leaders in each country engage in broad social and political actions. The experience of working with leaders from the three Balkan countries suggests that talking together about the nature of obligations yields insights concerning leadership and reform that can be helpful in locations marked by differing challenges and opportunities.

Conclusions

1. Mental health reform in postwar countries depends on the role of psychiatric leaders in strengthening the public mental health system.
2. The leader's reform work involves reconciling institutional, professional, personal, and especially humanitarian obligations. This reconciliation is often very taxing on the leaders, requiring courage, patience, perseverance, and sacrifice.
3. Collaborative conversations are one way for internationals to facilitate the reform work of psychiatric leaders, and these conversations should include a focus on the reformer's sense of their humanitarian obligations.

Recommendations

1. Local psychiatric leaders of reform should embrace humanitarian obligations and strive to reconcile these with competing institutional, professional, and personal obligations.
2. International mental health initiatives in postwar countries may assist the reform work of local psychiatric leaders through collaborative conversations that facilitate two-way exchange and learning on the subject of reform, especially the personal, professional, institutional, and humanitarian obligations that shape their roles as reformers.

Note

1. All quotations (in italics) and observations come from tape recordings and field notes of meetings and conversations. All participants gave their permission and reviewed this text.

References

Bourdieu, P. (Ed.). (1993). *The weight of the world: Social suffering in contemporary society.* Stanford, CA: Stanford University Press.

Das, V., Kleinman, A., Lock, M., Ramphele, M., & Reynolds, P. (2001). *Remaking a world.* Berkeley: University of California Press.

de Jong, J. (Ed.). (2002). *Trauma, war, and violence: Public mental health in socio-cultural context.* New York: Plenum.

Kekezi, H., & Hida, R. (Eds.). (1991). *What the Kosovars say and demand.* Tirana, Albania: 8 Nentori.

Malcolm, N. (1998). *Kosovo: A short history.* New York: New York University Press.

Rieff, D. (2002). *A bed for the night: Humanitarianism in crisis.* New York: Simon & Schuster.

Silber, L, & Little, A. (1995). *Yugoslavia: Death of a nation.* New York: TV Books.

Urbina, L. (1999). *Report on mental health in Kosova.* Geneva: World Health Organization.

Weisstub, D. N., & Arboleda-Florez, J. (2000). An international perspective on mental health law reform (pp. 189–210). In A. Okasha, J. Arboleda-Florez, & N. Sartorius (Eds.), *Ethics, culture and psychiatry*. Washington, DC: American Psychiatric Press.

World Health Organization. (2001). *World health report 2001: Mental health: New understanding, new hope*. Retrieved February 23, 2005, from http://www.who.int/whr/ 2001/en/

CHAPTER 5

THE HEALING POWER OF FORGIVENESS AND THE RESOLUTION OF PROTRACTED CONFLICTS

Eileen R. Borris

Forgiveness is a focus on the present which frees us from the past and opens up the future.

—S.E. Fillipaldi

To practice forgiveness is one of the most challenging tasks asked of us. Challenging, yet necessary if we are to break destructive cycles of hatred, violence, and fear in our families, communities, and nations. In a century that has witnessed "ethnic cleansing" and the use of terrifying weapons of mass destruction, forgiveness may well be more crucial to the resolution of volatile conflicts than conventional diplomacy and bargaining. How else, except through processes of forgiveness, can we allow healing to occur at its deepest psychological levels? How else can we repair broken relationships, rebuild our communities, and coexist among diverse cultures in an atmosphere of mutual understanding?

In the current global community, we can readily see events and situations in which the past holds so firm a grip on the present as to choke off possibilities for living anew. This death grip manifests itself in such places as the former Yugoslavia, the Middle East, and Rwanda. Here, people kill each other violently because of their inability to forget a painful collective past and their unwillingness to chart a new course into the future. For some peoples, such as the Serbs, Croats, and Muslims of the Balkans, grievances date back to before World War I, and in some cases, even further back in time to the fourteenth century. In the recent crisis in the Balkans, we have seen the living willingly become the indignant and vengeful ghosts of the dead. In many instances, past intercommunal grievances have been artificially revived in order to realize political and economic goals, but the point remains: People everywhere are susceptible to such cynical demagogic appeals as long as their collective memory contains unhealed wounds.

Shortly after the liberation of France, the philosopher Merleau Ponty wrote about the dangers of being frozen in history, history such as that of the Holocaust, which many claim must not be forgotten. "A man who has lost a son or a woman he loved does not want to live beyond that lost. . . . The day will come, however, when the meaning of these books and these clothes will change. . . . To keep them any longer would not be to make the dead person live on, quite the opposite: they date his death all the more cruelly" (Weschler, 1993, p. 7). Is our enmeshment with the past rooted not only in unhealed pain, but also in our fear of forgetting the past and thereby betraying the dead and all that they have suffered? Perhaps we need to remember the past in a new way, in a manner that allows for the release of its burdens so that we can live in a more constructive manner. The challenge before so many peoples and nations at the end of the twentieth century is to honor the past while being released from its psychological and political shackles. This release can be accomplished through acknowledgment and forgiveness.

In her remarkable book *The Human Condition*, the German-Jewish philosopher Hannah Arendt, writing just 13 years after the end of World War II and the Holocaust, discussed the importance of forgiveness and its potential role in our public, political realm: "Without being forgiven, released from the consequences of what we have done, our capacity to act would, as it were, be confined to a single deed from which we could never recover; we would remain the victims of its consequences forever, not unlike the sorcerer's apprentice who lacked the magic formula to break the spell" (1958, p. 237). If those who hold onto grievances cannot forgive, they will never have the freedom of vision nor the political capacity to create a different society. It takes courage, strength, and spiritual struggle to rise above the battlefield of our emotions and see the world through the eyes of compassion; it takes a spiritual warrior to go beyond fear and hatred to see the soul of the enemy. If we do not learn how to forgive, we will remain trapped in the quagmire of anger, pain, and grief, perpetuating mutual suffering and thus causing more death and destruction, as the many civil wars raging throughout the world currently attest. Until individuals and polities learn to forgive—not turn their backs, not remain passive, not condone, but forgive—fear and resentment will continue to be the harsh masters whom so many dutifully obey.

The Meaning of Forgiveness

Throughout their lives, most people learn about forgiveness in a variety of contexts, formal and informal. The word "*forgiveness*" itself evokes many different images, from weakness and passivity to noble moral standards. What one may not have learned is that forgiveness is an essential part of psychological and communal healing. Forgiveness entails and requires a personal release of anger, pain, and suffering that brings, as its gift, inner peace. This process asks us to look at the totality of who we are, to accept the darkness within ourselves, and to embrace that truth with compassion, understanding, and unconditional love. As we face ourselves with courage and acceptance, we become aware of our own humanness. The gift of self-acceptance helps us grow in understanding and compassion, which we can then, ideally, extend to others in the form of tolerance and forbearance.

According to *Webster's New International Dictionary* (Third Edition), to forgive is "to cease to feel resentment against on account of a wrong committed, to give up the claim to requital from or retribution upon an offender." Thus, forgiveness refers to a voluntary act on behalf of an individual, in which the individual makes a conscious decision and a deliberate choice about how he or she will deal with a past event. One of these choices may be based on the belief that a person can adequately and absolutely judge events, and can thus measure the magnitude of an offense and decide that an equal measure of retribution will balance an uneven account. This belief is part of the ancient philosophy of "an eye for an eye, a tooth for a tooth."

Another choice is to practice an attitude of forgiveness. This attitude allows one to let go of anger and resentment by deciding to absolve what are perceived as wrongs committed against one by another (Hope, 1987). This choice entails recognition of the ways attitudes and beliefs color situations. These attitudes and beliefs arise from our judgments and perceptions, which, in turn, arise from our individual emotions, memories, needs, and desires at the time of the event. They are not objective facts, although we want to interpret them as such. The attitude of forgiveness is founded on the understanding that one screens and creates the past through the process of judgment in the same way that one screens and creates the present through the process of perception. Therefore, it is our interpretive filters of judgment and perception that dictate our reality.

A fuller definition of forgiveness, drawn primarily from the work of North, is the following: "Forgiveness is the overcoming of negative affect and judgment toward the offender, not by denying ourselves the right to such affect and judgment, but by endeavoring to view the offender with compassion, benevolence and love while recognizing that he or she has abandoned the right to them" (Enright, Gassin, & Wu, 1992). There are a few important points to make about this definition. First, the one who forgives has suffered a deep hurt and loss, such as a betrayal or a violation, which elicits anger and resentment. Although it is clear that the offended person has a right to this resentment, he or she chooses to overcome it. Because of this choice, a new response emerges that results in a change in perception based on understanding, compassion, and love. This response occurs because of a free choice, not because of an obligation. The paradox is that, as an individual lets go of his or her feelings of anger, hatred, and the corresponding desire for revenge, it is he or she who is healed. By accepting and coming to terms with damaging past events, those who can see the situation from a perspective of understanding and compassion can ultimately transcend the past.

Enright and the Human Development Study Group (1994) developed a process model of forgiveness (see Table 5.1). This particular model describes

Table 5.1
Psychological Variables Engaged in the Process of Forgiving Another

---

1. Examination of psychological defenses (Kiel, 1986)

2. Confrontation of anger; (the point is to release, not harbor, the anger; Trainer, 1981)

3. Acknowledgment of shame, when appropriate (Patton, 1985)

4. Awareness of cathexis (Droll, 1984)

5. Awareness of cognitive rehearsal (the thoughts we repeat to ourselves) of the offense (Droll, 1984)

6. Insight that the injured party may be comparing self with the injurer (Kiel, 1986)

7. Insight into a possibly altered "just world" view (Flanigan, 1987)

8. A change of heart/conversion/new insights that old resolution strategies are not working (North, 1987)

9. A willingness to explore forgiveness as an option

10. Commitment to forgive the offender (Neblett, 1974)

11. Reframing, through role-taking, who the wrongdoer is by viewing him or her in context (Smith, 1981)

12. Empathy toward the offender (Cunningham, 1985)

13. Awareness of compassion, as it emerges, toward the offender (Droll, 1984)

14. Acceptance/absorption of the pain (Bergin, 1988)

15. Realization that self has needed others' forgiveness in the past (Cunningham, 1985)

16. Realization that self has been, perhaps, permanently changed by the injury (Close, 1970)

17. Awareness of decreased negative affect and, perhaps, increased positive affect, if such an affect begins to emerge, toward the injurer (Smedes, 1984)

18. Awareness of internal, emotional release (Smedes, 1984)

Source: Adapted from Enright & Human Development Study Group, 1994, p. 66.

and integrates the cognitive, affective, and behavioral strategies formulating a moral response. The model begins with the preforgiveness experiences, such as working with the psychological defenses and strong emotions, while mentally going over the event in one's mind. Then elements are subtracted from each of these three systems. In the affective system, so-called negative emotions such as anger, hatred, contempt, and sadness are relinquished (Richards, 1988). These emotions are gradually released, in a slow process, depending on the individual and the circumstances of the wrong suffered. The next part of the model introduces to a person's awareness that a new solution may be required. It involves the processes of change leading toward forgiveness including reframing processes and developing empathy. The individual gradually stops judging, condemning, and planning revenge. The cognitive changes that take place in the wake of the affective transformations then filter to the behavioral system: The individual no longer feels impelled to act out his or her revenge.

As one continues with this process, one finds a continuum from destructive behaviors to neutral behaviors, finally ending in constructive behaviors. The individual eventually reaches the point of desiring to help others as a result of his or her own development of compassion, whether or not he or she has received acknowledgment and apologies from the offender. At a cognitive level, the offended individual may come to the realization that he or she has a right to all of his or her destructive emotions, yet he or she is willing to let them go (Enright et al., 1992).

With regard to the behavioral system, the individual begins to develop a more harmonious communion with others, including the offender. Instead of refusing to communicate with the offender, the individual is now willing to meet with the offender and develop a new relationship. As the forgiver completes the forgiveness process, he or she experiences an inner release of negative thoughts and destructive emotions, signaling the healing of a damaged relationship (Augsburger, 1981).

The following are some important observations about forgiveness as a multidimensional process (Enright, 1991).

1. Forgiveness occurs only between individuals. Even though catastrophes can create deep pain in a person's life, one does not forgive a natural disaster, an epidemic, or an inanimate object. The power and effectiveness of forgiveness lies in the fact that it transpires between individual human beings.

2. Forgiveness follows a deep, personal, and long-lasting injury or hurt inflicted by another person or persons (Kolnai, 1973; Murphy, 1982). For example, one does not forgive the Nazis for the Holocaust unless one was personally hurt by this event (Gingell, 1979). The willingness to deal with the pain is the beginning of growth and healing. In fully experiencing his or her pain, the individual learns to open up his or her heart to humanity and empathize with the sufferings of others at a deeper level; in other words, the individual learns compassion.

3. Some researchers believe that the offense is an objective reality and not just a perception of the offended party. There are others, however, who believe that the event is neutral and that the individual gives meaning to the event according to his or her perceptions and personal history (Enright et al., 1989). This is an important point, since our unconscious motivations are strong factors in how we react to the world. Our projections, those unacceptable and painful thoughts and feelings that we unconsciously hold about ourselves, yet only see and condemn in others, shape our perceptions and responses. We see the world through particular lenses, which serve as filters for our unconscious needs and desires, and which thus give form to our life's stages. This dynamic is central to the way we create the face of the enemy. Part of the forgiveness process involves acknowledging and owning our projections. In embracing the totality of who we are, our perceptions of the world can indeed change. Even though we cannot change painful past events, we can alter the meanings we ascribe to such events. This is a key stage in the forgiveness process.

4. Forgiveness is only possible if the individuals involved have a strong sense of justice. One cannot feel a deep sense of moral injury and outrage without a corresponding sense of fairness (see also Brandsma, 1982; Hunter, 1978; and Kohlberg & Power, 1981). Justice itself takes on new and more subtle meanings as one gains a deeper understanding of forgiveness; one begins to see new dimensions of one's own and another's humanity. Pope Paul II, in Encyclical no. xiv, emphasized this understanding when he said: "The command to forgive does not precede the objective demands of justice, but justice in the correct sense of the word is actually the ultimate aim of forgiveness. Justice is not punishment but restoration, not necessarily to bring things back to the way they were, but to the way they should be. It is about restoring harmony." What kind of justice is it if some crimes are so unforgivable that we chose vengeance in place of healing and return of peace? Perhaps justice, like forgiveness, can be seen in terms of a change of perception. Justice can only happen when an inner shift has occurred within those in charge of justice.

5. The offender need not apologize in order for the forgiveness process to take place. Otherwise, the injured party's healing would depend entirely on the offender's regret. Were the offender to die before a change of heart, the offended party would be trapped in a permanent state of unforgiveness, pain, and anger. For some, this conclusion demonstrates the unconditional character of forgiveness (see also Cunningham, 1985; Downie, 1965; Smedes, 1984; and Torrance, 1986; for opposite view see Dobel, 1980; and Domaris, 1986).

6. Forgiveness is relational; it is possible to have an offended offender (see Beatty, 1970). There is nothing logically to prevent victims from also being victimizers, as the history of the Lebanese civil war and the recent carnage in the Balkans attests.

7. Forgiveness, in some cases, may not only restore the relationship to its original quality, but may even improve it. Here, we find the healing quality of forgiveness and its ability to transform our relationships from connections based on mutual fear and hatred to a communion based on mutual acceptance, compassion, and tolerance.

The critical dimension of forgiveness is a shift in one's understanding of, and relationship to, the other person, oneself, and the world. The hurt is seen differently, and as a result of someone else's woundedness. The shift permits us to see a larger perspective where the injury becomes a shared pain with other human beings. We see someone else's suffering and struggles, and therefore feelings of victimization make way for feelings of compassion. No longer is there only one possible connection with the other person. There are choices. A new vision creates feelings of interconnectedness that empowers us. It is with this backdrop that the stage is set for reconciliation to take place.

Although there is great debate surrounding the concept of forgiveness there has also been a consensual agreement with specific points regarding the general meaning of forgiveness. Enright and the Human Development Study Group (1994) spelled out these points very clearly, for they bring up many different issues that at times are hard for people to accept.

1. Forgiving another person occurs in the face of deep, unjust hurt (Kolnai, 1973; Murphy & Hampton, 1988).
2. In forgiving such offense, the person gives up resentment, hatred, and/or anger toward the other, and instead tries to take a stance of compassion (North, 1987).
3. The forgiver understands that the offender has no right to such benevolence, but nonetheless offers it. Forgiveness thus is an unconditional gift given to one who inflicts the hurt.
4. Forgiveness is distinguished from reconciliation (Horsbrugh, 1974; Kolnai, 1973). Forgiveness is an internal process and is the psychological response to injury. Reconciliation is a behavioral coming together of two or more people. It is possible to forgive and not reconcile and very difficult to reconcile and not forgive.
5. The forgiver is aware that injustice has occurred and yet takes a stance of benevolence toward the offender.

A Structural Model of Forgiveness

A team of graduate students at the University of Wisconsin–Madison led by Dr. Robert Enright formed the Human Development Study Group to discuss and focus on issues concerning forgiveness. Their work together led them to the development of a structural model on forgiveness that is strongly influenced by Kohlberg's model with respect to justice. Enright, Santos, and Al-Mabuk (1989) began by studying people's perception of conditions that made forgiveness easiest for them. They used as example justice dilemmas from Rest's (1979) Defining Issues Test. The dilemma used was a story about Heinz and a druggist. Heinz's wife was dying and needed to obtain a drug, which he could not afford. The greedy druggist would not give it to him. In the original Rest dilemma, Heinz must decide whether or not to steal the drug in the first place. Heinz's wife dies. The question asked is, "Can Heinz forgive the greedy druggist for not helping him save his wife's life?"

The subjects used in Enright's study were from grades 4, 7, 10, and college. Their ages were 9, 12, 15, 18–21, and adults. Everyone was interviewed regarding the influence of revenge, restitution, peer and authority pressure, and/or restored social harmony on the decision of Heinz to forgive. Unconditional forgiveness was also assessed. The team developed six "soft stages" as a result of the information gathered. Table 5.2 presents the findings of the

Table 5.2
Developmental Progression in the Understanding of Forgiveness

---

Soft stage 1:	Revengeful forgiveness

I can forgive someone who wrongs me only if I can punish him or her to a similar degree to my own pain.

Soft stage 2:	Conditional or restitution forgiveness

If I get back what was taken away from me, I can forgive. Or, if I feel guilty about withholding forgiveness, I can forgive to relieve my guilt.

Soft stage 3:	Expectational forgiveness

I can forgive if others put pressure on me to forgive; I forgive because other people expect it.

Soft stage 4:	Lawful expectational forgiveness

I forgive because my religion or similar institution demands it.
(Note that this concept differs from stage 2 in which I forgive to relieve my own guilt about withholding forgiveness.)

Soft stage 5:	Forgiveness as social harmony

I forgive because it restores harmony or good relations in society.
Forgiveness decreases friction and outright conflict in society; it is a way of maintaining peaceful relations.

Soft stage 6:	Forgiveness as love

I forgive because it promises a true sense of love. Because I must truly care for each person, a hurtful act on his or her part does not alter that sense of love. This kind of relationship keeps open the possibility of reconciliation and closes the door on revenge. Forgiveness is no longer dependent on a social context, as at stage 5. The forgiver does not control the other by forgiving, but releases him or her.

---

study. The term *soft stages* was chosen because many of the subjects exhibited reasoning at two adjacent levels rather than the single stage reflective of structured wholeness.

If we are to include the concept of self-transcendence in which forgiveness enables us to transcend our consciousness beyond ego, then perhaps one more stage should be considered. The last stage of forgiveness one finds that there really is no "other" to send forgiveness toward but only a sense of shared being. At this stage when people experience forgiveness at its deepest levels, it takes on a mystical quality. Although we may feel that forgiveness is humanely impossible, yet in our hearts we remain open. This experience is so transformative that our sense of oneness cannot be denied.

There were some interesting findings concerning the developmental progression. In reviewing the responses, Enright et al. (1989) found the following: (1) the two lowest stages tend to confuse justice and forgiveness because something is required of the offender before "forgiveness" is granted; (2) although people reasoning on the middle two stages do not confound forgiveness and justice, they grant forgiveness only when significant social pressures emerge; (3) conditions are still imposed by those reasoning on stage 5, but those conditions must occur after forgiveness is granted, and (4) only reasoning on stage 6 captures the understanding of the unconditionality underlying forgiveness.

Ultimately, forgiveness can become a way of life. Its transformational power moves us from being helpless victims of unpleasant circumstances to powerful co-creators of our emotional, social, and political realities. We learn how to view ourselves and other people with fresh eyes, seeing our shared humanity in terms of its future potential, not just in reference to our past misdeeds.

Rethinking Forgiveness

Before one can attain a clearer understanding of the social and political applications of forgiveness, it is necessary to examine some commonly held misperceptions about the implications of forgiving. Some of these misperceptions center on the concepts of "pardoning," "reconciliation," and "condoning."

First and foremost, forgiveness is *not* pardoning. Forgiveness is an inner emotional release. Pardoning is a public behavioral release, which may or may not be correlated with affective transformations, and which usually entails an authority overseeing laws by which the degree of punishment is established for violations. When a lawbreaker has his or her punishment reduced or suspended, we may say he or she has been pardoned. When officials pardon a criminal for his or her wrongdoing, they always reassert that a wrong was committed. The Judeo-Christian tradition long ago understood forgiveness in this light of legal pardon (Frost, 1991): It is a way of affirming norms in the very process of seeking to lift from wrongdoers the full penalty due them for their violation of those norms. Here we find one of the most common misunderstandings of forgiveness: To forgive the wrongdoer does not mean that one abolishes the punishment for what was done.

Forgiveness is *not* condoning. Certain behaviors, such as unprovoked violence, abuse, and aggression, are always unacceptable. Sometimes the most compassionate acts require taking firm action to stop such behaviors or preventing the behavior from recurring. Forgiveness does not entail support for behaviors that cause pain and suffering. What is important to remember is that forgiveness is a process that happens internally on a personal level. One does not have to accept or condone a wrongdoer's behavior in order to forgive.

Forgiveness is *not* reconciliation. Forgiveness is a personal, individual, internal release, which only involves oneself. Forgiveness, thus understood, may well be an indispensable step in preparing conflicting parties for reconciliation, but it only involves individuals, not groups. Reconciliation is a coming together of two or more people. I can forgive someone and demonstrate as much in my behavior, but I may choose not to reconcile until changes in the offender's behavior take place. We can forgive another without having to reconcile.

The Process of Forgiveness

Forgiveness requires taking responsibility for our thoughts and beliefs by transcending our psychological defenses in order to change our perceptions. There are certain psychological tasks one must complete to accomplish this process. This transcendence and change happens gradually and idiosyncratically, as the forgiveness process is influenced by many factors, such as the severity and history of the offense. People enter into this process at different stages of readiness, depending on the circumstances and the traumas involved. For example, to encourage forgiveness immediately after someone has just been raped, tortured, and imprisoned would be detrimental to the entire forgiveness process, on both the psychological and social levels.

The forgiveness process begins only when we can allow ourselves to look objectively and critically at our own psychological defenses and feel the anger, hurt, and pain we have stored up inside. Until we are able to do this, we remain immobilized by strong emotional undercurrents. In our willingness to look at our pain and inquire as to its cause, we are taking the first step in breaking the cycle of hatred and fear. This process of self-inquiry presupposes a readiness to explore the workings and origins of our own defense mechanisms, especially denial and repression, even when confronting severe psychological trauma and abuse or situations of violent, internecine conflict that appear unresolvable.

As we walk through our personal psychological gateways, we approach what Carl Jung termed the "shadow," a psychological complex that is present in all human beings (1969). This complex functions as an inner opponent with which we struggle throughout our lives. What renders a part of our psyche a shadow is not its dangerousness, but rather, its hiddenness; the fact that we are unaware of it lends the shadow its potential destructiveness. As such, the shadow possesses an emotional charge and presents a significant moral opposition to the ego-personality. Owning our shadow is a critical step, for when we deny our hidden aspects, we can all too easily perceive the world in stark, "black-and-white" terms, as being either all good or all bad. This dichotomization is often superimposed on other dualities. For example, when these judgments are superimposed on religious, racial, cultural, or national differences, the result is racism, and the prejudices separate and antagonize people, thus deepening the schisms between "us" and "them." By not recognizing our shadow in operation, it is easy to judge and attack others, not realizing that what we have attacked in another we have already unconsciously condemned in ourselves. Consequently, we can only see our own unacceptable parts in others. Hence, we engender situations of discrimination, scapegoating, victimization, war, and even genocide.

The role of the shadow in victimization hinges upon a combination of mental, emotional, and social mechanisms by which a person or people claim righteousness and purity for themselves while attributing hostility and evil to their enemies. A major function of the shadow's role in victimization is to enable a person, or a group, to escape from guilt and responsibility and place blame on others. To consistently blame others is rooted in arrested psychological development. By blaming, one denies both one's responsibility and one's potency. Blame produces further blame, creating a feedback system based on shared delusions. Adversaries engage in a process of dumping their psychological "toxic" waste on one another, never realizing that all, which they hate in the other, is but a reflection of what they hate and fear in themselves. The process of unconscious projections of negative emotions and images onto one's enemy is universal. It explains why we need enemies: We form a hate bond, an adversarial symbiosis (see Keen, 1988), which guarantees that neither party will be forced to confront his or her own disturbing shadows.

Victimization is always reactionary. It is a drama that takes place between two or more parties who feel powerless to do anything except respond to aggressive initiatives of the other in order to demonstrate their "superiority." Yet, just because we project our vices onto the enemy does not automatically mean the enemy is innocent of these projections. Nevertheless, we can never determine the extent of our own complicity in the perpetuation of suffering unless we are willing to study the sources of the projections and examine our own motives (Keen, 1988).

The chief psychological defense that prevents our knowledge of our feelings and motivations is denial, the refusal to accept things as they are. We do not want to see what is true about ourselves or the situations in which we find ourselves, as individuals or members of a collective. Our self-righteousness, pride, feelings of insecurity, and fear are some of the obstructions that block our clear view of ourselves and our circumstances. The dynamics of denial are important to understand since one of the first psychological tasks we must master in learning to forgive is the task of accepting ourselves, others, and situations as they truly are. When we learn to accept, we learn to forgive, for acceptance is the path of forgiveness.

If one has no awareness of his or her unacceptable feelings and desires, he or she is using the defense mechanism of repression. One does not necessarily choose to repress feelings; psychological editing takes place on an unconscious level whenever a person senses that it would be unsafe or terrifying to allow particular memories and emotions to surface. Unfortunately, when we repress our emotions, they usually manifest themselves in other ways, for example, in anxiety attacks, psychosomatic illnesses, or as powerful and illogical negative emotions toward others.

One of the most difficult defense mechanisms to counteract is projection. When we use projection, we disown our feelings by unconsciously attributing them to others. For example, if we feel hatred toward ourselves and cannot accept these feelings, we place these feelings outside of ourselves and say that some person or group hates us. As Jung once commented, "Projections change the world into the replica of one's own unknown face" (1969). What we attribute to the world is actually what we are hiding from ourselves; what we see outside of ourselves, in the actions and intentions of others, is a reflection of our own inner feelings.

One of the most difficult feelings to accept in ourselves is guilt. Even as victims, we have a part of us, a part that many of us are totally unaware of, that makes us feel we have deserved what has happened to us. If we are honest with ourselves, we can recognize that we have had a hand in what we are experiencing. As one proceeds in the forgiveness process, he or she eventually needs to acknowledge his or her feelings of guilt. Guilt refers to the psychological experience of everything we have judged as being unacceptable in ourselves. It is a strong belief that there is something inherently wrong with us and that, because of our reprehensible nature, we need to be punished. Guilt is one of the strongest motivating factors of human behavior. Just experiencing the slightest twinge of guilt and its attendant feelings of unworthiness, inadequacy, and insecurity causes most people to feel excruciating discomfort. We will do just about anything to avoid the stinging experience of guilt. Thus, we employ our defense mechanisms to hide the pain that threatens us with feelings of separateness. We deny our feelings of guilt, and instead only see moral deficiencies in someone else. Consequently, we attack and blame others for our own weaknesses and flaws, to which we are willingly blind.

Another distraction that can prevent us from self-exploration is holding on to the past and its regrets and mistakes, especially other people's mistakes. Here again, if we focus on their guilt, we do not have to look at our own guilt. Being stuck in the past means that we are not taking responsibility for the present. Regardless of our reasons and justifications, when we hold on to the past, we are saying that we want to remain a victim; we are choosing not to have peace.

As we continue in the forgiveness process, we begin to reexamine the relationship we have with ourselves and with our higher nature. This reexamination is the turning point in the forgiveness process. As long as we believe ourselves to be separate from our higher nature and thus, victims to guilt and fear, it becomes psychologically impossible to experience anything else. The compassion that is within us and that can be given to others is hidden behind veils of guilt and hatred, just as peace cannot coexist with fear and conflict.

At this point, we begin to look at our relationship to our higher natures differently. We begin to examine the premises of the ego in relation to our spiritual self, which is the source of our compassion. The idea that there is a part of ourselves that does not condemn us and that is composed of compassion can be threatening to our ego, that part of our psychological makeup that strives always to be in control. We can abandon our investment in the logic of the ego, choosing instead to identify with our truer, spiritual self.

As we take responsibility for our feelings, thoughts, and behaviors in this way, we learn to accept life as it is. We do not look toward others for change and answers; thus, we stop using others as an excuse for our lack of growth. If change comes at all, it comes from within, growth being our own responsibility. Once we become more aware of our feelings and how we use our various defense mechanisms, we gradually realize the extent to which our emotions, particularly our fears and desires, influence what we perceive, believe, and do. The more we understand desire and fear, the more capable we are of disentangling ourselves from their compulsions.

As we begin to grow in spiritual understanding, we will recognize that forgiveness entails seeing through the eyes of compassion rather than through the eyes of fear. This recognition heralds a more objective way of looking at the world, without being attached to what we see. With increasing insight and awareness, we eventually realize that there are many ways of looking at any situation, and our personal perspective is but one of them. Listening to others and respecting their ideas and experiences helps us to open up to a wider spectrum of reality, while minimizing the possibility of violent, automatic emotional reactions. As Ferrini notes, "Forgiveness enables us to open up the doors of our conceptual prison and walk free into the light of day. It helps us understand the limits of our knowledge so that together we can move into the unknown" (1991).

This recognition is the crucial point at which compassion develops and has a direct impact on the forgiveness process. There must first be a sense of compassion if an individual is to understand the other side of any conflict in which he or she finds himself or herself embroiled. As Muller-Fahrenholz writes, "Compassion bears the pain of the past. It no longer tries to accuse, to suppress, to condemn, to refuse. It allows the memories to uncover the origins of shame and hurt. Such memories will bring deep sorrow. But it is through such sorrow and grief that we set each other free from the chains of past wrongs so that we may freely move towards a new future together" (1989).

Through the insights born of compassion and humility, we begin to see the wrongdoer differently. We are able to let go of our need for control and our need to be right, and we begin to walk the path of forgiveness by recognizing that we and the wrongdoer are more similar than different. Given the same circumstances, we might all react in similar ways.

The forgiveness process ultimately involves both sides of any wrongdoing: the injured and the injurer. How that process begins is different for each one of us. In some cases, a third party may be able to provide the necessary trust and protection, leading to dialogue and change. Whatever the process, and whatever the nature of the wrongdoing, it is always the victim who forgives, and by this act of forgiving, he or she, who had been made into an object by loss, violation, or injury, once again becomes a subject, and thereby the master of his or her own destiny, perhaps for the first time.

Although forgiveness is essentially a dyadic process transpiring between injured and injurer, it is also necessarily triadic in nature. Because we are each so enmeshed in our ego, we need an external, or "third," factor to enable us to step outside of a system of thinking based upon fear and guilt and to adopt a radically different way of thinking and feeling. The willingness to call upon the services of this third factor completes the forgiveness process. This third factor may be a specific element of strength, faith, or trust that makes us sufficiently free from feelings of guilt, shame, anger, and fear so that we can be at peace with ourselves. This third factor requires us to transcend ourselves, the other, and our mutual history. It provides the spark of courage to open up, it describes a moment of daring and trusting that moves heart, mind, and will in a new direction. This factor is the surprising energy that dismantles the seemingly solid barriers between us and within us. Call it God, or grace, or the Holy Spirit, call it compassion, faith, or transformation—we need this factor to complete the forgiveness process. We cannot force this factor into existence; we can only prepare ourselves mentally by recognizing what we do not want, and by being willing to let this third factor assist us in the transcendence of our fearful and destructive ways of perceiving, feeling, and acting. Through our experience of this third force, we achieve the necessary emotional release that frees us from the past and brings inner peace to our lives.

Forgiveness in Politics: The Gift of Starting Over

Can forgiveness be a political virtue? Politicians search for new relations with each other all the time. Although they rarely speak in terms of understanding, compassion, or forgiveness, this absence does not mean that these virtues are not to be constantly striven for in the public realm of political action. The question is often posed, especially in our current blood-drenched century, concerning what steps humanity must take in order to recover from past sufferings and develop more constructive and creative ways of solving the multifaceted and increasingly dangerous problems that now confront the human race. Finding answers to this question is particularly crucial given the perils of continued warfare in a world full of weapons of mass destruction. One of the most cogent replies to this question came from Hannah Arendt, who identified two key requirements for the sustenance of a creative and constructive political life: The first is the ability of people to make agreements to live reciprocally in new ways that contrast with those of the past, and the second is the freedom to enter into these agreements with integrity, setting aside not memory, but the continuing hostility and need for retribution associated with the memory of a painful past. This "setting aside" Arendt termed "forgiveness" (1958). Forgiveness viewed in this light describes a process that goes beyond social integration and facilitates social change.

American poet Robert Frost once observed that "to be social is to be forgiving" (1979). The political scientist Brian Frost comments that achieving justice in politics is often complicated, if not rendered impossible, because the agents and victims of past injustices cannot repair the breach between themselves through strictly legal or political means. Forgiveness, however, can repair such a breach. Forgiveness does not guarantee that we will survive each other, but without its transformative processes, our capacity to bring pain to ourselves and others only increases.

Forgiveness requires community and participation; it cannot be accomplished in isolation. We have created our own world and our own realities, but we have created these with little thought or consideration. The survival of humanity will require that we emerge from the darkness of our own individual minds and find the courage to embrace our true, common nature. The challenges now confronting the human race are so dire and threatening that we may have to undergo nothing less than a comprehensive transformation of consciousness if we are to survive. The psychological and political processes of forgiveness are key components of such a transformation.

References

Arendt, H. (1958). *The human condition.* Chicago: University of Chicago Press.

Augsburger, D. (1981). *Caring enough to not forgive.* Scottsdale, PA: Herald Press.

Beatty, J. (1970). Forgiveness. *American Philosophical Quarterly, 7,* 246–252.

Bergin, A. E. (1988). Three contributions of a spiritual perspective to counseling, psychotherapy, and behavioral change. *Counseling and Values, 33,* 21–31.

Brandsma, J. M. (1982). Forgiveness: A dynamic theological and therapeutic analysis. *Pastoral Psychology, 31,* 40–50.

Close, H. T. (1970). Forgiveness and responsibility: A case study. *Pastoral Psychology, 21,* 19–25.

Cunningham, B. B. (1985). The will to forgive: A pastoral theological view of forgiving. *The Journal of Pastoral Care, 39,* 141–149.

Dobel, J. P. (1980, January/February). They and we have not paid dues. *Worldwide,* pp. 13–14.

Domaris, W. R. (1986). Biblical perspectives on forgiveness. *Journal of Theology for Southern Africa, 54,* 48–50.

Downie, R. S. (1965). Forgiveness. *Philosophical Quarterly, 15,* 128–134.

Droll, D. M. (1984). Forgiveness: Theory and research (Doctoral dissertation, University of Nevada–Reno). *Dissertation Abstracts International, 45/8-B,* 2732.

Enright, R. D. (1991). The moral development of forgiveness. In W. Kurtines & J. Gewirtz, (Eds.), *Handbook of moral behavior and development, Volume I* (pp. 123–152). Hillsdale, NJ: Erlbaum Press.

————, Gassin, L. A., & Wu, C. R. (1992). Forgiveness: A developmental view. *Journal of Moral Education, 21*, 99–114.

————, & Human Development Study Group. (1994). Piaget on the moral development of forgiveness: Identity or reciprocity? *Human Development, 37*, 63–80.

————, Santos, M., & Al–Mabuk, R. (1989). The adolescent as forgiver. *Journal of Adolescence, 21*, 95–110.

Ferrini, P. (1991). *The twelve steps of forgiveness.* Brattleboro, VT: Heartways Press.

Flanigan, B. (1987). *Forgiving.* Workshops held at the Mendota Mental Health Institute, Madison, WI.

Frost, B. (1991). *The politics of peace.* London: Darton, Longman and Todd.

Frost, R. (1979). The star-gazer. In E. Connery (Ed.), *The poetry of Robert Frost.* Latham, NY: Holt, Rinehart and Winston.

Gingell, J. (1979). Forgiveness and power. *Analysis, 35*, 113–117.

Hope, D. (1987). The healing paradox of forgiveness. *Psychotherapy, 24*, 240–244.

Horsbrugh, H. J. N. (1974). Forgiveness. *Canadian Journal of Philosophy, 4*, 240–244.

Hunter, R. C. A. (1978). Forgiveness, retaliation and paranoid reactions. *Canadian Psychiatric Association Journal, 23*, 167–173.

Jung, C. J. (1969). *On the nature of the psyche.* Princeton, NJ: Princeton University Press.

Keen, S. (1988). *Faces of the enemy: Reflections of the hostile imagination.* San Francisco: Harper and Row.

Kiel, D. V. (1986, February). I'm learning how to forgive. *Decisions*, pp. 12–13.

Kohlberg, L., & Power, C. (1981). Moral development, religious thinking and the question of a seventh stage. In L. Kohlberg (Ed.), Essays on moral development. Vol. 1. The philosophy of moral development (pp. 311–372). San Francisco: Harper & Row

Kolnai, A. (1973). Forgiveness. *Proceedings of the Aristotelian Society, 74*, 91–106.

Muller-Fahrenholz, G. (1989). On shame and hurt in the life of nations: A German perspective. *Irish Quarterly Review, 78*, 127–135.

Murphy, J. G. (1982). Forgiveness and resentment. *Midwest Studies in Philosophy, 7*, 503–516.

————, & Hampton, J. (1988). *Forgiveness and mercy.* Cambridge: Cambridge University Press.

Neblett, W. R. (1974). Forgiveness and ideals. *Mind, 83*, 269–275.

North, J. (1987). Wrongdoing and forgiveness. *Philosophy, 62*, 499–508.

Patton, J. (1985). *Is human forgiveness possible?* Nashville, TN: Abingdon.

Rest, J. R. (1979). *Revised manual for the defining issues test.* Minneapolis, MN: Minnesota Moral Research Projects.

Richards, N. (1988). Forgiveness. *Ethics, 99*, 77–97.

Smedes, L. B. (1984). *Forgive & forget: Healing the hurts we don't deserve.* San Francisco: Harper & Row.

Smith, M. (1981). The psychology of forgiveness. *The Month, 14*, 301–307.

Torrance, A. (1986). Forgiveness: The essential socio-political structure of personal being. *Journal of Theology for Southern Africa, 56*, 47–59.

Trainer, M. (1981). *Forgiveness: Intrinsic, role-expected, expedient, in the context of divorce.* Unpublished doctoral dissertation, Boston University.

Weschler, L. (1993, April 9). Getting over. *The New Yorker*, p. 7.

CHAPTER 6

PERSONAL REFLECTIONS ON TREATING TRAUMATIZED REFUGEES

J. David Kinzie

One is never totally sure of all the personal experiences that, combined over a lifetime, cause one to devote professional energy to treating traumatized refugees. However, several early images in my professional career stand out. In 1964, I was a general physician working with civilians in Vietnam.

> Our team at the clinic was treating mostly South Vietnamese army soldiers and their families in a small village. At the end of the day, someone took me to a little hut where a prisoner was being kept. He was a young boy with a bullet wound through his arm. He had a very primitive sling to hold it and apparently had been there for some time. Clearly he needed to be in a hospital, and I started to load him on a bus. There was a large and apparently acrimonious discussion about what to do and finally I was told he couldn't go to the hospital because he was a prisoner and could escape. We have had other prisoners in the hospital, however. I gave him some pain medicine and eventually made several visits back to see him. He was courteous and polite and told a little about his life. He had come from the north, traveled two months on foot to come to the south before he was shot and captured. We developed sort of a friendship speaking through my interpreter, and I felt with a cast and perhaps antibiotics, his arm could be healed. But in the second week, he was not there, and no one seemed able to tell me what happened to him. A week later, a nurse said he had been beheaded. This act seemed to capture to me the utter fatality and cruelty of the Vietnam War.

I made no commitment to help Vietnamese or any other refugees, but the sense of guilt for America's involvement never really left me. This sense was magnified by many of the cruelties told to me, and some I have witnessed, by Americans on Vietnamese. When the war got too difficult for civilians, I was transferred to Malaysia and worked with the Orang Asli, the aborigines who lived in the jungle. A unique program was set up there by Dr. Malcolm Bolton, who had organized an elaborate system for treating 40,000 aborigines spread throughout the jungle interior of Malaysia (Kinzie, 1966). He had taken the brightest, young people from the villages, given them basic training in medical care, and put them back in the villages, supplying them with simple medicines. A radio contact with the central hospital of 200 beds was established with all the villages. Emergency patients could be transferred out through arrangement with the Malaysian air force. This system defused the hostility of the native healers and provided much creditability from modern medicine; it was a model that I was later to incorporate in the Intercultural Psychiatric Program.

> In one aboriginal village medical visit, I was struck by a screaming woman in a wood cage. They said that she was crazy, which seemed to be correct. The husband had to fight his way into the cage, sit her down, and force her to eat, or else she would have starved herself to death. Even then, we had effective antipsychotic medicine, which the husband forced down her, and she was able to become calmer. Eventually, we got her back to the hospital and over the next few weeks, she greatly improved, appearing normal. I was impressed by the severity of her psychosis and wondered what would have happened to her if we had not been available.

Later, Dr. Bolton and I wrote an article on psychiatric disorders in Malaysian aborigines. Perhaps our article was one of the earliest ones on psychiatric disorders among very isolated peoples (Kinzie & Bolton, 1973).

The Intercultural Psychiatric Program Begins

In 1976, I became the director of Psychiatric Residency Training at Oregon Health & Science University. The next year, we took in a special resident, a former Vietnamese surgeon, Dr. Kiet Anh Tran. Dr. Tran had a desire to help Vietnamese refugees, and we decided to start a clinic at that time for the refugees from the Vietnam War, who were just starting to enter into the United States. Originally the plan was to start a small clinic with Dr. Kiet Anh Tran and myself, and I hoped that with his four years of training, he would be able to continue the clinic on his own. I foresaw it as a five-year project. We had no idea of the need of the program nor anticipated its growth.

After beginning our work, we soon realized that there was a need to treat other refugees from the Vietnam War besides the Vietnamese. These included Lao and the hills people, the Hmong and Mien, and later, the Cambodians. At that time, we became aware of a cultural counseling training program in town that had counseled each of these ethnic groups. We then used them as interpreters and treated some of the difficult patients (Kinzie, Tran, Breckenridge, & Bloom, 1980). Eventually, many of the counselors became permanent members of the Department of Psychiatry staff and along with faculty psychiatrists, began treating a variety of patients with severe mental illness. As we recruited new counselors, we consciously picked warm, empathetic, and respected members of the ethnic community and then provided an intensive and indeed long-term training program so that they could be counselors and case managers in their own right.

The role of the counselors is (1) to be interpreters for the psychiatrists, (2) to be a liaison of the community they represent, and (3) to be a case manager and eventually a counselor both in group and individual sessions for the patients. The overall care remains under the direct supervision of the psychiatrists, who continue to see the patients regularly. Three of the psychiatrists have been with the program almost since its inception: myself, Dr. Paul Leung, and Dr. Jim Boehnlein. Unfortunately, Dr. Kiet Anh Tran died a few years after completing training.

This model now has endured for 25 years and currently there are 1,100 patients, including 50 children in the clinic, treated by 10 part-time psychiatrists and 25 ethnic counselors and mental health workers. The program can accommodate 17 different languages. The groups that have expanded beyond the Indo-Chinese program include Russian; Bosnian; Somalian (whose counselor also speaks Swahili); Ethiopian (Oromo and Amharic); Farsi- and Kurdish-speaking people from the Middle East; and Spanish-speaking people, displaced mostly from the civil wars of Central America. Members of our staff can also speak Mandarin, Cantonese, and French. We are able to serve patients from the French-speaking areas of Africa.

Early on, the refugees predominately presented depression, and we felt that it would be valuable to develop a Vietnamese language depression scale. The scale used both Western and Vietnamese concepts of depression and has proved to have a great deal of specificity and sensitivity (Kinzie et al., 1982). We still get requests for the scale, although in the day-by-day clinical situation, it is not used often since the clinic interview is more valuable. In addition to depression, we saw a surprising number of chronically mental ill people with psychosis and schizophrenia. These patients, of course, have remained with us, and about 15 to 20 percent of our patients currently have chronic mental illness related to both trauma and other factors. The idea that psychosis can come from massive trauma, although not documented in the literature, is clearly a clinical phenomenon.

> He was a bright, young Vietnamese male, son of a prominent Vietnamese family, in which his brothers and sisters had attended prestigious American colleges. He appeared kind of shy and awkward as he asked about a job. His thoughts seemed confused and illogical at times. It was several weeks later when I received a report that he had been standing naked in the park. At this time, his psychosis was quite evident: paranoia regarding his family, loose association of speech, and auditory hallucination. In the 20 years since he originally came to the clinic, he has shown a great deal of deterioration in his personal and social life. His

family had fled immediately after the fall of Saigon in 1975, but he reported no direct trauma from that event. He's generally socially intrusive and difficult to follow in his speech. Medication has prevented him from being hospitalized, and his behavior has not been so bizarre as to bring on the police, as was the first time. Nevertheless, he is a tragic example of mental illness.

The presentations of the Vietnamese, as with other Asians, have often been described as somatically preoccupied, unresponsive to medication, and perhaps lacking in insight, that is, psychological mindlessness.

This patient is a Vietnamese woman in her mid-thirties who, through our counselor, complained of backaches, headaches, and poor sleep. Nothing helped her improve. The counselor was really supportive of her since she had lost her husband during the Vietnam War and was undergoing a severe grief reaction. On about the fourth session, the counselor was called out of the office to answer the phone. The patient immediately switched over into fairly good English. She lifted up her skirt and showed a badly burned leg. She described how her husband had constantly abused her and had thrown boiling water on her leg in a fit of anger. Indeed, she was quite relieved when he was killed in the war—an expression that she could not voice to the Vietnamese counselor, who represented a tradition of value of devotion to her husband. When the counselor came back, the patient switched back into Vietnamese and complained of headaches and backaches. As we were leaving, she asked that I not tell the counselor what had happened to her.

Treatment of refugees, perhaps like the treatment of other people, is full of surprises, and usual prejudices and stereotypes are often highly inaccurate.

The Cambodians

From 1975 to 1979, the Khmer Rouge regime of Pol Pot controlled Cambodia. There were rumors and indications that things were not well, but information had been sparse and not publicized well until the movie *The Killing Fields* (Joffè, 1984), which came much later than the influx of patients from Cambodia. We were surprised by their appearance and presentation. They seemed different from the Vietnamese. Muted in response, taciturn in words, and blunted in affect, and in retrospect, they showed much of the numbing of severe post-traumatic stress disorder. This diagnosis was not known to us at first, partly because we did not expect it and partly because the diagnosis of post-traumatic stress disorder was not official until 1980 with DSM-III.

He was a distinguished looking Cambodian male, with grey hair and relatively tall. He showed very little emotion as he described many symptoms including pervasive sadness, very poor sleep, nightmares, and intrusive thoughts of the Khmer Rouge. He had once been a judge and as a member of the old regime was singled out particularly for persecution. For four years, he and his wife had labored at a "reeducation camp" where they were frequently starved and were forced to witness indiscriminate murder during "indoctrination sessions." The saddest events were when two of his eight children were executed and two died of starvation. As he sat working in the field one day, he began to cry as he thought of his losses. A friend rushed to him and told him, show no tears. It will show that you belong to the past and you will be killed immediately. "They even took tears from me," he said.

Every week with a new Cambodian, the stories seem to be worse than before. Beatings; children, husbands, wives killed in front of people, sometimes in a savage way; starvation; no medical attention for severe disease or wounds. Long hours of labor, malnutrition, and no end in sight. Gradually, it dawned on us that this presentation was a qualitatively different clinical one than most Vietnamese had displayed. We made a simple questionnaire out of the diagnosis of post-traumatic stress disorder, and I think we were surprised to find that all of the Cambodian patients we had seen suffered from post-traumatic stress disorder (PTSD) (Kinzie, Fredrickson, Ben, Fleck, & Karls, 1984), one of the earliest reports of PTSD in a civilian non-Western population. We had an initial success in treating this group and wrote that with modern treatment, the prognosis is not as pessimistic as was described with Holocaust victims. Indeed, over half seemed to be improved within a year (Boehnlein, Kinzie, Rath, & Fleck, 1985). Subsequently, all those who showed initial improvement later relapsed, and now we have recognized that complex or severe PTSD in severely traumatized refugees is a chronic relapsing disorder.

During this time, the schools in Portland became aware of some disturbing behavior of some Cambodian children. We then were able to do a survey of 40 Cambodian high school children, using a psychiatric interview. We found a prevalence rate of about 50 percent of PTSD and a depression rate almost as high. Surprisingly, despite being academically behind, they were not disruptive in school nor did they manifest antisocial behavior (Kinzie, Sack, Angell, Manson, & Rath, 1986; Sack, Angell, Kinzie, Manson, & Rath, 1986). Most, despite their symptoms, were suffering privately. A three-year follow-up of these children indicated a drop-off in depression but not partially in PTSD, indicating they had separate prognostic categories. Indeed, of those who had PTSD before, some do not have it now, but others did develop it in the meantime (Kinzie, Sack, Angell, Clarke, & Rath, 1989; Sack, et al., 1993).

Socialization Groups

We eventually determined that individual therapy and medication was not sufficient to treat the Cambodians and, to a lesser extent, the other groups. The numbing and avoidance left them quite isolated, even from other Cambodians. We started group therapy of a special sort with the

Southeast Asian populations. We were aware that they were reluctant to speak about personal information in groups; therefore, we defined the group meetings as part of their treatment and included the doctor in the original sessions, and they obediently complied. We later found that just doing activities together, such as cooking, planning, outings, and education on English or citizenship was extremely valuable. Such activities became the major approach in the group therapy, which technically was called a socialization group experience (Kinzie et al., 1988).

Once a month, I came to the Cambodian group to do American-style therapy, that is, just talking. They immediately delved into their past, almost obsessed with the Pol Pot experience. For the first year, getting them away from their past was difficult. As a therapist, I wasn't sure if that reluctance was good or bad. After about two years of once-a-month meetings, they could lighten up and get into other topics toward the end of the hour. The intensity, which was so severe at times that some patients had to leave the group, had diminished; perhaps some healing or desensitization had occurred. For the future, I recommended sticking to a less threatening socialization experience, which would be just as, if not more, beneficial.

PTSD in the Clinic

Since practically all of the Cambodians had PTSD and depression, plus psychosis in some cases, we wondered how common these illnesses were, not just in the clinic but also in the entire population. Therefore, the physicians started to do systematic surveys of PTSD questions with their patients. We were surprised to learn that patients we thought we knew had neither remembered nor felt comfortable about talking about their traumas or their experiences, even their symptoms. We found a much higher rate of PTSD than had previously been recognized by the physicians. The rate was almost 90 percent among the Mien hill tribe people in Laos and 50 percent among the Vietnamese. Knowing this factor greatly enhanced our ability to help and also gave us some concept of the chronicity of many patients (Kinzie et al., 1990).

> She was a rather shy, plain Vietnamese workingwoman. It was thought that she was mentally retarded. By a Western intelligence test, her IQ was rated 64. On the other hand, I saw her prepare and organize five other Vietnamese women to prepare a five-course Vietnamese lunch, at which she appeared more than competent and completely in charge. Her symptoms had been primarily those of depression, but I asked her after several years of treatment if she had had any traumas. She reluctantly and quite shamefully mentioned that she had been a servant girl for a Vietnamese family in Vietnam. On several occasions, she was raped by the man of the house. She felt shamed and powerless to do anything about it. After this discussion and my reaction of acceptance and sorrow for her, she seemed to brighten up in the subsequent meetings, and there was no further indication of mental retardation.

Medication

Clinical folklore says that Asians require lower dosages of psychotropic medications than Americans. To test this opinion, we decided to test the blood tricyclic levels of our Asian patients. Indeed, most of the Asians in the 1980s were on tricyclic antidepressants. After we had tested about 20 persons, the lab called to tell me that they couldn't get the equipment working because they could find no traces of the antidepressant in their blood levels. At first, I was shocked, because these patients were known to me and kept their appointments.

What was not apparent until later was that although they kept their appointments, they did not take much of the medicine. Indeed the blood levels were extremely low in all groups. After discussing these results with the patients, I assured them that they would not have to leave the clinic or be punished for not complying, and provided them with further education on the value of medicine. In turn, the compliance rate greatly improved among Cambodians, partially improved among Vietnamese, and did not improve at all among the Mien (Kinzie, Leung, Boehnlein, & Fleck, 1987).

After testing, we determined that Asians as a rule did not need a lower dose of medicine than Caucasians. Once they received and took the appropriate dose to achieve the appropriate blood levels, the depression did remarkably improve. During this testing, we also became aware that some of the symptoms of post-traumatic stress disorder, particularly hyperarousal, irritability, nightmares, and poor sleep, were very similar to the symptoms of drug withdrawal.

Noting this similarity led us down a new route: Drug withdrawal, particularly from cocaine, has been treated with clonidine. We therefore started treating our PTSD patients with clonidine and found a marked reduction in nightmares (Kinzie & Leung, 1989). We followed this course of treatment with all-night polysomnograph sleep studies on clonidine. We did two all-night studies in the patients' homes. We gave them two weeks of clonidine and repeated the study. Although only four patients participated in the studies, we were able to demonstrate that the report of nightmares almost entirely disappeared in those patients. They did seem to feel more relaxed, but their depressive symptoms remained the same (Kinzie, Sack, & Riley, 1994).

Psychopharmacology among the various ethnic groups is complicated. Some complications may be a result of cultural differences. Adding trauma to the refugee experience increases the complication (Kinzie, 1998; Kinzie & Friedman, 2004). Clearly, though, medication is extremely beneficial and can provide a great reduction in suffering.

Prognosis

The course of PTSD is remitting and unpredictable. As mentioned before, most of the patients would have an exacerbation of their symptoms with current stresses. These stresses may be simple reminders such as war or violence on TV or a new threat, such as an assault, robbery, or an accident. Severe medical illness can also reactivate symptoms that had been apparently quiescent. After a new trauma, most of the symptoms reflected the severe previous trauma, that is, concentration camp or war experiences. These memories can reactivate under intense pressure despite years of treatment.

The most recent study event was the destruction of the World Trade Center on 9/11, which was displayed on TV repeatedly in the hours after the event. The patients seemed mesmerized, unable to stop watching television and also not comprehending exactly what was happening. Many patients appeared to have a reactivation of their symptoms, and we were motivated to do a survey of many of them (Kinzie, Boehnlein, Riley, & Sparr, 2002). The Bosnians and Somalians had the most immediate reactions. Possible reasons for this prevalence include (1) the Bosnians' and Somalis' war was more recent (as one Somali said, "I came to the United States to get away from war and now it has come to the United States; I have no other place to run"), and (2) they may have felt more vulnerable, since they had lived in the United States for less time and were of a Muslim background. The reactivation of their symptoms stayed for a couple of months but then slowly decreased as the security and safety of the clinic gave them confidence that a war in the United States was not imminent.

The reaction among Cambodians and Vietnamese was less strong, but still notable.

> This patient is a poised Cambodian woman raised in a rather upper-class family. Her husband was a merchant, and she had an equivalent of a high school education. When Pol Pot came to power, her husband was immediately killed and during the time of Pol Pot's reign, her parents died and two children died of starvation. She was threatened repeatedly with execution and forced labor for four years. In treatment, she remained calm, poised, and gracious. She developed a more thorough interest in Buddhist meditation and became a lay Buddhist monk. She provided a great deal of help to others, including patients and also some Americans new to Buddhism. She remained in treatment for 10 years and with some encouragement finally left treatment with assurance that she could return if symptoms renewed.

> The second patient came from a well-to-do Cambodian family. Her husband was active in the previous government and politically well connected. When Pol Pot came to power, he was executed. One of her children died at childbirth and another died of starvation. She underwent four years of forced labor and starvation. She came to the United States with one child. She married again and had another child. She appeared always well-dressed, groomed, and sociable. Every time she attempted a new social activity, however, she developed increased symptoms. Any kind of work pressure that reminded her of Pol Pot became symptomatic. Her children's difficulties academically and socially greatly increased her stress. She developed hypertension and early signs of diabetes. The nightmares have never gone away, and she continues to have multiple symptoms of depression and post-traumatic stress disorder.

Analysis of these and 23 other patients who have been seen for more than 10 years reveals a bimodal pattern. About half the patients improved dramatically, having very low symptoms and very low Clinician Administered PTSD Scale (CAPS) scores. Another group continued to have a high rate of symptoms, with high CAPS scores and social impairment (Boehnlein et al., 2004). Despite analysis of all the trauma, demographic variables, education, marital status, and ongoing stress, there was no apparent difference between the two groups. The most information we have at this point is that unknown factors account for the resiliency of some patients and the chronicity of others.

Psychotherapy Issues

I have both struggled with the difficulties of and experienced the pleasures of interacting with patients from other ethnic groups. In theory, the problems are immense. Different values, expectations of treatment, and various (or lack of) psychology theories of disorders increase the challenges of working interculturally. Multiple social problems and of course traumas complicate the issues of treatment when therapists and patients are from different cultures. Various aspects of these topics have been examined, from the theoretical models to evaluation and psychotherapy techniques with Indo-Chinese; more recently articles dealing with trauma and countertransference and ethical issues have been published (Kinzie, 1978, 1981; Kinzie & Boehnlein, 1993; Kinzie & Fleck, 1987).

The cultural issues seem less complicated to me now than when I started in the field. I almost never think of my patients in terms of their ethnicity. Besides focusing on our relationship, I think more of their personal life stories, their individual struggles. The issue of trauma is different. The stories are horrendous, the suffering endured tremendous, and their problems unrelenting at times. Taking the first history is often difficult since it is necessary to go over many of the traumas the patient endured. They are simply terrible stories. They have the effects of human cruelty that best can be described as evil acts.

Clearly, all who work with human trauma will have some reaction and indeed, the countertransference problems and burnouts among practitioners are quite great. In our own clinic, we found that psychiatrists were aware of feeling irritable, sometimes depressed, and a experiencing a sense of personal vulnerability. There also was a sense of failure of the education system, which failed to teach about the problems of dealing with massive psychic trauma. This sense was acute among some counselors, ones who oftentimes reexperience their own traumas as they interpret the history of patients.

Finding the right emotional distance for both therapist and counselor takes a great deal of both experience and support. The tendency is both to run (i.e., deny the seriousness of the problems) or objectify and trivialize them in an intellectually and remote manner. Studies indicate that empathic strain (the term used by Wilson & Lindy, 1994) is a huge problem.

Patients do get better and are grateful. Their problems do not have to endure. The problems can become more mundane every day instead of catastrophic and overwhelming. Nevertheless, the problem in therapy should not be minimized. In my own case, a liberal arts education, medical school, five years of residency, and practice in multiple cultures had left me generally unprepared for the massive physical and psychological trauma told by our patients. I had assumed, reinforced by every educational experience, that progression of human knowledge since the Age of Enlightenment will lead to progression in human well-being: less poverty, less crime, less war, less disease. The trajectory is onward and upward. Perhaps the Nazis' experience was an aberration, and we can expect that the species will continue to improve.

Clearly, a trajectory that goes only onward or upward is not the case. Vietnam, Cambodia, Somali, Bosnia, Rwanda, Afghanistan, and perhaps scores of other places in the world have indicated that wars, torture, indiscriminate killing, looting, and raping continues, if not at an increased pace, then certainly at a better-documented pace than before. Something is terribly wrong and some responses are called for, but it is unclear what the responses should be.

One solution may be the simple relationship between a doctor and the traumatized patient. Without becoming too theoretical, listening to a suffering human being telling a story, and staying and sharing the experience can be deeply moving for both parties, and alternatively therapeutic and uplifting. The dialogue becomes an interactive dance where both experience pain and joy, and sometimes relief and peace. The therapist no doubt becomes wounded somewhat in the process and must guard against cynicism and bitterness, and monitor the therapist's own subjective response, particularly those of anger and hostility.

Why have we, those of us who devote professional time and energy to working with severely traumatized patients, been able to go so long? One possibility is because those of us involved in our particular work see it as a mission. A new psychiatrist from the program observed, "You are all involved in a mission of love." Another possible factor is a connection between professional dedication and strong religious belief (Protestant, Catholic, Jewish, Buddhist). Strong faith does seem to sustain people for the long haul and give their own lives some personal centering and guidance.

In my most recent writings on the subject (Kinzie, 2001), I observed that the psychotherapy of the traumatized individual seemed to center predominately around technique exposure and cognitive behavioral therapy. I feel that this focus on technique has missed the variable of the therapist's own self and the interaction, the interrelationship between the patient and therapist. There are several aspects of this interaction that I should summarize.

Initially, patients have a need (or not) to tell personal trauma stories. Therapists must have the ability to listen, not to run away, not to become objective or detached but to stay together, and to stay with the patient. Patients need constancy over time, and therapists must have the ability to be consistently the same person without deviating, thus providing a constant source of stability. As patients improve, they often feel a need to give, and their need to give must be matched by the therapists' ability to receive. Doctors give a lot in terms of time, skills, and treatment abilities, but the patients need to give too, and the sign of giving is one of the most important aspects of improvement in therapy.

Finally, there is indeed a problem with evil. Both patients and therapists may be searching for something sacred to believe in a profane world. The hallmark of a spiritual life as defined by Karasu (1999) is belief: belief in the sacred, belief in unity, and belief in transformation. At some level, all of us in this work must believe that there is something sacred in life, that we are all united, and that there is a possibility of transformation of human beings even from the most desperate situations. The search for this sacredness, unity, and transformation is the private and subjective growth necessary for maintaining oneself while dealing with traumatized patients.

> In my quiet regular meditative moments, I often reflect on my long-term work with refugees. It has been difficult, challenging, painful, and immensely rewarding. For every moment of pain I have experienced, there have been more moments of joy and grace. These moments come back periodically: the prayer by the Cambodian Buddhist nun wishing us a safe journey to a trip to Asia; the very private, personal description by an African woman of a brutal gang rape never revealed without a counselor present; a schizophrenic Somali patient in the middle of a very confrontational interview stopped and said, "I sorry what happened to your people in 9/11." These moments are very touching and rewarding.

It is said that once you learn there is no Santa Claus you can never get him back. The same is true, in reverse, about evil. Once it is seen, it won't go away. The age of innocence is lost. We struggle with it and seem unable to overcome it, seem unable to diminish it, stop it, or even mitigate its effects. But we can be there to help those who come to us with the scars and wounds from human destructiveness. Listening, reducing symptoms, being there for them, and providing continuity of care are the core of the treatment. These actions are not only helpful but are what those of us who take up this profession are required to do.

In the last 25 years, much has been done to help traumatized refugees. Programs have been established in many countries, and there have even been attempts to help victims at trauma sites. Some have been more clinically sound than others, and a few have been subjected to scientific study. This field is still one of improvisation and experimentation. There have been technical advances in approaches to groups and families, and in the use of medicine. To me, the constant in each recovery has been that of one person relating to another, offering support, hope, consistency, and expertise during these troubled times. Other help, such as assisting people to gain access to housing, financial aid, and schooling and/or job retraining is essential, but success often comes down to one-on-one relationships.

Suggestions for professionals beginning work with traumatized refugees include the following:

1. Aim to develop the highest level of clinical competence. One must be well trained as a psychiatrist or psychologist. This work is difficult and requires more experience, training, and personal maturity than dealing with middle-class Americans.

2. Develop a tolerance and empathy for trauma stories. As painful as they are to hear, one must stay with the patient, without running away into a "professional" distancing stance, trivializing the problem, or becoming overprotective and overinvolved. Avoiding these pitfalls takes a great deal of experience of sitting with a patient, feeling the pain, and mutually developing realistic plans for help.

3. Be respectful and appreciate people from other cultures. Culture variations are a unique aspect of human life, but clearly what we have in common is much greater than cultural difference. Human contact— respectful, warm, and genuine—overcomes some cultural stereotyping and allows a real encounter. Flexibility in the interaction is the key. It is not time for a diagnostic theoretical approach or an operationalized manualized approach. Treating traumatized refugees is neither formula-bound nor simple.

4. Reduce symptoms. Many symptoms can easily be decreased—especially those of depression and hyperarousal and reexperiencing—by medications (Kinzie & Friedman, 2004). These should be used in conjunction with supportive dynamic therapy. Socialization group activities greatly reduce isolation and avoidance behavior.

5. Expect a long course. Traumatized refugees have marked symptoms when adjusting to the United States in addition to the chronic course of PTSD. Long-term therapy is indicated. Short-term or time-limited therapy is inappropriate and may be counterproductive, producing a sense of abandonment after the patients have opened up.

6. Take care of yourself. Burnout is a major issue for therapists working with traumatized patients. Countertransference or empathetic strain means the tensions and pressure within the therapist have become so severe that the therapist can no longer be effective. Even worse, interaction may become hostile and dismissive to the patients with very destructive results. Therapists need to have fulfilling nonprofessional lives, have support (and therapy) from colleagues, and take joy from the gains the patients make. Limits on the number of patients treated may be necessary as well as maintenance of a balanced professional caseload. Above all, remember we are to serve patients and the first rule of medicine is "do no harm." When we or our colleagues feel we are harming patients, it's time to change work.

References

Boehnlein, J. K., Kinzie, J. D., Rath, B., & Fleck, J. (1985). One-year follow-up study of posttraumatic stress disorder among survivors of Cambodian concentration camps. *American Journal of Psychiatry, 142*, 956–960.

———, Kinzie, J. D., Sekiya, U., Riley, C., Pou, K., & Rosborough, B. S. (2004). A ten-year treatment outcome study of traumatized Cambodian refugees. *Journal of Nervous and Mental Disease, 192*, 658–663.

Joffè, R. (Director). (1984). *The Killing Fields* [Motion Picture]. United States: Warner Studios.

Karasu, T. B. (1999). Spiritual psychotherapy. *American Journal of Psychotherapy, 53*, 143–162.

Kinzie, J. D. (1966). Malaysia aborigine medical program, Letter to the Editor. *Journal of American Medical Association, 197*, 163–164.

———. (1978). Lessons from cross-cultural psychotherapy: The Malaysian experience. *American Journal of Psychotherapy, 32*, 510–520.

———. (1981). Evaluation and psychotherapy of Indochinese refugee patients. *American Journal of Psychotherapy, 35*, 251–261.

———. (1998). Ethnicity and psychopharmacology: The experience of Southeast Asians. In S. Okpaku (Ed.), *Clinical methods on transcultural psychiatry*. Washington, DC: American Psychiatric Press.

———. (2001). Psychotherapy for massively traumatized refugees: The therapist variable. *American Journal of Psychotherapy, 55*, 475–490.

———, & Boehnlein, J. K. (1993). Psychotherapy of victims of massive violence: Countertransference and ethical issues. *American Journal of Psychotherapy, 47*, 90–102.

———, Boehnlein, J. K., Leung, P., Moore, P., Riley, C., & Smith, D. (1990). The prevalence of post traumatic stress disorder among Southeast Asian refugees. *American Journal of Psychiatry, 147*, 913–917.

———, Boehnlein, J. K., Riley, C., & Sparr, L. (2002). The effects of September 11 on traumatized refugees: Reactivation of posttraumatic stress disorder. *Journal of Nervous and Mental Disease, 190*, 437–441.

———, & Bolton, J. D. (1973). Psychiatry with aborigines of West Malaysia. *American Journal of Psychiatry, 130*, 769.

———, & Fleck, J. (1987). Psychotherapy with severely traumatized refugees. *American Journal of Psychotherapy, 41*, 82–94.

———, Fredrickson, R. H., Ben, R., Fleck, J., & Karls, W. (1984). Post–traumatic stress syndrome among survivors of Cambodian concentration camps. *American Journal of Psychiatry, 141*, 645–650.

———, & Friedman, M. (2004). Psychopharmacology in treatment of traumatized refugees. In J. Wilson & B. Drozdek (Eds.), *Broken spirits: The treatment of asylum seekers and refugees with PTSD*. New York: Brunner-Routledge.

———, & Leung, P. (1989). Clonidine in Cambodian patients with post traumatic stress disorder. *Journal of Nervous and Mental Disease, 177*, 546–550.

———, Leung, P., Boehnlein, J., & Fleck, J. (1987). Antidepressant blood levels in Southeast Asians: Clinical and cultural implications. *Journal of Nervous and Mental Disease, 175*, 480–485.

———, Leung, P., Bui, A., Ben, R., Koepraseuth, K. O., Riley, C., et al. (1988). Cultural factors in group therapy with Southeast Asian refugees. *Community Mental Health Journal, 24,* 157–166.

———, Manson, S. M., Vihn, D. T., Tolan, N. T., Anh, B., Pho, T.N., et al. (1982). Development and validation of a Vietnamese-language depression rating scale. *American Journal of Psychiatry, 139,* 1276–1281.

———, Sack, W., Angell, R., Clarke, G., & Rath, B. (1989). A three-year follow-up of Cambodian young people traumatized as children. *Journal of American Academy of Child and Adolescent Psychiatry, 28,* 501–505.

———, Sack, W. H., Angell, R., Manson, S., & Rath, B. (1986). The psychiatric effects of massive trauma on Cambodian children I: The children. *Journal of American Academy of Child and Adolescent Psychiatry, 25,* 370–376.

———, Sack, W. H., & Riley, C. M. (1994). The polysomnographic effects of clonidine on sleep disorders in posttraumatic stress syndrome: A pilot study with Cambodian patients. *Journal of Nervous and Mental Disease, 182,* 585–587.

———, Tran, K. A., Breckenridge, A., & Bloom, J. D. (1980). An Indochinese refugee psychiatric clinic: Culturally accepted treatment approaches. *American Journal of Psychiatry, 137,* 1429–1432.

Sack, W., Angell, R., Kinzie, J. D., Manson, S., & Rath, B. (1986). The psychiatric effects of massive trauma on Cambodian children II. The family and school. *Journal of American Academy of Child and Adolescent Psychiatry, 25,* 377–383.

Sack, W. H., Clarke, G., Him, C., Dickason, D., Goff, B., Lanham, K., et al. (1993). A six-year follow-up study of Cambodian adolescents. *Journal of American Academy of Child Psychiatry, 32,* 431–437.

Wilson, J. P., & Lindy, J. (Eds.). (1994). *Beyond empathy: Managing affect and countertransference in treatment of post-traumatic stress disorder.* New York: Guilford Press.

CHAPTER 7

CHALLENGES IN INTERNATIONAL DISASTER MENTAL HEALTH RESEARCH

Paul Bolton

Introduction

This chapter describes some of the major challenges I have faced in designing and conducting mental health research in developing countries and how these challenges were addressed. The challenges included issues ranging from cross-cultural suitability to logistical problems. Most of my experience has been in sub-Saharan Africa, and all of the examples discussed here come from that part of the world. However, on the basis of more limited recent experience in Asia and Latin America, I believe that many of the problems and solutions discussed here also apply to studies conducted in other regions.

All of the research on which this chapter is based is applied research, done in collaboration with humanitarian nongovernmental organizations (NGOs). The projects form part of an ongoing collaborative effort by our group to build research, needs assessment, and project evaluation capacity among these organizations. Therefore, the approaches that we have developed and used with our NGO partners are abbreviated (compared with full-scale research projects) to match the typical NGOs more limited resources while aiming to preserve scientific rigor.[1] Organizations attempting to conduct basic (as opposed to applied) research without local collaborators may well confront different obstacles in addition to those described in the present chapter.

The main challenges we have faced in working in developing countries are listed in Table 7.1. The first two bulleted items refer to ethical concerns that our research would not be harmful and would in fact be likely to benefit the communities being studied. The next two issues concern which aspects of mental health should be assessed and how to design an approach that

Table 7.1
Major Challenges

- Assuring that no harm is caused to participants
- Assuring that the research will have a practical application
- Deciding what to assess
- Addressing cross-cultural differences
- Distinguishing mental illness from environmental effects

---

would be culturally appropriate and yield meaningful results. Where Western mental health concepts form the basis of the research, the issue is whether these concepts are valid in other cultures. The last bulleted item refers to the observation that assessment of mental illness in Western countries assumes a healthy physical environment. The issue here refers to attempts to assess the presence of mental illness: How can this presence be detected in stressful environments that produce apparent symptoms in persons without mental illness? This chapter describes each of these issues in detail and how I have sought to address them.

"First, Do No Harm"

Issue

This principle originally comes from medical practice and has since been adapted to the public health sphere. With regard to mental health research, our concern has been that interviewing people about mental health, particularly asking about traumatic events, could be distressing and even harmful. There remain conflicting opinions on this perspective. Some experts I have consulted suggest that recalling traumatic events is more cathartic than harmful, but others are very concerned. There are also concerns about the impact of these interviews on the interviewers, particularly where they are local people who have also experienced traumatic events. Repeatedly talking with people about their experiences might be a constant reminder of their own experiences and be distressing.

Approach

The approaches to this issue are summarized in Table 7.2. On reflection, there appear to be no compelling programmatic reasons to interview people about traumatic experiences. Psychosocial and mental health needs are based on current problems rather than exposure, and many persons exposed to trauma do not require interventions. Even when interviewing for post-traumatic stress disorder (PTSD), where record of traumatic experiences is required for a diagnosis, the presence of the symptoms of PTSD are enough to determine whether a person has a specific problem or not. For those situations where interviewees want to talk about events, interviewers are given brief training on empathetic (i.e., emotionally perceptive) listen-

Table 7.2
Approach to Avoiding Harm to Respondents and Interviewers

- Avoid asking about traumatic events
- Train interviewers in listening and empathy
- Provide follow-up if available
- Provide debriefing for interviewers where indicated

---

ing. This listening style includes allowing interviewees to talk at length about their experiences before gently bringing them back to continue the questionnaire. In most cases, referring disturbed persons for further attention has not been an option, due to lack of appropriate services. In those situations, interviewers would ask people who felt they needed to talk if they would like them (the interviewer) to return later for further conversation. Requested return visits usually occurred the following day and, to permit these repeat visits, additional time was budgeted into the studies.

Additional resources have been required to address concerns about the interviewers' needs. During a study of depression in Rwanda in 1999, the interviewers were local people, many of whom had been present when the 1994 genocide occurred. At the end of each day a clinical psychologist working for the NGO met with the interviewers as a group (and individually as required) to discuss their experiences during the same or previous days. During a later study of mental health among displaced persons in northern Uganda, the interviewers did not reside in the displaced persons camps and therefore were not considered to be at increased risk of mental distress or of overly identifying with the interviewees. In that study, no special arrangements were made to provide psychological support to the interviewers.

Despite our concerns, in the Rwanda study participants with depression generally welcomed the opportunity to discuss their experiences and problems. Many spontaneously stated that the interview had helped them and asked for further visits. However, concerns for the interviewers were justified. There was a significant need for debriefing, and some were quite disturbed by their interviewing experiences. Those who were most disturbed were not the ones who had previously witnessed violence. Rather it was those with little experience who expressed the most distress at hearing of the severity of interviewees' experiences and symptoms. These interviewers said that the daily debriefings—both the individual and group discussions—were helpful in dealing with their distress. My impression was that the debriefings had this effect, with interviewers demonstrating improved mood after discussing their interviewing experiences.

This experience was repeated during a recent ethnographic study of the impact of human immunodeficiency virus (HIV) among HIV-positive women in Zambia. My colleagues found that reports of domestic violence appeared to be more disturbing for those local interviewers who had not been aware of these issues than for those who had knowledge and experience of the same. The interviewers also benefited from debriefing. In contrast, in Uganda, during studies of both children and adults, we did not find significant problems among the interviewers. In most cases, interviewees expressed problems related to grief and depression and to social problems resulting from displacement of the population. The emphasis was therefore on symptoms and on precipitating events that were within the range of normal experience (death of loved ones due to disease) and nonviolence (displacement). At this time, based on experience to date, it appears that listening to reports of terrible events outside the interviewer's experience, rather than reports of symptoms and signs, is most disturbing for interviewers. Therefore, future studies after violent events will continue to include psychological support for interviewers.

Practical Application

Issue

When first beginning health research, I decided that each study must benefit the community being studied. As with concerns about harming participants, this issue is considered an ethical one. If participants are asked to contribute their time, risk emotional upset, and relinquish some of their privacy, there should be tangible benefits to be gained. These requirements effectively disqualified research designed only to expand general human knowledge of mental health problems or simple assessment of prevalence without further beneficial action.

Approach

In each case, the Applied Mental Health Research (AMHR) group and I conduct applied research in collaboration with NGOs or other implementing organizations working with the local population. Rather than being stand-alone projects, these studies function as needs or impact assessments or both; the NGO partners commit to executing programs to address the major issues identified in the study, and the interventions should be followed by repeat assessments, to assess program impact.

What to Assess?

Issue

There are two distinct but complementary approaches to addressing mental health problems at the population level. One focuses on well-being and on persons who are distressed but not clinically ill (the psychosocial approach), while the other focuses on those with clinical illness. The decision of which to focus on, or whether to address both, is still controversial among organizations implementing mental health intervention programs (Bracken & Petty, 1998; Neugebauer, 2001; Silove, Ekblad, & Mollica, 2000; Summerfield, 1999).

Approach

In each population, our group's decision on what to focus on is based on three factors:

1. Public health importance
2. Measurability
3. Assessing the need for interventions requiring mental health expertise

Public health importance refers to both the prevalence and the severity of a condition. Therefore, a common severe problem would be a greater priority than a rare severe problem or a common mild problem. The technical issue of measurability refers to ability to accurately identify and measure the mental health variables of interest. If a problem cannot be measured then it cannot be determined whether interventions have made any difference, or even whether they are helpful or harmful. Regarding the need for mental health interventions, many mental health problems are relieved by non–mental health interventions (for example, creating schools and jobs or reuniting families). Therefore, assessing problems that respond to these interventions is not a priority for NGOs, not because they are not important, but because these interventions are already being implemented in most programs as part of normal community recovery or development efforts. Generating additional reasons for doing programs that will go ahead anyway is not important to programmatic planning. Instead, the major concern of assessment is whether there are problems not currently being addressed by existing programs.

For some mental illnesses, the fundamental diagnostic criteria are well established across at least some cultures, so that changes in illness status, prevalence, and incidence can be measured. Investigation of these illnesses would help define the need for specific mental health expertise. Examples include depression and PTSD, both of which can have a severe impact on those affected. Therefore, where they are common, they likely to represent public health priorities and be suitable for cross-cultural assessments, and lessons learned in one population may be relevant to others.

In both Rwanda and Uganda, the author's NGO partner felt that they could not address both categories of problems—both psychosocial and clinical. Based on the above considerations, I decided in each case to focus on assessment of clinical illness, specifically depression-like symptoms, rather than on nonclinical distress. Table 7.3 (left column) summarizes the major reasons for focusing on mental illness in these sites.

The right column of Table 7.3 refers to potential issues with focusing on mental illness that were of concern. The first three issues relate to the importance of cross-cultural differences, while the fourth issue addresses fears that only a small portion of the community would benefit from such a program. On reflection, the latter was dismissed as an issue. In other cultures where mental illness has been studied, it has been found to significantly affect other family members, because of problems with stigma and the need to care for

Table 7.3
Advantages and Disadvantages of Assessing Mental Illness

Advantages	Disadvantages
Depression and PTSD found to be common among a variety of populations	Not yet known if depression and PTSD occur across most cultures
Well-defined criteria	Unknown how appropriate these criteria are across cultures
Require mental health interventions	Lack of evidence for effective interventions in most cultures
Known to cause intense suffering and dysfunction	May require excessive focus on selected individuals

the individual. In populations where mental illness is common (e.g., in both Rwanda and Uganda), I found that 20 percent of adults in the communities studied had depression-like illness (Bolton, Neugebauer, & Ndogoni, 2002); this prevalence would result in many more people affected—both directly and indirectly—and ultimately helped by interventions.

Assessing Functioning

In addition to which types of mental health problems to assess, there is also the issue of assessing their impact on individuals and the population. The major reason mental health problems are important is their impact on individual and community function. Therefore, in each study we assessed the level of functioning of participants, including changes between initial and subsequent assessments (e.g., after a mental health intervention).

Existing instruments for assessing function are unsuitable for cross-cultural adaptation. Most instruments include questions on tasks that are biased toward the Western experience, such as shopping or playing golf (Ware, 1993). Even tasks that are commonly performed across cultures, such as cleaning house, may differ greatly in key aspects (e.g., cleaning a hut compared to cleaning an urban apartment). Other questions attempt to address this problem by asking about universal components of tasks, such as lifting a certain weight or walking a certain distance. But the lack of reference to any particular task that a person needs to do makes it difficult to assess the impact of dysfunction. The appropriate cutoff point for these activities also varies by culture—the ability to walk only one mile might be considered adequate in developed countries, but grossly dysfunctional among nomads. Finally, the impact of inability to do these components varies by culture and situation: Inability to lift a certain weight may be much less important to an office worker than an agricultural laborer. An approach was needed that could be used across cultures, yet give a better assessment of the important elements of function for both the individuals and those around them. To achieve both needs, we decided to abandon the goal of a single instrument that could be used across cultures. This forsaking of the goal was made easier by our conclusion, for the reasons described above, that existing instruments meant for cross-cultural use were achieving semantic but not real-world comparability. For each new population being studied, our approach is to identify tasks that local people consider important and to use these to construct a locally appropriate function assessment instrument (see *Ethnographic Methods* below) (Bolton & Tang, 2002).

Cross-Cultural Differences

Issues

Despite the support in the literature for the cross-cultural occurrence of mental illnesses such as depression and PTSD, few cultures have actually been studied. Evidence from one culture or another does necessarily support existence of the same phenomena in cultures not yet studied. Even for those populations that have been studied, there are problems with the quality of evidence: Many of the existing studies used only quantitative survey methods employing translated Western instruments. These often consist of questions with "yes or no" answers (closed questions) so that a person could be diagnosed as ill simply by saying yes to every symptom. There is a real risk that refugees and other groups in need (who are the subjects of many of these studies) may try to appear sick or badly off if they suspect it might win them increased assistance. Therefore, the use of closed questions alone is inadequate evidence for the presence of a specific mental illness or problem among these groups.

There are other instrument issues apart from the use of closed questions: Should a new instrument be created for each population, or can instruments used in other populations be adapted? If an existing instrument can be adapted, how can adequate translation be ensured? How can the instrument be validated among the local population (i.e., does the instrument measure what it is supposed to measure)?

Approach

Ethnographic Methods

Meeting these challenges requires a means of investigating by interview (independently of a quantitative survey) whether these illnesses really occur locally and, if so, how they are understood. Another aim is to conduct the investigation in a way that would not provide clues or suggestions to the respondent as to what these problems are or what the interviewer expects them to look like. In other words, the development of an open and nonleading method of investigation is required to precede the survey.

Ethnographic (or qualitative) methods provide the necessary approach. These methods are open ended in the sense that interviewees are encouraged to say whatever they want about a topic. They are nonleading in the sense that they are designed to obtain information from informants without providing verbal or other cues as to what the interviewer may expect to hear. When these methods are conducted correctly, the interviewee is allowed to present personal views while having no idea of what the interviewer thinks about that topic.

We incorporated a short ethnographic study into the research design to investigate local perceptions of mental health, prior to the use of quantitative instruments. The resulting information is then examined to determine whether the problems or illnesses in question occur in this population, and how they differ from these problems elsewhere. This information is then also used to design and test the quantitative instrument before using it to assess individuals.

The ethnographic study has three stages:

1. Free listing: A sample of the population of both sexes and various ages are each asked for a list of the problems affecting people in the community and a brief description of each problem. Once the list is complete, the interviewer reviews it for mental health problems. For each problem, the interviewee is asked for the name and contact information of someone in the community who is knowledgeable about that problem. Adult male respondents are then asked to list the important tasks that adult men do regularly to care for themselves, the tasks they do to care for their families, and the tasks they do to care for (or contribute to) their communities. Adult female respondents are asked for similar lists of tasks for adult women. In the case of children, both children and their caretakers are asked to describe normal behaviors for children, including both tasks and play.[2]

2. Key informant interviews: These interviews are detailed and open, with persons identified in the free lists as knowledgeable about specific mental health problems. The aim is to develop more detailed information about the problems given in the free lists, as well as to learn about other mental health problems not mentioned in the lists. Often several interviews are necessary with a respondent to record all their relevant information.

The data from methods 1 and 2 are studied to determine if any of the local problems (or combinations of problems) are substantially similar to specific mental problems or illnesses known to occur in Western countries. If no such similarities can be found, this absence is regarded as evidence that these Western mental illnesses either do not occur locally or are not very important. In either case, they are considered to be unsuitable as the basis for interventions and therefore are not studied further. On the other hand, if close similarities are found, this parallel is preliminary evidence that these illnesses occur and are important locally, which makes them suitable candidates for further assessment (by survey) and intervention (if found to be common).

Sometimes a clear picture of significant local problems fails to emerge from the free lists and key informant interviews. For example, for a particular local syndrome there may be disagreement on what are the important features. In this case, interviewing more key informants may make the picture clearer. Another option is to use a third method:

3. Pile sorts: A set of cards is created, each card representing a mental health symptom or problem that emerged in the free listing and key informant interviews. A new sample of local people, drawn in the same way as for the free listing, are asked to sort these cards into as many piles as they like, and then to explain why the cards in each pile belong together. All the pile sort results are summarized in a single table, showing which symptoms and problems frequently go together and which do not. These results are used to try to gain a consistent picture of the local disorder(s).

At the end of the ethnographic study, the researchers should have the following information:

- Do local versions of specific Western mental problems or illnesses exist?
- What are these problems called locally and how do they differ from their Western counterparts?
- What are the local terms and descriptions for other (non-Western) mental health symptoms and problems?
- What are the important tasks or behaviors that local people do regularly (adults, children, or both)?

Where the ethnographic study suggests the presence of a particular Western problem or illness, and an instrument is available for assessing it, it is simpler to adapt the existing instrument rather than to create a new one. In Rwanda, the ethnographic study supported the local occurrence of both depression and PTSD. We assessed depression by adapting the depression section of the Hopkins Symptom Checklist (HSCL) (Derogatis, Lipman, Rickels, Uhlenhuth, & Covi, 1974). We chose the HSCL because it has been used for many years in a variety of cultures and found to work well. All the symptoms assessed in the HSCL were mentioned in the ethnographic ministudy as part of local syndromes, which supported its validity for local use.

Function

At this stage, we also analyze the results of the free listing exercise on tasks. Interviews are collapsed into summary lists of what men, women, and children do. For men and women, these lists are reviewed for the tasks mentioned most frequently and for which inability to perform a task clearly affects others. These tasks are included in the quantitative instrument. For example, in Rwanda, prayer was listed frequently as an important task that men and women do to care for themselves. However, it was removed as it was not clear that the inability to pray would cause problems for others.

Washing oneself was retained because others would have to do this task for the person if they could not do it themselves. This difference does not imply that tasks like praying are not important to the individual and that the inability to perform them is not distressing. In the case of children, the most frequently mentioned tasks and behaviors were chosen.

Using these criteria, 10 tasks are chosen for men, 10 for women, and 10 for children. These are included in a draft function instrument that has separate sections for men, women, and children. For each task or behavior, respondents are asked the amount of difficulty they have in performing it, compared to others of their age and sex. The function instrument is combined with the adapted (or created) instrument assessing local mental health problems, to form a draft survey instrument.

Translation

The standard approach to translation of quantitative survey instruments involves either a sequential translation/back-translation method or group translation. In the former, one individual does translation into the desired language and another person also fluent in both languages then translates the result back into the original language. Both work in isolation. Comparison of the original version with the back-translated version allows the investigator to assess the accuracy of the initial translation. In group translation, translators work together to produce a consensus version.

We have had problems when using these approaches, even when used together. In developing countries, particularly poor rural areas where people are less educated, translators are different from most of the community. They are usually more educated or have a higher socioeconomic status than most local people. Even if they come from the local area, they frequently have lived for an extended time away from the community (to seek education or work); they may not even come from the community being studied. These differences result in different word usage from most of the community, especially the poorer members. The result can be translation of key concepts into terms that local people do not share or whose meaning if different from that of the translators. In practice, we have found that group translation and translation/back-translation cannot address or even detect these problems. This incapability is because both methods only use translators to check each other's work.

To enhance the quality of the translation, we have continued to use both these approaches, but then compared the resulting translation of key concepts with the terms used by participants in the ethnographic study. This consultation includes the translators. Where the translators have used a term that differs from the local term, the local term is substituted. The draft instrument is then pilot-tested on community members as part of the validity study and tested for understandability. This evaluation is done after the interview by asking the participant what questions, if any, were difficult or confusing. Interviewers then meet to compare notes. For those questions for which multiple respondents reported difficulties, the questions are reviewed with the translators and the key concepts checked again against the ethnographic data.

Validity

The final cross-cultural issue is how to test the local validity of the draft instrument. This evaluation is done after the pilot-testing. Validity refers to whether the instrument measures what it is supposed to measure. In this context, the issue is whether an instrument that accurately assesses a particular mental health problem among Western populations does the same among another population. Even with accurate translation, validity may be poor and must be checked separately. The objective is to establish "criterion validity," which is accomplished by comparing the newer instrument with another method (referred to as a "gold standard"), which is already known to be valid among the local population. When assessing mental health problems, the gold standard is often an assessment by a mental health professional familiar with the population of interest. For most of the populations that NGOs work with, this information is not available. Therefore, an alternative method for testing criterion validity is needed.

We have used a modified approach for testing validity without a gold standard (Bolton, 2001). For example, in our studies in Rwanda and Uganda, we determined which of the local problems described in the ethnographic study was closest to the Western concept of depression. Knowledgeable persons were then asked to name community members who definitely had this local problem and those who definitely did not. A short validity study was then conducted: These community members were interviewed by using the instrument, without the interviewers knowing whether or not they were said to have the illness. At the end of the interview, respondents were asked if they thought they had the illness.

In the analysis, only those interviews were used in which the knowledgeable person and the respondent agreed that they had or did not have the illness. This requirement was to decrease the likelihood of misdiagnosis of the local problem. For the remaining cases, the association between diagnosis with the local problem by the respondent and others was compared with diagnosis of depression by the instrument. In both Rwanda and Uganda, a strong relationship was found between depression and report of a depression-like illness, supporting the validity of the instrument to diagnose depression.[3] Once all these tasks had been completed, the survey instrument was ready for use in a standard survey.

Separating Mental Illness from Environmental Effects

Issue

The final issue is how to diagnose a mental illness, particularly depression and PTSD, in environments likely to produce symptoms even among those without these disorders. For example, many people will temporarily express symptoms of distress and depression as part of a normal time-limited reaction to traumatic events and loss. Persons may continue to manifest abnormal symptoms for long periods when the environment remains stressful. For example, individuals could be expected to exhibit depression symptoms such as depressed mood, loss of appetite, difficulty sleeping, and loss of interest as part of a normal response to situations where families have been split up and people reside in areas of poverty and crowding. Refugees who reside in dangerous or insecure environments might exhibit many of the symptoms of PTSD and anxiety disorders (such as heightened anxiety and exaggerated startle reactions) as a matter of survival.

Approach

Little work has been done in Western countries to identify symptoms that indicate illness regardless of circumstances, and we have been unable to find any work in this area for other cultures. Lacking a way to reliably identify illness in these stressful environments, we have opted to delay assessments until the situation has improved and after the normal grieving period has passed. This choice is consistent with our contention that the best initial mental health interventions are those focused on improving the person's environment. Once improvements are done to the extent possible, it is appropriate to conduct assessments to determine those whose symptoms are persisting and therefore require additional specific interventions.

Conclusions

- Ethical considerations require linking research with mental health interventions.
- Mental illness is an appropriate (but not the only) focus for mental health research in developing countries, particularly among trauma-affected populations.
- We have attempted to address the major cross-cultural assessment issues through applied ethnographic methods combined with quantitative assessment.
- Issues in differentiating illness from environmental effects require that assessment be delayed until the normal grieving period has passed and the environment has improved. This preference is consistent with focusing assessment on issues that require specific mental health expertise.

Notes

1. Manuals describing all the methods used by the author and AMHR and mentioned in this chapter can be obtained from the author on request at pbolton@bu.edu.
2. This approach has so far been successfully used for children from 10 to 17 years of age.

3. Where the issue is validity in assessing the presence of a local syndrome without a Western equivalent, a slightly simpler approach was used: Responses to questions about the local syndrome's symptoms were compared directly against report of the respondent and others as to whether they have the syndrome.

References

Bolton, P. (2001). Cross-cultural validity and reliability testing of a standard psychiatric assessment instrument without a gold standard. *Journal of Nervous & Mental Disease, 189*, 238–242.

———, P., Neugebauer, R., & Ndogoni, L. (2002). Prevalence of depression in rural Rwanda based on symptom and functional criteria. *Journal of Nervous & Mental Disease, 190*, 631–637.

———, & Tang, A. (2002). An alternative approach to cross-cultural function assessment. *Social Psychiatry and Psychiatric Epidemiology, 37*, 537–543.

Bracken, P. & Petty, C. (Eds.). (1998). *Rethinking the trauma of war*. New York: Free Association Books.

Derogatis, L. R., Lipman, R. S., Rickels, K., Uhlenhuth, E. H., & Covi, L. (1974). The Hopkins Symptom Checklist (HSCL): A measure of primary symptom dimensions. *Modern Problems in Psychopharmacology, 7*, 79–110.

Neugebauer, R. (2001). Minding the world's health: World Health Day 2001 [Editorial]. *American Journal of Public Health, 91*, 551–552.

Silove, D., Ekblad, S., & Mollica, R. (2000). The rights of the severely mentally ill in post-conflict societies. *Lancet, 355*, 1548–1549.

Summerfield, D. (1999). A critique of seven assumptions behind psychological trauma programmes in war-affected areas. *Social Science & Medicine, 48*, 144–162.

Ware, J. E., Jr. (1993). *SF-36 health survey manual and interpretation guide*. Boston, MA: The Health Institute, New England Medical Center.

CHAPTER 8

DEVELOPMENT OF THE RAPID ASSESSMENT OF MENTAL HEALTH: AN INTERNATIONAL COLLABORATION

Gerard A. Jacobs, Jean Pierre Revel, Gilbert Reyes, and Randal P. Quevillon

Introduction

The present chapter is intended to provide the reader with a sense of the process involved in a collaboration among two major international organizations and a small academic institution. The purpose of this project was to develop a method of assessing the mental health needs of people who were displaced from their homes due to armed conflict or its consequences (i.e., refugees and displaced persons). The World Health Organization (WHO) undertook this endeavor and enlisted the assistance of the world's largest humanitarian nongovernmental organization (NGO), the International Federation of Red Cross and Red Crescent Societies (IFRC). To provide the technical assistance necessary for developing an approach consistent with the scientific literature on mental health needs and assessments, they turned to the Disaster Mental Health Institute (DMHI) at the University of South Dakota (USD).

The present chapter describes the most instructive elements of the collaborative process between these global humanitarian organizations and a team of psychology professors and doctoral students housed within an academic institution. The operational roles and the challenges faced by all three parties to this partnership are mainly viewed from the academic perspective of those at the DMHI. Collaborations between large organizations and academic institutions are nothing new, of course, and there are many different types of partnerships depending on the goals and the institutions involved. Typically the details of such collaborations are kept private, making it difficult for others to learn from examples such as the one illustrated in the present chapter. In the interest of transparency, the present chapter outlines the process that unfolded and highlights the most salient and instructive aspects for the purpose of informing others who may wish to forge similar partnerships.

Since the beginning of their activity, humanitarian organizations have focused on the provision of assistance to victims of disasters or conflicts. Such assistance consists mainly of food and nonfood items such as shelter, water, sanitation, and health care. At the end of the 1980s, in Western Europe and North America, a series of disasters and transport accidents raised the issue of "nonmaterial needs." Mass casualty disasters in the Baltic Sea and in the United States, and a rash of very large-scale natural disasters in the United States, were experienced as traumatic events both by those who were directly affected and by the disaster response workers. A number of Red Cross national societies began to discuss the need for some form of systematic psychological support for those affected by disasters.

In May 1991, the First International Conference on Psychological Support was convened by the IFRC in Copenhagen, Denmark. The participants were representatives of Red Cross or Red Crescent national societies. Among the recommendations produced by the participants was a call to launch an IFRC Psychological Support Programme (PSP).

As these programs developed in various countries and as psychological support began to become a more common part of humanitarian assistance, similarities to and differences with other forms of assistance emerged.

Psychological support needed to be tailored to each individual culture to a much greater extent than the provision of food, water, shelter, and so forth. Initially there were questions about whether some cultures would need or even permit psychological support. Over time, however, it has become evident that a need for psychological support is as widespread as the need for food, water, and shelter.

As with any scientific endeavor, methodology with regard to psychological support became progressively more rigorous. Funding agencies began to demand greater accountability for resources invested in psychological support, including accurate assessment of needs and evaluation of outcome. The need for food, water, and shelter can be accurately calculated with a minimum of knowledge about the situation (e.g., how many people are affected), and the effectiveness of such assistance can be measured through obvious means (e.g., how many pounds of food, gallons of water, and cots and blankets have been distributed; even the impact of this assistance on the condition of those affected is subject to monitoring through indicators such as mortality, morbidity, and nutritional status). But for psychological support, the assessment of needs is not as straightforward, and it is very difficult to measure how much psychological support has been delivered in a relief operation and what its impact was. There was a growing need for scientifically validated tools for psychological support program management.

The World Health Organization is the United Nations' specialized agency for health. In humanitarian situations, WHO works with government ministries of health to bring about the highest possible level of health. WHO's definition of health was set forth in its constitution in 1946: "Health is a state of complete physical, mental and social well-being and not merely the absence of disease or infirmity" (WHO, 2004). In humanitarian situations and especially in complex emergencies, WHO often serves to coordinate health services and related programs being provided by various government and nongovernment agencies and organizations.

Mary Petevi was the Coordinator for the Mental Health of Refugees and Displaced Persons in the Programme on Mental Health, Division of Mental Health and Prevention of Substance Abuse at WHO in 1999. She had reviewed efforts to assess the need for psychological support in several previous complex emergencies. In her analysis, she concluded that assessments of the psychological support needs of refugee populations in the early stages of events had exhibited several shortcomings.

These assessments had been primarily clinical in nature rather than population oriented. In other words, they had focused on the clinical pathology in individuals rather than on the psychological needs of the entire affected community. Since there are limits to available resources, the humanitarian response to such events seldom has the capacity to serve the specific clinical needs of individuals. Assessment instruments used that *were* validated had rarely been revalidated for the culture or even language in which they were being used. Assessments used generally focused on deficits and provided little information about resources. The assessments usually were very focused, examining only a limited specific component of the overall situation. The assessments were conducted by expatriates and only rarely involved local partners. Furthermore, the communities that were the focus of the assessments were rarely directly consulted about how the assessment could best be conducted. The variety of strategies used in the assessments and the shortcomings mentioned above made it difficult to compare data from different assessments of the same emergency or between emergencies. Finally, assessments were generally conducted in isolation, providing very little information about the evolution of needs and resources across time within an event or across different events.

Among those in leadership roles in both government and nongovernment organizations, these shortcomings had resulted in resistance to programs for psychological support. It was difficult to document the need for psychological support, which, in turn, resulted in a lack of credibility, and the consequential loss of political and financial support. Moreover, this uncertainty and inconsistency had also resulted in a lack of adequate agency policies regarding psychological support and limited cooperation between different sectors of responses to events and between different agencies providing psychological support in the response operations.

At the operational level, these shortcomings had also had an impact on efforts to provide effective psychological support. Inconsistent support for the concept and inconsistent funding led to poor preparedness. Agencies generally did not have a plan for "capacity-building" for psychological support. Programs were not fielded in all operations, and when psychological support was provided, the programs seemed to be too narrow or even inappropriate to meet the needs of the communities they were intended to serve. In addition, psychological support programs were generally structured as independent operations, and they had limited interaction with the public health community, which had responsibility for the ongoing care of the community. Programs were seldom community based, focusing rather on clinical interventions with a very small portion of the affected communities. Often these were psychiatric programs involving the short-term use of psychotropic medications. The sustainability of such programs was limited, due to both the lack of involvement of community members in the program and the high cost per individual served. These operational problems, in turn, further limited the political acceptance of psychological support as a standard part of humanitarian response to complex emergencies.

Moreover, this analysis was discussed at a meeting of WHO emergency humanitarian assistance partners in 1998. The partner organizations generally agreed with these conclusions, and the WHO Department of Mental Health and Substance Dependence (MSD) decided to develop a tool to provide a more standardized method of assessment. An initial Work Group was formed, including the WHO MSD, IFRC, and the International Centre for Migration and Health (ICMH). ICMH is a nonprofit association of institutions and people committed to improving the health of people in the context of migration of all kinds. ICMH has been designated as a WHO Collaborating Centre for Health-related Issues.

Development of the RAMH

Early in their discussions, the working group recognized that its members had extensive field experience, but limited academic/scientific background. They also decided that there was a need for a fresh perspective from outside the community of those who provided humanitarian assistance to refugee communities. The members of the working group were aware of the Disaster Mental Health Institute's (DMHI) work with the IFRC's psychological support program. In January 1999, Petevi contacted Gerard Jacobs, Director of the DMHI at the University of South Dakota (USD). Petevi said that the DMHI's work with the American Red Cross and the IFRC, as well as the USD Clinical Psychology Training Program's reputation for excellence in community and cross-cultural theory, and the Program's firm academic/scientific perspective were key elements for the invitation. She asked if the DMHI would join the working group, to provide an academic/scientific perspective. Specifically, her initial request was that the DMHI conduct a critical review of the extant literature on refugee mental health and summa-rize what was known regarding effective assessment of the mental health needs of refugees in the early stages of an event.

The DMHI is a fairly small entity. It is comprised of three full-time and two part-time faculty who are all clinical psychologists holding PhD degrees and six doctoral fellows in the USD Clinical Psychology Training Program. It provides both graduate and undergraduate academic curricula. All of the DMHI faculty are members of American Red Cross disaster response teams and serve as volunteers in disaster mental health during disaster relief opera-tions. Two are also members of the IFRC International Roster for Psycho-logical Support. The DMHI had no experience in the field of refugee mental health; the DMHI's work had been exclusively in the field of disas-ter psychology and preparedness activities.

Joining the Work Group represented a significant diversion from the work in which the DMHI had thus far been involved. An invitation from a major UN organization or an NGO can be a seductive opportunity, but needs to be considered with care. The faculty and students held a series of meetings to discuss the implications and ramifications of taking on this role. For academic faculty and doctoral students, it represented more than simply taking on a new project. It had implications for the faculty's research pro-grams, and for the untenured faculty, it also had importance for progress toward promotion and tenure. For faculty and students, it meant becoming familiar with an entirely new field of research. It meant abandoning, at least temporarily, projects that had potential for external funding. In return, there were other possibilities for funding if the DMHI were able to develop a good reputation in its work with WHO, and the potential for positively impacting humanitarian assistance strategies was evident.

The DMHI's commitment to WHO could not be in name only. Four of the five faculty and five of the six doctoral fellows committed significant por-tions of their workload to this project. This acceptance also entailed encum-bering a major portion of the DMHI budget, both in the form of personnel and in the actual costs of conducting a thorough review of the literature. Other than the DMHI's fixed academic curricula, nearly the entire produc-tive capacity of the DMHI became focused on the collaboration with WHO.

The task given the DMHI by the Work Group was to quickly conduct a review of the relevant literature and to develop a practical field assessment instrument to document the needs of refugees for psychological support. This instrument was intended to be equally effective in any refugee event anywhere in the world. The DMHI was to deliver a draft document in three months. It was made clear that this first assignment was a test of the DMHI's working capacity and professional savvy. The Work Group gave the DMHI little guid-ance, hoping to achieve a genuinely fresh look at the issues. The time frame did not allow a thorough search of the literature. The doctoral fellows obtained and summarized the relevant literature, which were reviewed by the faculty.

In addition, the faculty discussed theoretical issues in assessment, field operations, community theory, trauma, resiliency, and cultural/ethnic/religious awareness and sensitivity. First, a set of principles emerged for the assessment tool. Then, an outline was developed, laying out the essential elements. Strategies for assessing those elements were selected. Finally, the specific method of fulfilling each strategy was agreed on.

About halfway through this process, WHO forwarded to the DMHI literature that the Work Group felt was important to have included. Much of this material overlapped with the sources garnered through the DMHI literature searches, but in addition there were also UN and NGO reports and program evaluations that were technically in the public domain, but not visible through traditional literature search techniques. Such sources are sometimes referred to as "gray literature." This material hinted at issues that the Work Group felt were important, and these were consistent with the DMHI's approach from the beginning. The reports also provided some valuable documentation of the challenges to be faced and the relative utility of various strategies.

In April 1999, the DMHI forwarded its first formal draft of the Rapid Mental Health Assessment (RAMH) to WHO. It included a critical review of the literature, a point-by-point rationale based on that review, the actual proposed instrument, and suggestions for training that would be required to effectively employ the tool. This process was a very anxious one for the DMHI faculty and fellows. They had worked in a relative void, trying to develop a refined strategy and instrument from an amorphous mass of literature and theory. In the same time frame, the other members of the Work Group had been discussing the necessary components and characteristics of the rapid assessment, based on their extensive field experience in refugee events. Therefore, when they received the DMHI draft, they had expectations of what would be included and how the content would be structured.

Second Phase of the Development of the RAMH

The feedback to the DMHI was that it was obvious that the DMHI had no field experience in refugee situations. This statement was not news to either the DMHI or the other members of the Work Group. Concerns regarding the practicality of the application of the instrument in the field were detailed, with suggestions for alternate strategies. The DMHI was asked to have a more thorough review of the literature completed and a more practical form for the instrument prepared by July.

Despite the intensity of the first phase, in the second phase of the development of the RAMH, the efforts of the DMHI doubled. All fellows were committed to the project and two faculty focused almost completely on the effort. Another faculty member was asked to make the review of the literature his sole commitment for the next four months.

The electronic search engines Psyclit and Medline were used. Search terms were related to field assessment of mental health, refugee mental health, community-based interventions, and cross-cultural issues in assessment. Letters were sent to noted authorities in the field, explaining the WHO project to them and soliciting their input regarding the most important resources to examine, including, if possible, copies of any "gray literature" materials they might be able to share. Because of the limited resources of the DMHI, the search was limited to English-language literature or materials with at least an English abstract.

All books that were identified as important were purchased, and all articles identified were obtained. (The United States has an interlibrary loan system that makes it possible to obtain copies of any material held at any of the participating libraries in the nation.) Each source obtained was subjected to an "umbrella search," scanning the document for any other relevant resources, which were then ordered. All materials were annotated in a uniform systematic process. All annotations were reviewed by Reyes and then passed on to the other faculty. Reyes took on the task of writing a review of the literature, while the other faculty focused more on refining the instrument based on the feedback from the Work Group and the ongoing review of the literature. In the end, some 650 sources were identified and obtained, of which roughly 200 were considered significant for the immediate work.

Community Principles in Development of the RAMH

The community principles brought to bear in the development of the DMHI draft instrument were nearly mirror images of the problems identified by Petevi in her initial evaluation that had begun the entire process, even though that assessment had not been shared with the DMHI. The development of the RAMH was heavily influenced by the principles and values of community psychology. The fabric of this approach is woven from the threads of numerous concepts (e.g., Dalton, Elias, & Wandersman, 2001; Levine, Perkins, & Perkins, 2005; Rappaport, 1977). Community theory, though not monolithic, has strong consistent emphases on the need for cultural sensitivity and respect for diversity, capacity building and empowerment, consideration of strengths as well as weaknesses, collaboration and active participation by those being served, and advocacy.

More than many other forms of humanitarian assistance, assessing the need for or providing psychological support to refugees and internally displaced persons demands a high level of cultural sensitivity and respect for diversity. A culturally informed assessment process is critical to the validity of the information gathered. It is also a safeguard against the assessment itself being a source of further stress or victimization. The disruption of social norms produced by the event, for example, must be assessed with cultural competence, including knowledge of the target population's social structure, norms and mores, and diversity. To gauge disruptions of maternal roles, for instance, a culturally informed knowledge of the range of typical maternal roles is necessary.

Procedurally, the assessment process needs to fit within the cultural context as well. For example, if interviews with key informants are being used in the assessment, the indigenous customs regarding who may disclose information to whom (e.g., whether a child can talk directly to an adult stranger, if men may ask questions of women directly, etc.) must be known and followed. A careful, consultative, and deeply respectful approach is needed to yield the most accurate and useful data possible and to avoid negatively impacting people who may already be traumatized.

The RAMH also employed an ecological perspective (see Kelly, 1966; Kelly, Ryan, Altman, & Stelzner, 2000). In community psychology, the ecological approach includes a focus on the interdependence of systems as well as the cycling of resources, including resources for stress relief and psychological support. An important element of the RAMH is documenting areas of strength, such as specific resources and cultural practices for stress relief and resilience. In addition, it was considered tremendously important for the RAMH to obtain information regarding the complex interaction of political, social, and cultural factors within the displacement event and its context.

The model of trauma that shaped the RAMH was also a reflection of community psychology principles. Traditional psychology, psychiatry, and public health have often employed a disease model in assessing and treating psychological problems. This model tends to employ categorical views of who felt the impact of events. That is, displacing events would be seen as causing, both at the time of the event and in the future, a given number of individuals who would show enough symptoms to qualify as a "case" or a diseased or impaired individual (i.e., one who meets criteria for a diagnosis such as post-traumatic stress disorder or major depression). Unfortunately, this categorical approach focuses those providing assistance on a narrow range of human responses, can severely limit the number of persons who receive assistance, and increases the likelihood of unfortunate and needless stigma (see Scheff, 1999).

The model used in the development of the RAMH, consonant with many community psychology theorists and psychological first aid approaches of humanitarian organizations, employs a stress model as its prime explanatory conceptual framework for describing psychological impacts of disastrous events (see, for example, Dohrenwend, 1978). One of the most salient aspects of this model is that it is a dimensional model. Instead of relying on clinical "caseness," the model provides services to individuals who do not currently, and may never, meet diagnostic criteria—it broadens the range to anyone who might reasonably benefit from psychological support. This expansion also helps reduce the stigma associated with mental health assessment and intervention.

This stress model emphasizes contextual factors of the stress response, not just what happens within the individual. Social support and other beneficial resources are emphasized, which focuses attention on several potential sources of benefit for those affected by the event. Consequently, assessments need to include information regarding various social structures that might be sources of resilience (e.g., family patterns and religious or spiritual practices), which could be supported as part of a community-focused psychological support program, as well as documenting those context elements that might have a negative influence on the psychological well-being of those affected.

While many other community psychology-influenced concepts guided the development of the RAMH, the need for a culturally informed and respectful process, the use of an ecological perspective, and the employment of a dimensional model of psychological reactions to the events were the most significant in shaping the final tool.

These community principles were employed in considering the levels of analysis that were needed, the consideration of context in the assessment, the use of indicators, the assessment of resources as well as deficits, and in considering how the information would best be used. Consideration was also given to the assumption that the rapid assessment would be only one piece of a larger assessment package that would include an ongoing needs assessment, assessment of program conceptualization and design, monitoring program operations and service delivery, evaluating program outcomes or impact, and assessing effectiveness (including cost effectiveness).

Third Phase and Field Review of the RAMH

The DMHI team submitted a second draft to WHO in July 1999 and received fairly rapid feedback, together with a request to revise and resubmit within just two weeks. The feedback focused primarily on the practical application of the instrument in a field setting. The DMHI team struggled to incorporate the feedback from the Work Group and in August 1999 submitted its third draft to WHO.

This draft was submitted by WHO to 25 authorities in the field, representing high- and low-income countries and countries coping with both conflict and nonconflict events. Their feedback was reviewed in September 1999 by the Work Group and used to modify the RAMH. This draft was reviewed internally by WHO and sent again to the field reviewers. It was also used for a pilot test in East Timor in December 1999. Further adjustments were made by the Work Group before the tool was sent for a third major external review. This final review was conducted by a larger group of authorities in the field nominated by the Work Group and invited by WHO to participate.

In September 2000, the Work Group met for five days virtually around the clock, reviewing the very detailed commentary from the reviewers. This discussion was very frank and animated, and it explored and genuinely evaluated each suggestion that was made. A final draft was produced based on these discussions. One tiny aspect of this session, the naming of the tool, highlighted some of the challenges of working in an international political context. Politically correct language becomes more difficult when many UN agencies and international NGOs are involved. The title wound up being 22 words long (Petevi, Revel, & Jacobs, 2001).

Final Review and Endorsement

Thirty-five authorities in the field participated in the International Consultation on Mental Health of Refugees and Displaced Populations in Conflict and Post-Conflict Situations, which was held at WHO world headquarters in Geneva in October 2000. Relevant UN agencies and NGOs also sent observers.

The opening session of this event was fairly overwhelming in its majesty. Held in the board room of WHO in Geneva, the participants were seated at a circular table, while the gallery of the chamber was nearly filled with observers. Dr. Gro Harlem Brundtland, Director-General of WHO, and Ms. Mary Robinson, United Nations High Commissioner for Human Rights, and other dignitaries addressed the session. Over the next three days the participants made minor changes to the document and, in the end, endorsed the use of the RAMH in refugee situations worldwide. The tool was officially released by WHO in January 2001. The RAMH is available for downloading from the Internet at http://www.who.int/disasters/repo/7405.pdf.

In the months that followed, plans were made for further field testing of the RAMH and for the development of the remainder of the comprehensive assessment package of which the RAMH had only been intended to be the initial component. By October 2001, WHO and the DMHI had laid out a five-year plan for the development and testing of a Detailed Assessment of Mental Health, which was to be the ongoing tool for assessment of changing aspects of the situation, for determination of the effectiveness of any psychological support program, and for the development of a program to train people in the appropriate use of the tools.

Intervening disaster responses delayed contact with the WHO office for the Mental Health of Refugees. In January, calls to that office by the DMHI were not answered. After some effort, queries through other offices at WHO revealed that the Mental Health of Refugees office had been closed at the end of 2001. The entity funding the office chose not to renew the funding, and the office simply ceased to exist—as did the collaboration with the DMHI and the five-years of work to which the DMHI had agreed.

Lessons Learned

Working with major international agencies and NGOs has some impressive benefits and advantages. But there are also some major caveats that come with the territory.

The reputation and resources of WHO are fairly amazing. They enabled WHO to draw together 35 of the best minds in refugee mental health in the world for the international consultation. How many university programs or independent NGOs could convince many of the top experts in the field to conduct a detailed review of a draft tool without monetary compensation? In addition, a recommendation from WHO carries considerably more power than it would from a typical NGO.

In working with such large and powerful organizations, however, politics will often dictate the terminology that is used—and even the mission, goals, and objectives of a project. One day a project involves "mental health," the next day "psychology," and the following day "psychosocial support." The project can fluctuate from conflict situations to nonconflict situations. The program everyone is collaborating on can be the most important thing to the organization one moment, but suddenly becomes only one of a dozen the next. A detailed five-year collaboration can dissolve at the whim of a funding agency or government or because of some organizational restructuring.

It is also important to realize that such organizations often do not give authorship to individuals or share organizational credit for documents published under their logo. That means that an organization or individual can spend many months on a scholarly endeavor and receive not so much as an acknowledgment in the resulting product. If an organization or individual depends on recognition for funding or for credit toward promotion and tenure, it is important to realize that these organizations probably are not the professional path to seek.

In the case of the RAMH, people familiar with WHO found it extraordinary that the names of the Work Group were included as authors and that both the DMHI and IFRC were listed as developing the project jointly with WHO. Despite the extensive contributions of some other DMHI faculty and staff, however, they received only acknowledgments in the final product. For tenure-track faculty, it would be useful before undertaking such tasks to ensure that their university recognizes this aspect of international humanitarian work and can accept a letter from the agency assuring them that a scholarly product without the faculty member's name on it is nevertheless evidence of scholarly achievement.

From the perspective of major international agencies and NGOs, on the other hand, collaborating with high-quality small NGOs and academic institutions has distinct advantages as well. These smaller organizations often have the flexibility to respond quickly to requests, a flexibility that larger organizations often do not have. Academic institutions have a particular advantage in the availability of well-educated highly trained doctoral students who can take on aspects of research and scholarly work for their own projects, theses, and dissertations.

In conclusion, before deciding to work with a major NGO, UN agency, or some similar entity, examine both the advantages and the disadvantages. In addition, be certain to have alternate plans that can be substituted for projects that may simply disappear or change dramatically in nature overnight—an especially important consideration for tenure-track faculty who intend to remain at their institutions.

References

Dalton, J. H., Elias, M. A., & Wandersman, A. (2001). *Community psychology: Linking individuals and communities.* Belmont, CA: Wadsworth.

Dohrenwend, B. S. (1978). Social stress and community psychology. *American Journal of Community Psychology, 6,* 1–14.

Kelly, J. G. (1966). Ecological constraints on mental health services. *American Psychologist, 21,* 535–539.

———, Ryan, A. M., Altman, B. F., & Stelzner, S. P. (2000). Understanding and changing social systems: An ecological view. In J. Rappaport & E. Seidman (Eds.), *Handbook of community psychology* (pp. 133–159). New York: Kluwer Academic/Plenum.

Levine, M., Perkins, D. D., & Perkins, D. V. (2005). *Principles of community psychology: Perspectives and applications* (3rd ed.). New York: Oxford University Press.

Petevi, M., Revel, J. P., & Jacobs, G. A. (2001). *Tool for the rapid assessment of mental health needs of refugees, displaced and other populations affected by conflict and post-conflict situations: A community-oriented assessment.* Geneva, Switzerland: World Health Organization.

Rappaport, J. (1977). *Community psychology: Values, research, and action.* New York: Holt, Rinehart & Winston.

Scheff, T. J. (1999). *Being mentally ill: A sociological perspective* (3rd ed.). New York: Aldine de Gruyter.

World Health Organization. (2004). Constitution of the World Health Organization. Retrieved November 29, 2004, from http://policy.who.int/cgi-bin/om_isapi.dll ?hitsperheading=on&infobase=basicdoc&record={21}&softpage=Document42

CONCLUSIONS AND RECOMMENDATIONS FOR FURTHER PROGRESS

Gilbert Reyes

A frequently expressed concern in humanitarian circles is that we are chronically engaged in the inefficient process of "reinventing the wheel." Frustrations regarding this issue seem justified, given the tendency of humanitarian organizations to operate in a more territorial and insular manner than is either necessary or wise. Counterarguments point to frequent conferences among these NGOs, but such meetings seldom result in substantive changes in policies or operations, and cooperative agreements are the exception rather than the rule. A reasonable inference can be drawn that some humanitarian organizations would rather take a proprietary stance toward "wheel development," preferring the autonomy and distinctiveness of creating their own "wheel" to the efficiency and communality involved in working cooperatively with others of their kind. Similar observations can be made regarding mental health professionals, who are sometimes better rewarded for relabeling borrowed "wheels" than they would be for adopting existing wheels with minimal adaptations to suit the particular conditions of their situation. One might say that, rather than reinventing the wheel (i.e., the general model of psychological support), a more efficient procedure is to adapt elements of wheels successfully used by others to fit the characteristics of one's own particular terrain. The responsibility for ensuring that a modified "wheel" (i.e., a situation-specific model) will be culturally congruent rests with the people in the affected areas, who are free to select what to keep or discard and choose the placement and timing of its use. Thus, what gets adopted in any given situation will be generally useful principles, but the operational details and practices will vary in accordance with needs, cultures, and conditions.

A major intention of the *Handbook of International Disaster Psychology* has been to establish a sufficiently diversified base of information on when, where, why, and how disaster psychosocial services are implemented, as well as what is done and by whom. Accordingly, the contributing authors have articulated many of the most important ideas that have influenced the development of psychosocial humanitarian operations over the past decade. They have also shared their own activities and experiences in a transparent manner so that others might learn from their successes and failures. Their descriptions of the practices and principles that have been employed to help heal the psychological and social wounds among populations affected by potentially traumatic events offer a rich resource from which others with similar goals may borrow to formulate their own programs and practices.

Volume 1 provided an overview of the field and addressed the fundamentals issues and principles of concern to those who design and implement psychosocial programs for disaster survivors. Volume 2 described a variety of programs conducted around the world and the recommended practices for promoting effect healing at both individual and collective levels. Volume 3 focused specifically on mental health issues of refugees and the favored approaches to needs assessment and psychosocial care under a complex set of conditions and stages of migration. Volume 4 identified several populations whose special needs and circumstances tend to be overlooked and thus require conscientious consideration to ensure adequate care. The authors, all of whom are experienced members of the international humanitarian community, represent a broad spectrum of nationalities, cultures, and viewpoints. The stories told in these pages should prove instructive and inspiring to anyone concerned with promoting the psychosocial welfare of people who have endured the fear and loss that accompany widespread violence and social upheaval. Readers are encouraged to glean from these works the most useful and inspiring ideas from which they can develop their own skills, practices, and programs.

Politics, Cultures, and Controversies
Cannot Be Ignored

International psychosocial support activities have not unfolded without controversy. Some have argued that the humanitarian psychosocial movement reflects Western ideology with a vision of life and its norms that is at odds with native cultures indigenous to those places where catastrophic events are most likely to occur. Critics invoke images of cultural imperialism perpetrated by the former colonial aggressors against the relatively innocent and primitive captives of their misguided ministrations. There is certainly some truth in these accusations, given the asymmetry of a humanitarian community dominated by lighter-skinned people of the Northern Hemisphere "serving" the darker-skinned peoples of the Southern Hemisphere in a present version of *White Man's Burden* (Kipling, 1899). But the comparisons employed by these critics are commonly as dramatic, overwrought, and anecdotal as the claims their adversaries use to compel the forces of "compassionate" action. In the absence of reliable evidence, what poses for truth may be unfounded but persuasive claims which better serve the political or religious agendas of their purveyors than they do the psychosocial needs of their targets.

Cultural differences are often invoked as obstacles to effective helping. Cultures do have expectations and values that set boundaries around actions and influence the effectiveness of our means and the appropriateness of our goals. But that does not mean that intercultural collaboration is all about obstacles (Marsella & Christopher, 2004; Szegedy-Maszak, 2005). Cultures are also resilient and malleable to conditions, and can be understood as resources rather than obstacles. Moreover, because the most prominent voices against disseminating "Western models" of psychological support are often Western intellectuals (Pupavac, 2001; Summerfield, 1999, 2005), the discourse is suspiciously devoid of non-Western voices. That is, it would appear to be an argument among "Western" factions, rather than between Western and non-Western voices. This invites a comparison with the colonial era, during which factions within the dominant powers argued over what was in the best interest of the cultures and people whom they held in subordination. The time for Western speakers to serve as proxies for non-Westerners should be passing, and the fact that non-Western speakers often call for more collaboration casts suspicion on the claims of the anti-Western Westerners.

This state of affairs is not specific to the debates over models or intervention strategies, but instead cuts across almost every issue and area of concern in humanitarian intervention. Representatives of developing nations are shamefully underrepresented in the discourse of assertions, arguments, and deliberations that converge to influence the development of humanitarian psychosocial policies affecting their regions. Moreover, even when governments and ministries from the developing world are somewhat represented, the same cannot be said for less affluent groups with little access to state power. This means that women, religious and ethnic minorities, indigenous tribes, and underclasses may have little say in the planning, implementation, and distribution of psychosocial services. Thus, a strong recommendation is presently expressed for greater inclusion of non-Western voices and perspectives in the discourse over which psychosocial beliefs and practices are appropriate, welcome, or desirable for use among disaster survivors in developing countries. Beyond this, it is also important to seek the insight and wisdom of groups at the margins of national and international power circles. Of particular concern is the muted influence of women from the least developed nations, whose lives (and those of their children) are among those most frequently and severely affected by war and other disasters.

Concerted International Efforts Are Needed

Humanitarian stakeholders share values and interests that should improve their prospects for collaborating toward commonly held aspirations.

Nevertheless, it is a widely held perception that they often function with a greater emphasis on autonomy than on cooperation. While it is understandable and predictable that the social psychology of these organizations would mirror those of governments and corporations, it is unfortunate that humanitarian organizations would rather tolerate waste and duplication than pursue cooperative partnerships that might allow a more efficient division of efforts and responsibilities. For example, psychosocial support for expatriate delegates has received considerable attention, and some, but not all, organizations have the requisite resources to provide mental health care for their field personnel. Cooperative agreements would allow psychosocial delegates from one NGO partner to share their services with personnel from another, resulting in better distribution of preventive care without the need for each NGO to develop its own psychosocial services.

As recently as 2001, the World Health Organization issued a declaration requesting that the international community agree to consensual guidelines for improving cooperation in the best interest of serving the psychosocial needs of refugees and other displaced populations (WHO, 2001). Such cooperation and collaboration would require division of roles and activities, a consequence of which would be to limit the autonomy of any given signatory organization. Unfortunately, the sovereignty of governments and NGOs alike tends to supersede such noble ideals as cooperative action or the placing of a beneficiary's interests above organizational politics. Nevertheless, leaders in the humanitarian community, faced with inadequate funding and an escalating spiral of mission objectives, should take a progressive route toward the forging of collaborative agreements that would improve efficiency and decrease unnecessary duplication of services.

International Standards of Care Are Needed

Psychosocial services have become a staple part of humanitarian relief operations around the world. Much of this progression has been driven by an increasing emphasis on the psychologically "traumatic" impact of war, disasters, and other tragic events. The fundamental propositions of international disaster psychology begin with the belief that extreme psychological distress and trauma predictably follow from events in which death, injury, and massive loss are involved. Specific claims are seldom made regarding the magnitude of the psychosocial consequences, but the impact is expected to include profound distress and substantial impairment of adaptive behavior among a large proportion of the population. A sense of extreme urgency is also evident in the alarming tone of news reports quoting claims by international mental health experts that major portions of populations affected by the 2004 Indian Ocean tsunami will develop trauma or other mental disorders (e.g., WHO, 2005). The responses to these alarms vary, with some ad hoc psychosocial emergency teams responding within the first few weeks (e.g., Kuriansky, 2005), while larger organizations take a more cautious, measured, and deliberative stance (Anderson, 2005).

Given the generally predictable occurrence of disasters, wars, and other catastrophic events, there would seem to be a third alternative in which planned action strategies are prepared well in advance. Once an activating event occurs, the strategy can quickly be reviewed and revised to fit any unanticipated conditions and the action plan can then be implemented without unnecessary delay. In fact, many governmental and nongovernmental organizations do exactly that with regard to material supplies such as food, water, medicines, munitions, and plastic sheeting. Indeed, this policy of preparedness for the unexpected is quite common for most goods that are considered essential to survival or social stability. Countless institutions, from police and fire departments to hospitals and insurance companies, exist to respond quickly when chronic problems arise, and many communities now have emergency mental health response capacities as well. Yet the global community, after more than a decade of experience with international disasters, remains relatively unprepared to respond to the psychosocial aspects of a major disaster in any systematic and concerted manner.

After nearly a decade of discussion regarding "best practices," no widely accepted standards of care have emerged. Contributing to this problem is the paucity of real research in this area. The present author recommends that humanitarian psychosocial organizations and experts (e.g., Psychosocial Working Group, 2004), convene not only to establish consensual endorsement of interventions, but also to develop action strategies for responding with all deliberate speed and coordination to address the psychosocial needs of disaster survivors. Organizations with an historical head start in developing psychosocial programs can help to inform others, and the sharing of lessons learned and approaches to delivering services can be exchanged in the service of all concerned. A more provocative suggestion would include establishing an international NGO dedicated specifically to providing psychosocial support in a manner analogous to that of Médecines Sans Frontières (Doctors Without Borders) in the arena of medical care.

Rapid Assessment of Psychosocial Needs Should Be a Standard Practice

Recent efforts directed toward the rapid assessment of psychosocial needs in disaster-affected populations have been helpful and instructive (e.g., Dodge, 2006; Jacobs et al., 2006), but episodic and limited in scope. The history of medical and psychosocial interventions demonstrates the importance of accurately assessing problems and resources before devising a plan to provide services. In the rush to relieve human suffering after catastrophic events, there is a danger in assuming the nature and magnitude of psychosocial needs while ignoring existing resource capacities in favor of imported experts. Although it is true that some presuppositions based on past experience are likely to prove true, important information may be missed or delayed unless needs assessment is granted a formal role in the overall service plan. To ease the succession from needs assessment to intervention, it is possible to begin assessing very early and in tandem with the deploying and tailoring of services (i.e., listening to the beneficiaries and tailoring the service model). It is also crucial to build an evaluation component into the service model so that the lessons learned are less subject to global appraisals that suit political rather than developmental aims.

Psychological Trauma versus Disaster Psychology

The international humanitarian community must operate on assumptions that are either self-evident or adapted from analogous circumstances. Thus, it is self-evident that supplies of clean water will be critically needed in remote regions where refugees often assemble, and it stands to reason that the emotional needs of people displaced by a wildfire will be analogous to those of people displaced by an earthquake. Historical trends in the mental health fields have elevated the concept of psychological trauma to a position from which it eclipses any other explanatory framework or descriptive terminology. This has led to a condition where psychological trauma is treated as though its existence and importance are self-evident across every type of human catastrophe, from war to flood and famine to disease. In turn, the proper response to these events must center foremost on preventing or alleviating the formation of a traumatic disorder. Evidence to support the proposition that refugees (Fazel, Wheeler, & Danesh, 2005), torture survivors (Silove, 1999), and others who have suffered terribly in disasters often develop trauma-related symptoms and clinical disorders is abundant and convincing. But there are many psychosocial consequences other than trauma that carry great importance and that are often more amenable to change without intrusive interventions that may not be welcomed or valued by disaster survivors. Thus, the emphasis on trauma may inadvertently obscure the importance of less dramatic issues that are not as "sexy," compelling, and provocative in tone. Nevertheless, what is actually provided in many instances is not "trauma-focused treatment," but instead consists of more mundane-sounding approaches such as education, stress management, and crisis intervention, which are often what is most useful for prevention activities and immediate relief of acute stress.

Disaster psychology, while closely connected to traumatology, is also distinct in several ways, including a decidedly normalizing stance toward short-term responses to acute stress and a pronounced emphasis on community-based interventions. In contrast to the clinical therapies typically applied in cases of post-traumatic stress disorder, the techniques preferred by disaster psychologists are more akin to crisis intervention and stress management and emphasize reduction of emotional arousal with brief support for problem solving and other effective coping strategies. Disaster survivors are not referred to as either clients or patients, and no "case" is ever formulated or assigned to a particular provider. Privacy is almost impossible, confidentiality is very limited, and no formal therapeutic relationship is either acknowl-edged or terminated. Rather, if the disaster psychologist detects the need for "clinical" services, a referral is made to an appropriately skilled provider who need not be experienced in disaster mental health. More often, the approach taken could best be described as a "public health" approach, with the purpose of taking steps to prevent the need for more targeted interven-tions by reducing the impact of known risk factors. This proactive model is superior in many ways to reactive models, but it requires very different skills and objectives from those needed for working with a more select group of survivors who display symptoms of clinical disorders. Thus, the qualifica-tions for disaster psychologists are substantially different from those of trau-matologists, and these areas of expertise are not interchangeable. Therefore, while skilled trauma-clinicians have much to offer in response to disaster survivors, they should also acknowledge the need to develop the pertinent skills for disaster field assignments.

Humanitarian Assistance and Military Aggression Are Incompatible

Interventions can take countless forms, and it is debatable whether the aims are indeed wholly altruistic and compassionate (i.e., humanitarian), or if there is another, more selfish agenda being disguised. The secular human-itarian movement has long been encumbered by the historical example of religious charities that blended compassionate deeds with missionary indoc-trination. Selective governmental humanitarian efforts in the late twentieth century were often suspected of being part of a global propaganda struggle between the opposing powers of communism and capitalism during the Cold War. These examples illustrate the fragile credibility of altruistic acts across national and cultural boundaries and should inform true humanitari-ans of the dangers of blended agendas. In a spate of publications over the past decade, contributors have called the humanitarian community to task over its questionable behavior or suspect motives (Holzgrefe & Keohane, 2003; Moore, 1999; Smillie & Minear, 2004). Concurrently, the rates of intentional violence against humanitarian personnel have reached histori-cally high levels (Sheik, Gutierrez, Bolton, Spiegel, Thieren, & Burnham, 2000), as illustrated by the 2003 bombings of the United Nations and Red Cross offices in Iraq during the American occupation. In such a climate of scrutiny, criticism, and profound security concerns, it is more important than ever that humanitarian motives be kept wholly distinct from partisan politics and military adventures.

Since its inception, the Red Cross/Red Crescent movement has wisely promoted and subscribed to principles of neutrality and impartiality in the pursuit of humanitarian goals. Only the strictest adherence to such princi-ples can possibly serve to shield humanitarian workers and the people they seek to serve from becoming targets of terror, torture, and death. This is not to say that military means cannot be employed in the service of humanitarian ends. Indeed, the ostensible rationale behind many if not most wars is to serve the greater good of humanity while defeating some evil force. But in violence the ends are often believed to justify any means of achieving them, and this includes the resort to instrumental aggression in the service of geopolitical goals of domination, pacification, and exploitation. Conversely, in humanitarianism the means must conform to principles of compassion, dignity, and human rights if the ends are to maintain legitimacy. Anything less threatens to destroy the very foundation upon which the international humanitarian enterprise has been erected.

Psychosocial Issues Need Better Advocacy

In the competition for disaster relief resources, psychosocial concerns are given more lip service than action. Basic survival needs are so clear and compelling that humanitarian mental health advocates find themselves relegated to the margins while central planning concerns are pursued with fervor. This is to some extent a necessary and reasonable situation, since mental health is a relative luxury in the face of mass destruction and death. Nevertheless, if psychosocial interventions are ever to be both timely and effective, they must move from being marginal concerns toward being integral and influential in the overall scheme of disaster response planning.

At present the priorities are such that mental health and psychosocial support activities have more propaganda value than actual influence. This helps to keep the mental health sector in a reactive role, rather than supporting systematic, strategic development of responsive operational abilities and the undertaking of initiatives for building more resilient local capacity . Instead, the current state of affairs allows for a public voicing of compassion and vague claims of action for the anguish and trauma of the affected people, while the pace of response is more timid and tentative. This is to some extent due to legitimate doubts regarding the need for psychosocial interventions and an absence of evidence supporting the effectiveness of what is presently being offered. Thus, disaster mental health advocates will need to consider their steps carefully if they are to advance their cause while avoiding the temptation to overstate their importance at the risk of further undermining their precarious progress.

References

Anderson, N. B. (2005). The APA tsunami relief effort, part 2. *APA Monitor, 36*(4), 9.
Dodge, G. R. (2006). Assessing the psychosocial needs of communities affected by disaster. In G. Reyes & G. A. Jacobs (Eds.), *Handbook of international disaster psychology, Vol. 1. Fundamentals and overview.* Westport, CT: Praeger Publishers.
Fazel, M., Wheeler, J., & Danesh, J. (2005). Prevalence of serious mental disorder in 7000 refugees resettled in Western countries: A systematic review. *Lancet, 365,* 1309–1314.

Holzgrefe, J. L., & Keohane, R. O. (2003). *Humanitarian intervention: Ethical, legal, and political dilemmas.* New York: Cambridge University Press.

Jacobs, G. A., Revel, J. P., Reyes, G., & Quevillon, R. P. (2006). Development of the Rapid Assessment of Mental Health: An international collaboration. In G. Reyes & G. A. Jacobs (Eds.), *Handbook of international disaster psychology, Vol. 3. Refugee mental health.* Westport, CT: Praeger Publishers.

Kipling, R. (1899, February). The white man's burden: The United States and the Philippine Islands. *McClure's Magazine,* p. 12.

Kuriansky, J. (2005, February 21). Finding life in a living hell. Retrieved March 31, 2005, from http://www.nydailynews.com/front/story/283039p-242333c.html

Marsella, A. J., & Christopher, M. A. (2004). Ethnocultural considerations in disasters: An overview of research, issues, and directions. *Psychiatric Clinics of North America, 27,* 521–539.

Moore, J. (1999). *Hard choices: Moral dilemmas in humanitarian intervention.* New York: Rowman & Littlefield.

Psychosocial Working Group (2004). *Considerations in planning psychosocial programs.* Retrieved February 15, 2005, from http://www.forcedmigration.org/psychosocial/papers/PWGpapers.htm

Pupavac, V. (2001). Therapeutic governance: Psycho-social intervention and trauma risk management. *Disasters, 25,* 358–372.

Sheik, M., Gutierrez, M. I., Bolton, P., Spiegel, P., Thieren, M., & Burnham, G. (2000). Deaths among humanitarian workers. *British Medical Journal, 321,* 166–168.

Silove, D. (1999). The psychosocial effects of torture, mass human rights violations, and refugee trauma: Towards an integrated conceptual framework. *Journal of Nervous and Mental Disease, 187,* 200–207.

Smillie, I., & Minear, L. (2004). *The charity of nations: Humanitarian action in a calculating world.* Bloomfield, CT: Kumarian Press.

Summerfield, D. (1999). A critique of seven assumptions behind psychological trauma programmes in war-affected areas. *Social Science & Medicine, 48,* 1449–1462.

———. (2005). What exactly is emergency or disaster "mental health"? *Bulletin of the World Health Organization, 83,* 76.

Szegedy-Maszak, M. (2005, January 17). The borders of healing. *U.S. News & World Report, 138*(2), 36–37.

World Health Organization (WHO) (2001). Declaration of cooperation: Mental health of refugees, displaced and other populations affected by conflict and post-conflict situations. Author: Geneva.

———. (2005, January 19). Press release (SEA/PR/1384): WHO warns of widespread psychological trauma among Tsunami victims. Retrieved April 25, 2005, from http://w3.whosea.org/en/Section316/Section503/Section1861_8571.htm

EPILOGUE

Yael Danieli

This impressive, thoughtful *Handbook of International Disaster Psychology* succeeds in conveying and mapping many of the key issues and complex challenges that have confronted the field and influenced the development of psychosocial humanitarian operations over the past decade. The scope and depth of this superb compilation would not have been possible even a decade ago, demonstrating how far we have come as a field. But much of it is also a reminder of how far we have yet to go in a world that has unremittingly produced disasters that, despite growing awareness, are met at best by episodic and inconsistent response and a rather limited commitment to preventing them and their long-term—possibly multigenerational—effects.

Created on the ruins of the World War II, the United Nations (UN) was formed in a spirit of optimism. Never again would the world community permit such a devastating war to take place. The world organization was joined by numerous nongovernmental organizations (NGOs) in its efforts to create a new, intensified impetus to alleviate poverty, eradicate illness, and provide education to shape a better world. But despite 60 years of energetic action, problems abound, and are even increasing. Disasters and their consequences continue to torment individuals and societies, leaving trails of illness, suffering, poverty, and death. Life expectancy has increased in most countries, and the proportion of children in the world has risen dramatically as well, with a corresponding growth in the need for food, health care, and education.

Tragically, trauma is clearly as ubiquitous today as it was during and immediately following World War II, when the UN was created, in the words of the Charter, "to save succeeding generations from the scourge of war, which twice in our lifetime has brought untold sorrow to mankind, and to reaffirm faith in fundamental human rights, in the dignity and worth of the human person, in the equal rights of men and women and of nations large and small, and to establish conditions under which justice and respect for the obligations arising from treaties and other sources of international law can be maintained, and to promote social progress and better standards of life in larger freedom."

The end of the Cold War, and the vanishing of its ideological barriers, has given rise, not to a more peaceful world, but to a world in which nationalist and ethnic tensions have frequently exploded into conflict. International standards of human rights, although largely accepted by states, are discarded in the face of fanaticism and stored-up hatred. In addition, issues between states North and South—developed and underdeveloped—are growing more acute, and call for attention at the highest levels. The most recent recognition of this in the context of the UN is the Secretary-General's report, *In Larger Freedom: Towards Development, Security and Human Rights for All* (United Nations, 2005).

People today know more about what goes on in the world than ever before. Cameras transmit their revelations within minutes to living rooms around the globe. Modern mass communication has erased geographical distance and informs us of suffering immediately as it occurs. But increasing and intense coverage may lead to desensitization and apathy as efforts to cope with ever present, overwhelming news of disturbing events result in a psychological distancing from the suffering (Figley, 1995). With the parallel exposure to fictional film and video, the distinction between reality and fantasy becomes blurred. War and disasters may even become entertainment (note the proliferation of reality shows on television). The worst-case scenario occurs when the world is a helpless eye witness and its efforts merely symbolic, with the sole intention of giving the appearance that something is being done (among Sarajevo's 85,000 children, a symbolic group of 32 injured were evacuated). A contrasting scenario is the unprecedented, overwhelming generosity of pledges and outpouring of philanthropy, likely inspired by its proximity to gift-giving holidays, to the victims of the December 26, 2004, Asian tsunami. However, even if we accept that this response was due to the seemingly inherent political neutrality of natural disasters, how do we explain international neglect in the case of other natural disasters, as in El Salvador? The constant threat of terrorism and the aching persistence of war crimes, crimes against humanity, and genocide—previous, ongoing, and current—with the continued suffering of their victims, keep the international community ashamed.

Because the scars of traumatic stress can be both deep and long-lasting, their treatment is imperative. Such treatment, all too often neglected, is crucial in conflict resolution and in the building of peace—possibly the best preventer of further war and violence—among individuals and groups. Unless treated, the germ of hatred and holding on to the image of the enemy—both consequences of traumatic stress—may give rise to new conflicts and bloody clashes between ethnic or religious groups in an endless cycle of violence. Victims may become perpetrators as individuals, as members of families and communities, or as nations. Genuine peace cannot exist without the resolution of trauma. If traumatic stress constitutes one element in this terrible cycle, its interception could be one way to break the cycle.

The cessation of wanton violence and abuse of power without full multidimensional integration of trauma (e.g., political, psychological, social, legal) will impair a nation's ability to maintain peace, to rebuild so that sustainable development is possible.

International Response

In addition to documenting the ubiquity of exposure to extreme events, history has recorded a wide variety of sociopolitical efforts to intervene in ways that address the needs of those who have been exposed and to prevent or minimize the impact of future exposures. Since the creation of the United Nations in 1945, the response by the organized international community and in particular by the UN system has been largely political. The main political imperatives have been from two opposite poles of conflict in finding political solutions: on the one hand, the continued existence of international concern about human suffering, stimulated by the modern media, and on the other hand, conceptions of state sovereignty that lead states to resist international interference in matters that they consider to be under their control and within their jurisdiction. By and large, the joint arrival of intergovernmental and nongovernmental organizations has been able to bring much relief to many victims of disasters, even though such relief tends to be temporary, may not alleviate all the hardships suffered by the victims, and will frequently not address the psychosocial damage. This book should help in keeping attention focused on remedying this unacceptable situation.

Trauma and the Continuity of Self:
A Multidimensional, Multidisciplinary
Integrative (TCMI) Framework

In my own attempt to describe the diverse and complex destruction caused by massive trauma such as is examined in this volume, I concluded that only a multidimensional, multidisciplinary integrative framework (Danieli, 1998) would be adequate. An individual's identity involves a complex interplay of multiple spheres or systems. Among these are (1) the physical and intrapsychic; (2) the interpersonal—familial, social, communal; (3) the ethnic, cultural, religious, spiritual, natural; (4) the educational/professional/occupational; and (5) the material/economic, legal, environmental, political, national, and international. These systems dynamically coexist along the time dimension to create a continuous conception of life from past through present to the future. Ideally, the individual should simultaneously have free psychological access to and movement within all these identity dimensions.

Trauma Exposure and "Fixity"

Trauma exposure can cause a rupture, a possible regression, and a state of being "stuck" in this free flow, which I (Danieli, 1998) have called *fixity*. The intent, place, time, frequency, duration, intensity, extent, and meaning of the trauma for the individual, and the survival strategies used to adapt to it (see, for example, Danieli, 1985) as well as post-victimization traumas, will determine the degree of rupture and the severity of the fixity. Fixity can be intensified in particular by the *conspiracy of silence* (Danieli, 1982, 1998), the survivors' reaction to the societal indifference (including that of health care and other professionals), avoidance, repression, and denial of the survivors' trauma experiences (see also Symonds, 1980). Society's initial emotional outburst, along with its simultaneous yet unspoken demand for rapid return to apparent normality, is an important example. This *conspiracy of silence* is detrimental to the survivors' familial and sociocultural (re)integration because it intensifies their already profound sense of isolation from and mistrust of society. It further impedes the possibility of the survivors' intrapsychic integration and healing, and makes the task of mourning their losses impossible. Fixity may increase vulnerability to further trauma. It also may render *chronic* the immediate reactions to trauma (e.g., acute stress disorder), and, in the extreme, become lifelong *post-trauma/victimization adaptational styles* (Danieli, 1985, 1997). This occurs when survival strategies generalize to a way of life and become an integral part of one's personality, repertoire of defense, or character armor.

Viewed from a family systems perspective, what happened in one generation will affect what happens in the next, though the actual behavior may take a variety of forms. Within an intergenerational context, the trauma and its impact may be passed down as the family legacy even to children born *after* the trauma. The awareness of the possibility of pathogenic intergenerational processes and the understanding of the mechanisms of transmission should contribute to finding effective means for preventing their transmission to succeeding generations (Danieli, 1985, 1993, 1998).

The possible long-term impact of trauma on one's personality and adaptation and the *intergenerational* transmission of victimization-related pathology still await explicit recognition and inclusion in future editions of the diagnostic nomenclature. Until they are included, the behavior of some survivors, and some children of survivors, may be misdiagnosed, its etiology misunderstood, and its treatment, at best, incomplete.

This framework allows evaluation of each system's degree of rupture or resilience, and thus informs the choice and development of optimal multilevel interventions. Repairing the rupture and thereby freeing the flow rarely means going back to "normal." Clinging to the possibility of "returning to normal" may indicate denial of the survivors' experiences and thereby fixity.

Exposure to trauma may also prompt review and reevaluation of one's self-perception, beliefs about the world, and values. Although changes in self-perception, beliefs, and values can be negative, varying percentages of trauma-exposed people report positive changes as a result of coping with the aftermath of trauma (called "post-traumatic growth," by Tedeschi & Calhoun, 1996). Survivors have described an increased appreciation for life, a reorganization of their priorities, and a realization that they are stronger than they thought. This is related to Danieli's (1994) recognition of competence vs. helplessness in coping with the aftermath of trauma. Competence (through one's own strength and/or the support of others), coupled with an awareness of options, can provide the basis of hope in recovery from traumatization.

Integration of the trauma must take place in *all* of life's relevant dimensions or systems and cannot be accomplished by the individual alone. Routes to integration may include reestablishing, relieving, and repairing the ruptured systems of the survivor and his or her community and nation, and restoring the surviving community's or nation's place in the international community. For example, in the context of examining the "Right to restitution, compensation and rehabilitation for victims of gross violations of human rights and fundamental freedoms" for the United Nations Centre for Human Rights (1992), some necessary components for integration and healing in the wake of massive trauma emerged from my interviews with victims/survivors of the Nazi Holocaust, interned Japanese-Americans, victims of political violence in Argentina and Chile, and professionals working with them, both in and outside their countries. Presented as goals and recommendations, these components are organized from the following perspectives: (A) individual, (B) societal, (C) national, and (D) international.

A. **Reestablishment of the victim's equality, power, and dignity—the basis of reparation.** This is accomplished by (a) compensation, both real and symbolic; (b) restitution; (c) rehabilitation; and (d) commemoration.
B. **Relieving the victim's stigmatization and separation from society**. This is accomplished by (a) commemoration; (b) memorials to heroism; (c) empowerment; (d) education.
C. **Repairing the nation's ability to provide and maintain equal value under law and the provisions of justice**. This is accomplished by (a) prosecution; (b) apology; (c) securing public records; (d) education; (e) creating national mechanisms for monitoring, conflict resolution, and preventive interventions.
D. **Asserting the commitment of the international community to combat impunity and provide and maintain equal value under law and the provisions of justice and redress**. This is accomplished by (a) creating ad hoc and permanent mechanisms for prosecution (e.g., ad hoc tribunals and ultimately an International Criminal Court); (b) securing

public records; (c) education; (d) creating international mechanisms for monitoring, conflict resolution, and preventive interventions.

It is important to emphasize that this comprehensive framework, rather than presenting *alternative* means of reparation, sets out necessary *complementary* elements, to be applied in different weights, in different situations and cultures, and at different points in time. It is also crucial that victims/survivors participate in the choice of the reparation measures adopted for them.

To fulfill the reparative and preventive goals of psychological recovery from trauma, perspective and integration through awareness and containment must be established so that one's sense of continuity, belongingness, and rootedness are restored. To be healing and even potentially self-actualizing, the integration of traumatic experiences must be examined from the perspective of the *totality* of the trauma survivors' and family members' lives.

With survivors it is especially hard to draw conclusions based on outward appearances. Survivors often display external markers of success (e.g., occupational achievement or established families) that in truth represent survival strategies. Clearly, such accomplishments may facilitate adaptation and produce feelings of fulfillment in many survivors. Thus, the external attainments do represent significant adaptive achievement in their lives. Nevertheless, even survivors in the "those who made it" category (Danieli, 1985) still experience difficulties related to their traumatic past, suggesting that overly optimistic views of adaptation may describe defense rather than effective coping. In fact, it is within this category that we observe the highest rates of suicide among survivors as well as their children. Furthermore, these optimistic views and accounts may cause survivors, who may have already felt isolated and alienated from those who did not undergo similar traumatic experiences, to see themselves as deficient, especially when compared to their "supercoper" counterparts, and deter them from seeking help.

The finding that survivors have areas of both vulnerability and resilience is not paradoxical when viewed within a multidimensional framework for multiple levels of post-traumatic adaptation. And tracing a history of multiple traumas along the time dimension at different stages of development reveals that, while time heals ills for many, for *traumatized* people time may not heal but may magnify their response to further trauma and may carry intergenerational implications.

Future Directions

In the context of prevention, an absolutely necessary precondition is the creation of a network of early warning systems, which necessitates thorough familiarity with, understanding of, and genuine respect for the local, national and regional culture(s) and history (Danieli, 1998). The United Nations and its related organizations have developed such systems concerning environmental threats, the risk of nuclear accident, natural disasters, mass movements of populations, the threat of famine, and the spread of disease. It is now time to include the potential effects of traumatic stress in preparing to confront these and other events.

Comparing this book's conclusions with our conclusions of "International Responses to Traumatic Stress: Humanitarian, Human Rights, Justice, Peace and Development Contributions, Collaborative Actions and Future Initiatives" (Danieli, Rodley, & Weisaeth, 1996), I felt delighted with the editor's assertion that psychosocial services have become "a staple part of humanitarian relief operations around the world" (Reyes, 2006, p. XX). But I must agree with him that, despite this progress, psychosocial issues still need further and greater advocacy. We have a long way to go toward ensuring that mental health concerns become integral and influential in the overall architecture of disaster response planning, in order to support systematic, strategic development of operational capabilities and initiatives to build more resilient local capacity.

I am saddened by the inefficient process of "reinventing the wheel" that persists among both national and international humanitarian organizations. It might be helpful for humanitarian psychosocial organizations and experts, without sacrificing their diversity and richness, to endorse core, evidence-based standards of care and interventions. It would also be useful to develop coordinated action strategies for flexibly available psychosocial preparedness to enable speedy, systematic responses that address the psychosocial needs of disaster survivors.

Although mostly Western, the authors are experienced members of the international humanitarian community, representing a broad spectrum of nationalities, cultures, and viewpoints. I agree with the editors that the time for Western speakers to serve as proxies for non-Westerners should be passing and that *all* voices and perspectives—not only those of the imported experts—must be included in the discourse over which psychosocial frameworks and practices are appropriate for use among disaster survivors in developing countries. The resources, insight, and wisdom of groups at the margins of national and international power circles must be included as well.

Concurring with the guidelines generated by the Task Force on International Trauma Training of the International Society for Traumatic Stress Studies (Weine, Danieli, Silove, van Ommeren, Fairbank, & Saul, 2002), the editor argues for rapid assessment of psychosocial needs to become standard practice, and for building an evaluation component into the service to assess its effectiveness. Such assessment and evaluation practices will guarantee that lessons learned are less subject to appraisals that suit political rather than developmental aims. The concern over the incompatibility of humanitarian assistance, partisan politics, and military aggression is repeated in this book as well, and reinforced by the recognition of the cost paid by humanitarian aid workers and others on the front line (Danieli, 2002).

The five Cs of disaster work—Communication, Cooperation, Collaboration, Coordination, and Complementarity—apply here, too. So does the need for leadership strategies, such as compassionate articulation (Spratt, 2002), that can reduce chaos and terror and thereby diminish the effectiveness of terrorism.

Nongovernmental organizations must improve their efforts at coordination. The greatest obstacle still seems to be competition for visibility and credit, which is essential if they are to compete effectively for increasingly scarce resources. At both the organizational level and in the field, the desire to have highly visible, quantitatively impressive programs can lead to competitiveness and jealousies that work against unified efforts.

There is a risk that the uncritical use of concepts such as coordination, which creates the impression of easy, quick solutions irrespective of the complexities of traumatic stress, may result in the loss of an operational meaning for these concepts. For example, the result may be too many coordinators and too few doing the work, or the actual work may be being reserved to nonprofessional and insufficiently trained volunteers. Such volunteers may serve for short periods of time, with traumatic detriment to themselves, and without contributing to the pool of accumulated knowledge that ought to move the field forward.

It is essential for UN agencies and programs, and for NGOs, to further define and develop complementary roles in their responses to traumatic stress. Complementarity involves the tolerance of, respect for, and capitalizing on the differing strengths of the various partners—UN bodies, governments, NGOs, and the communities they serve.

Some of the programs described in this work are inspiring in their excellence. But what comes through most of all is that, however superb some programs are, they are too few, and the challenges they must face are overwhelming. Each of the noble examples of programs is dwarfed by the needs with which our world is faced. In fact, the most striking theme that keeps emerging in the field is the enormous gulf between what needs to be done and the resources available to do it with. Although difficult in the short term, providing the international community with this needed expertise will lessen long-term costs, and possibly prevent intergenerational effects and the resulting much larger costs—both human and financial.

Another resource-related issue is that available funds tend to be used for emergency shipments of food, medicine, housing, and the like in reaction to situations that have been widely publicized by the media. Once the emergency is no longer new, and the dramatic pictures are no longer on the nightly news, funds usually dry up and are not available for sustaining the short-term gains or for long-term care.

The work in this area radiates good will, idealism, and commitment, despite cynicism and despair, and despite the realization—emerging from situations such as those in the former Yugoslavia, Rwanda, Kosovo, East Timor, Democratic Republic of Congo, and Darfur/Sudan—that humanity has failed to learn the lessons and honor the commitments made after World War II.

The same world that created the circumstances for the crime, the victimization, has also created the circumstances for good and kind and compassionate people to be there for each other, for the victims in time of need. Viewing our work through the prism of traumatic stress, within the multidimensional, multidisciplinary integrative (TCMI) framework, should thus have not only a healing, but also a humanizing, effect on the victims and on society as a whole.

We must pursue primary, secondary, and tertiary prevention. We must continue efforts to reduce the stigma that still exists against the field of mental health while broadening its reach to join hands with other disciplines. We must partner with others in fields at and beyond the boundaries of mental health and extend our investigations and preventive suggestions also to the root causes of disasters.

The danger of bioterrorism, with medically unexplained physical symptoms challenging patients, clinicians, scientists and policy makers, necessitates special training for all public health professionals. Its psychological casualties far outweigh the physical ones (Flynn, 2004), and its long-term social and psychological effects are likely to be as damaging as the acute ones, if not more so (Wessely, Hyams, & Bartholomew, 2001). The threat of bioterrorism also calls for revamping the health/mental health systems on all levels/dimensions—before, during, and after such attacks.

Despite growing awareness and the accumulated body of knowledge, there are still policy makers who either deny the existence of the invisible, psychological wounds, or feel that they have a lesser priority in an era of dwindling resources. At every level, government policy has yet to fully comprehend and embrace the centrality of psychosocial issues in understanding and responding to disasters, particularly to terrorism. For any nation to become optimally prepared to cope, homeland security must include, integrate, and adequately fund psychosocial security (Danieli, Brom, & Sills, 2005) and the full participation of the social sciences in all aspects of preparedness. This book should certainly advance this undertaking.

References

Danieli, Y. (1982). *Therapists' difficulties in treating survivors of the Nazi Holocaust and their children.* Dissertation Abstracts International, 42(12-B, Pt 1), 4927. (UMI No. 949-904).

———. (1985). The treatment and prevention of long-term effects and intergenerational transmission of victimization: A lesson from Holocaust survivors and their children. In C. R. Figley (Ed.), *Trauma and its Wake* (pp. 295–313). New York: Brunner/Mazel.

———. (1992). Preliminary reflections from a psychological perspective. In T.C. van Boven, C. Flinterman, F. Grunfeld & I. Westendorp (Eds.), *The Right to Restitution, Compensation and Rehabilitation for Victims of Gross Violations of Human Rights and Fundamental Freedoms.* Netherlands Institute of Human Rights [Studie-en Informatiecentrum Mensenrechten], Special issue No. 12.

———. (1993). The diagnostic and therapeutic use of the multi-generational family tree in working with survivors and children of survivors of the Nazi Holocaust. In J. P. Wilson & B. Raphael (Eds.) *International handbook of traumatic stress syndromes* [Stress and Coping Series, Donald Meichenbaum, Series Editor]. (pp. 889–898). New York: Plenum Publishing.

———. (1994). Resilience and hope. In G. Lejeune (Ed.), *Children Worldwide* (pp. 47–49). Geneva: International Catholic Child Bureau.

———. (1997). As survivors age: An overview. *Journal of Geriatric Psychiatry, 30* (1), 9–26.

———, Rodley, N.S., & Weisaeth, L. (Eds.) (1996). *International responses to traumatic stress: Humanitarian, human rights, justice, peace and development contributions, collaborative actions and future initiatives.* Amityville, NY: Baywood Publishing.

———. (1998). *International handbook of multigenerational legacies of trauma.* New York: Kluwer Academic/Plenum Publishing.

———. (2002). *Sharing the front line and the back hills: International protectors and providers, peacekeepers, humanitarian aid workers and the media in the midst of crisis.* Amityville, NY: Baywood Publishing.

———, Brom, D., & Sills, J. (Eds.). (2005). *The trauma of terrorism: Sharing knowledge and shared care. An international handbook.* Binghamton, NY: The Haworth Press.

Figley, C. R. (Ed.). (1995). *Compassion fatigue: Coping with secondary traumatic stress disorder in those who treat the traumatized.* New York: Brunner/Mazel.

Flynn, B. W., (2004) Letters to the Editor: Behavioral Health Aspects of Bioterrorism. *Biosecurity and Bioterrorism: Biodefense Strategy, Practice, and Science, 2,* 232.

Green, B. L., Friedman, M. J., de Jong, J., Solomon, S. D., Keane, T. M., Fairbank, J. A., Donelan, B., & Frey-Wouters, E. (Eds.) (2003). *Trauma interventions in war and peace: Prevention, practice, and policy.* New York: Kluwer Academic/Plenum Publishers.

Reyes, G. (2006). Conclusions and recommendations for further progress. In G. Reyes & G. A. Jacobs (Eds.), *Handbook of International Disaster Psychology.* Westport, CT: Praeger Publishers.

Spratt, M. (2002, August 28). 9/11 media may comfort, terrify. Retrieved on August 29, 2002, from http://www.dartcenter.org/articles/headlines/2002/2002_08_28.html

Symonds, M. (1980). The "second injury" to victims. *Evaluation and Change* [Special issue], 36–38.

Tedeschi, R. G., & Calhoun, L. G. (1996). The posttraumatic growth inventory: Measuring the positive legacy of trauma. *Journal of Traumatic Stress, 9,* 455–471.

United Nations (2005). *In larger freedom: Towards development, security and human rights for all. Report of the Secretary-General.* Retrieved May 31, 2005, from http://www.un.org/largerfreedom/contents.htm

Weine, S., Danieli, Y., Silove, D., Van Ommeren, M., Fairbank, J. A., & Saul, J. (2002). Guidelines for international training in mental health and psychosocial interventions for trauma exposed populations in clinical and community settings. *Psychiatry, 65*(2), 156–164.

Wessely, S., Hyams, K., & Bartholomew, R. (2001). Psychological implications of chemical and biological weapons. *British Medical Journal, 323,* 878–879.

TOOL

Rapid Assessment of Mental Health Needs of Refugees, Displaced and Other Populations Affected by Conflict and Post-Conflict Situations

A Community-Orientated Assessment
WORLD HEALTH ORGANIZATION
Geneva 2002

RAPID ASSESSMENT OF MENTAL HEALTH NEEDS OF REFUGEES, DISPLACED AND OTHER POPULATIONS AFFECTED BY CONFLICT AND POST-CONFLICT SITUATIONS AND AVAILABLE RESOURCES

This document is a technical document on the Rapid Assessment of Mental Health Needs of Refugees, Displaced and Other Populations Affected by Conflict and Post-Conflict Situations and Available Resources (RAMH), jointly developed with the International Federation of Red Cross and Red Crescent Societies, and the Disaster Mental Health Institute, The University of South Dakota, USA, and further elaborated with contributions from Ministries of Health, Ministries of Cooperation, United Nations agencies, Humanitarian Agencies, NGOs, WHO Collaborating Centers, international mental health associations, international human rights societies, academic and research institutions, international humanitarian relief agencies, and with the participation of experts from countries in several WHO Regions, including countries in conflict and post-conflict situations. It is the final version of the document endorsed at the "International Consultation on Mental Health of Refugees and Displaced Populations in Conflict and Post-Conflict Situations", Geneva, 23-25 October 2000.

KEY WORDS: mental health/ community-oriented assessment/ humanitarian emergencies/ resources/ refugees/ forcibly displaced persons by conflict/ post-conflict/ mental health care.

Team of Mental Health Determinants and Populations
Department of Mental Health and Substance Dependence
WORLD HEALTH ORGANIZATION
in collaboration with
International Federation of Red Cross and Red Crescent Societies and
The Disaster Mental Health Institute, The University of South Dakota, USA

Geneva, January 2001

The tool was elaborated under the technical guidance of Ms M. Petevi, Technical Officer, Mental Health of Refugees, in collaboration with Dr R. Billington, Former Team Coordinator of Mental Health Promotion, Department of Mental Health and Substance Dependence, Noncommunicable Diseases and Mental Health, WHO Geneva. This document is based on the field experience of the authors, on a thorough critical review of articles and books on the topic (of which 200 are in an annotated bibliography), and on the participation and contributions of the reviewers.

AUTHORS:
Ms Mary Petevi, Technical Officer, Mental Health of Refugees, World Health Organization;
Dr Jean Pierre Revel, Former Senior Officer, Relief Health, International Federation of Red Cross and Red Crescent Societies (IFRC), currently in ICRC;
Dr Gerard A. Jacobs, Professor and Director, Disaster Mental Health Institute, The University of South Dakota, USA.

ACKNOWLEDGEMENTS
         This work would have not been completed without the substantial contribution of Drs R.P. Quevillon, T.L. Elliott, and G. Reyes, DMHI, USA. The contributions of J.V. Boero, M.D. Hiller, E.K. Johnson-Jimenez, K.L. Le Beaux, and S.E. McCaslin of the DMHI are gratefully acknowledged.

         WHO wishes to also thank and to acknowledge the active participation and contributions of the following in reviewing this document. The names of the experts, who in addition to having reviewed, participated at the "International Consultation on Mental Health of the Refugees and Displaced Populations in Conflict and Post-Conflict Situations", and endorsed the RAMH, are underlined:

         Dr F. Agani, Department of Neuropsychiatry, University Clinical Center, Kosovo; **Ms U. Agomoh**, Prisoners Rehabilitation and Welfare Action, Nigeria; **Dr F. Baingana**, Mental Health Specialist, The World Bank, USA; **Dr A. Baker**, Professor, Birzeit University, Palestine; **Prof. C. Ballas**, University of Athens and Advisor, Ministry of Health, Greece; **Dr H. Bamber**, Director, Medical Foundation for the Care of Victims of Torture; **Dr T. Baubet**, Médecins Sans Frontieres, France; **Ms L. Bremer**, Crisis Prevention Center, the Finnish Association for Mental Health, Finland; **Dr E. B. Brody,** Former Secretary General, World Federation for Mental Health (WFMH), USA; **Dr M. Dualeh**, Sr. Public Health Officer, Office of the United Nations High Commissioner for Refugees (UNHCR); **Dr S. Ekblad**, Chair, International Committee for Refugees and Migrants, WFMH, Sweden; **Dr M. Elmasri**, Algerian Society for Research in Psychology (SARP), Algeria; **Dr S. Fernando**, University of Kent and University of North London, U.K.; **Dr C. Garcia-Moreno**, Evidence and Information for Policy, WHO; **Dr A. Griekspoor**, Emergency Humanitarian Action, WHO, Switzerland; **Dr E. Hauff**, Deputy Secretary-General, World Association for Psychosocial Rehabilitation; **Dr P. Hypsier**, WHO Representative, Sri Lanka; **Mr R. Jayasinghe**, Program Manager, Mental Health of Refugees, Ministry of Health, Sri Lanka; **Dr J. de Jong**, Director, Transcultural Psychosocial Organization, Netherlands; **Dr M. Kastrup**, World Psychiatric Association (WPA), Denmark; **Mr N. Khaled**, SARP, Algeria; **Dr A. M. Kos**, Slovene Philantropy, Slovenia; **Dr G. Labellarte**, Italian Psychiatric Association, Italy; **Dr P. Lahti**, President, World Federation for Mental Health, Finland; **Mr J. Lavelle**, Director, International Programmes, Harvard Programme in Refugee Trauma (HPRT), Harvard University, USA; **Mr J. C. Legrand**, United Nation's Children's Fund, USA; **Dr I. Levav**, Former WHO Regional Mental Health Advisor, PAHO; **Dr B. Lopes Cardozo**, Center for Disease Control and Prevention, USA; **Dr S. Malé**, Sr. Public Health Officer, UNHCR; **Dr C. Mandlhate**, Regional Mental Health Adviser, WHO Africa; **Dr J-C. Metraux**, Director, "Appartenances", Switzerland; **Ms P. Mezzetti**, Office of the United Nations High Commissioner for Human Rights (UNHCHR), Switzerland; **Dr R. Mollica**, Director, HPRT, USA; **Dr E. Nahim**, National Coordinator for Mental Health, Ministry of Health, Sierra Leone; **Mr L. Ndahiro**, National Coordinator for Mental Health, Ministry of Health, Rwanda; **Dr F. del Ponte**, Senior Medical Advisor, Swiss Disaster Relief Unit, Federal Department of Foreign Affairs, Switzerland; **Mr F. Quesney**, Psychosocial Focal Point, United Nations Children's Fund, USA; **Dr N. Sartorius**, Former President, WPA, Professor, University of Geneva, Switzerland; **Dr E. Seheye**, National Coordinator for Mental Health, Ministry of Health, Burundi; **Dr H. Sell**, Former Regional Mental Health Adviser, WHO Regional Office for South-East Asia; **Dr B. Sharma**, Medical Director, Centre for Victims of Torture, Nepal; **Prof. D. Somasundaram**, University of Jaffna, Sri-Lanka; **Ms B. Stambul**, Medecins du Monde, France; **Dr N. Sveaass**, Secretary General, International Society for Health and Human Rights; **Dr L.H.M. van Willigen**, Honorary President of the International Society for Health and Human Rights, Netherlands; **Dr L. Weisaeth**, Division of Disaster Psychiatry, University of Oslo, Norway.

Portions of this document were adapted from *Rapid Health Assessment Protocols for Emergencies, Emergency and Humanitarian Action,* (1999), Geneva: World Health Organization.

RAPID ASSESSMENT OF MENTAL HEALTH NEEDS OF REFUGEES, DISPLACED AND OTHER POPULATIONS AFFECTED BY CONFLICT AND POST-CONFLICT SITUATIONS AND AVAILABLE RESOURCES

A TOOL FOR COMMUNITY-ORIENTED ASSESSMENT

VERSION FOR PILOT-TESTING

The creation of the tool became possible through the contributions of the Governments of Finland, Greece, and Cyprus

AUTHORS:
Ms Mary PETEVI, WHO
Dr Jean Pierre REVEL, IFRC
Dr Gerard A. JACOBS, DMHI

Issued by the
World Health Organization

Developed in collaboration with the
International Federation of Red Cross and Red Crescent Societies
and the Disaster Mental Health Institute, The University of South Dakota, USA

Geneva, 2001

TABLE OF CONTENTS

INTERNATIONAL CONSULTATION "Mental Health of Refugees and Displaced Populations in Conflict and Post-Conflict Situations"
From Crisis Through Reconstruction
WHO Geneva, 23-25 October 2000

WHO convened the International Consultation on Mental Health of Refugees and Displaced Populations in Conflict and Post-Conflict Situations, in WHO Headquarters in Geneva, on 23-25 October 2000. Thirty-five experts in this field were invited from low and high-income countries, including several which are currently in conflict or post-conflict situations. United Nations agencies, NGOs, academic and research institutions were represented. On the first day of the consultation, the assembled experts were addressed among others by four leaders in the worldwide protection and care of refugees.

Dr Gro Harlem Brundtland, Director-General of the World Health Organization told the assembly of the International Consultation,
"... To address the mental health needs of large populations, we need definite strategies and plans. Ad hoc arrangements and improvisations in response to each emergency will no longer be acceptable. Specific management ability, strong field experiences and evidence-based approaches are required... WHO strongly recommends the establishment of community-based mental health care from emergency through reconstruction. Earliest integration of mental health within the public health care system available in camps and national services is the most efficient, and cost-effective strategy. The concerned communities must be mobilized and actively involved to decrease psychiatric morbidity and increase sustainability."

Ms Mary Robinson, United Nations High Commissioner for Human Rights, said in her address,
"... The number of refugees and displaced persons in the world shames us all. We should be actively seeking ways of alleviating their suffering. I believe that your deliberations relating to the... practical tools for rapid assessment (RAMH)... which will be adopted at the end of this Consultation will be significant steps forward."

Mr Frederick D. Barton, United Nations Deputy High Commissioner for Refugees, to summarize the challenges that lay ahead, said,
"... Like so much we try to do, the immensity of this challenge can seem daunting. The numbers are huge, the locations are multiple, the resources are scarce, the needs are immediate and varied, and our approaches are often compartmentalised and paternalistic. Our certainty is that our work will produce as many questions as answers. As we go about this work, it is vital that we remain focused on those we seek to help, renewing our commitment to their futures. If we do that, we will advance the grand cause of peace - and begin to make progress on these huge mental health problems in conflict-torn places."

Ms Erin Mooney, stressed **on behalf of Dr Francis Deng**, Representative of the United Nations Secretary-General on Internally Displaced Persons that,
"... displacement impacts upon mental health in three major ways. First, there is the trauma associated with the occurrence of displacement, which not only may be induced by but also often involves serious violations of human rights. Second, once uprooted, the displaced suffer a tremendous sense of loss and dislocation, and an uncertain future for them and their children. Adding further strain, displaced persons may find themselves in a discriminatory, even insecure environment, such that they continue to be in a very precarious situation even in their places of refuge."

The expert participants in the Consultation reviewed, amended and endorsed the *Tool for Rapid Assessment of Mental Health Needs of Refugees, Displaced and Other Populations Affected by Conflict and Post-Conflict Situations, and Available Resources* (RAMH). They also called to integrate it in the United Nations Office for Coordination of Humanitarian Assistance (OCHA) Emergency Operations.

Part I: GUIDELINES

PREAMBLE

This tool is applicable to forcibly displaced populations in humanitarian crisis as a result of persecution, war, and conflict. Given the evolution of humanitarian relief work, peace keeping and peace enforcing operations, increasingly, humanitarian protection and assistance is extended to besieged and non-displaced populations. Therefore, in order to facilitate the reading, comprehension, and use of this document please note that the following terms as used herein include or mean the following:

"HEALTH" is a state of complete physical, mental and social well being and not merely the absence of disease or infirmity.'   (*WHO Constitution*)

"A REFUGEE" is a person who, "owing to a well-founded fear of being persecuted for reasons of race, religion, nationality, membership in a particular social group, or political opinion, is outside the country of his nationality, and is unable to or, owing to such fear, is unwilling to avail himself of the protection of that country."
(*1951 Convention Relating to the Status of Refugees*)

"FORCIBLY DISPLACED POPULATIONS " include asylum seekers, refugees, internally displaced, repatriated persons, and other non-displaced populations affected by persecution, war and conflict.

"MENTAL HEALTH RESOURCES" include individual, family, community, psychological, social, and economic strengths, which can help individuals and groups of people cope with stress, trauma and suffering. This also includes human, financial, and institutional resources (including policies and action plans) which can be mobilised to support the establishment of mental health programmes.

"CONFLICT" as used herein includes war, civil war, conflict (ethnic, military and religious), post-conflict, other unstable and violent situations and complex emergencies.

The tool is also applicable in situations resulting from **GENOCIDE.**

"COMPLEX HUMANITARIAN EMERGENCY" characterises a situation of political instability leading to unrest or civil strive, internal or cross border population movements, severe economic recession, and subsequent excess morbidity and mortality.   (*OCHA and Centre for Disease Control, Atlanta, USA*)

"MULTI-SECTORAL" means the collaboration in assessments, in development and implementation of responses between many professions within different ministries, NGOs, academic and research settings. These may include teachers, social workers, primary health care workers, physicians, nurses, psychologists, community health workers, counsellors, traditional healers, spiritual leaders, anthropologists, sociologists, economists, lawyers, leaders of the refugee community, associations, as well as others.

"MENTAL HEALTH PROFESSIONAL" as the term is used herein in a global context, includes a broad range of professionals with mental health knowledge and experience.

This tool is meant to be flexible, to permit its use in the above-mentioned situations, requiring an immediate qualitative assessment of mental health needs and resources. Adaptations might be needed to fit the context of future used. An effort was made to keep the language easily understood by mental health and non-mental health personnel worldwide and by those for whom English is a second language. Not all information called for in this tool will be possible to obtain in every situations. Much will depend on the timing of the Assessment. The information sought in this Tool is that considered as important in the professional literature and experience for the assessment of the mental health needs and resources in conflict and post-conflict situations.

USERS OF THE RAMH AND OVERALL SCOPE: Basic Considerations

This Tool for the Rapid Assessment of Mental Health Needs of Refugees, Displaced and Other Populations Affected by Conflict and Post-Conflict Situations and Available Resources (RAMH) is intended to be used by mental health professionals, non-mental health personnel, and others involved in mental and psychosocial community support. Since in any conflict or post-conflict situation, the community and health workers are among the first level of contact with forcibly displaced people, they need a basic tool to help them assess mental health needs in emergency situations.

The information collected through use of this tool will serve to set up immediate and longer-term community-based mental health programmes. Close collaboration with mental health professionals is necessary, when they are available. This will help in project design and capacity building, which will include training, establishment of services, ongoing supervision, monitoring and evaluation, care for chronic psychiatric clients, for traumatized persons, and for psychosocial rehabilitation of the community/ties concerned.

The RAMH tool can be used immediately in emergencies; at least one mental health professional should be included in the RAMH team.

Training will be necessary for personnel with little mental health knowledge and experience. As the RAMH will be field-tested during the year 2001, a training manual will be developed and training will be provided after the tool is validated. The Feedback Form attached to the tool enables teams using the RAMH during this pilot phase to provide valuable information to WHO, to refine the RAMH and to develop the RAMH training manual.

The Comprehensive Assessment of Mental Health (CAMH) which will be developed will help provide a more detailed and comprehensive picture of the mental health needs of populations affected by conflict. Because of the urgent need for mental health response in emergencies, all efforts will be made for simultaneous progress in the three above-mentioned goals.

NOTE FOR USER:

The rapid assessment of mental health needs and resources is a process that needs careful preparation. This publication includes this preparation and the actual assessment tool.

USERS MUST READ THIS TOOL THOROUGHLY BEFORE USING IT!

INTRODUCTION

1.   Conflicts and complex emergencies often result in the sudden creation of large numbers of refugees and internally displaced persons. They also subject large numbers of people who did not flee the country due to ongoing war, persecution, and violence. Conflicts involve various weaknesses in governments or even collapse of national authorities. This leads to loss of government control and can make it nearly impossible to provide vital services and protection to civilians. Conflicts result in widespread violence against people. Vulnerable groups such as the elderly, children, mentally ill and developmentally delayed, and the physically disabled pay a heavier price. Women caught in such situations become particularly vulnerable. Violence increases immediately the risk of psychological trauma within entire communities and nations. In conflicts with quickly shifting zones of combat, civilians are increasingly in the line of fire. Frequently, they become the primary targets of ethnic cleansing, murder, sexual violence, torture, and mutilation. In these situations, it is important to quickly obtain sufficient information to develop a community-based emergency mental health response, together with the affected and host communities.

2.   Although the two world wars took place in the first part of the 20th century, it is in the last 50 years that more than ever people have been displaced by conflicts. The consequences of conflict on public health will have a long-term negative impact on individuals and on their communities. In the long term, it delays efforts for socio-economic development, health, reconciliation and peace. Earliest response to needs for food, water, and shelter is a mental health response. But there must also be important efforts to mobilise and provide the resources needed to respond to immediate mental health and psychosocial needs. Until now in the field of health special emphasis has been put on nutrition, prevention, on management of infectious diseases, on maternal and child health. Much less attention has been given to mental health or to psychosocial needs. However, there is a growing recognition among donors, host government, and humanitarian agencies of the importance of mental health interventions in the early phase of emergencies.

3.   Another challenge is that most mental health projects have been based on psychiatric care only. It is true that within any refugee population there are chronically mentally ill and other severely traumatized because of the conflict. They must receive appropriate treatment and protection. Any traumatic event will result in distress and suffering that will have a powerful effect on individuals and communities. However, distress and suffering are not psychiatric illnesses. These reactions are normal (expected) reactions to extraordinary violent events and therefore generalized psychiatric care is inappropriate and thus must be prevented. Early and adequate mental health responses during the humanitarian emergency phase have proved to be cost effective. Such responses limit the impact of these events, and speed up coping and return to normal functioning of those affected. Any attempt to pathologize the situation must be avoided.

4.   There are a few mental health interventions that are broadly acknowledged as useful to start with even before a mental health assessment is completed. These include:

- Training of humanitarian aid workers of basic mental health skills, e.g., active listening, cultural sensitivity, trauma management, community-based activities, community empowerment;
- Providing recreational, cultural space in the design of refugee camps, e.g., playground, sports field, places for religious and cultural ceremonies and other community activities;
- Establishing and maintaining a flow of reliable information and making it available to the Communities concerned

----
"Rapid Assessment of Mental Health of Refugees, Displaced and Other Populations Affected by Conflict and Post-Conflict Situations, and Available Resources", WORLD HEALTH ORGANIZATION, Geneva, 2001

- Involving the concerned community/ies in decision-making processes, e.g., Where is the best location in the camp for schools, religious places, etc;

- Involving the refugee community, adults and adolescents, in concrete common interest activities, e.g., helping in camp construction and organisation, in family reunion, in food distribution, in agreed common discipline in the camp;
- Starting schooling for children, even partially;
- Support appropriate existing activities among the communities affected by conflict, within national/ camp services and informal settings;
- Organising creative and recreational activities for children as a means of strengthening the health and positive aspects of their personality as opposed to overemphasizing trauma and clinical activities (e.g., sports, theatre, singing, story-telling, dancing);
- Allowing for reestablishment of cultural and religious events;
- Facilitating creation of self-help groups;
- Facilitating inter-generational support mechanisms.

PURPOSE OF THE ASSESSMENT

1.   A Rapid Assessment of Mental Health Needs, and Available Resources (RAMH) must be organised as quickly as possible during the emergency phase. The RAMH tool is applicable and can be used to evaluate needs and available resources. This RAMH should within seven to ten days collect the qualitative and basic quantitative information necessary to design and start an emergency response. It must provide reasonably accurate general information on the mental health needs and resources of the communities concerned.

2.   It is important to keep in mind that the emergency RAMH should not remain the only assessment. The findings must be periodically updated. A more detailed evaluation of the needs of the vulnerable groups must follow. To this purpose, a "Comprehensive Assessment of Mental Health (CAMH: temporary name of a second tool) is under preparation by WHO.

3.   On the basis of the community-oriented data collected by the RAMH an appropriate community-based emergency mental health programme can be developed.   The more this programme corresponds to the needs of the people and respects their culture (religion, tradition, etc), the more effective it will be. Later on, an effective "CAMH" can provide the data necessary to refine the mental health programme and make sure that it remains both appropriate and cost effective. Periodic evaluations will indicate the progress made and will provide information to adjust to the changing needs of the populations concerned. In this document only the RAMH is developed.

4.   An RAMH is required whenever a conflict or a complex emergency strikes a community. It can be requested by the government concerned, by a UN agency, an NGO, a funding source, or suggested by WHO. The purpose of the RAMH is to:

"Rapid Assessment of Mental Health of Refugees, Displaced and Other Populations Affected by Conflict and Post-Conflict Situations, and Available Resources", WORLD HEALTH ORGANIZATION, Geneva, 2001

4.1 Describe the conflict[1], how it affects the area/s and the population, and identify actual and expected population movements;

4.2 Describe the affected populations[1] (estimated numbers, estimates of distribution by gender and age; estimates of numbers of orphans, unaccompanied minors, street-children, widows, raped, elderly, etc.);

4.3 Identify and rank the leading causes of mortality and morbidity among refugees[1];

4.4 Identify traumatic events experienced by the affected populations;

4.5 Identify the main characteristics in culture, religion, the socio-political organisation of the affected country/ies and community, and important differences with the host community;

4.6 Describe how people deal with the consequences of the violence and trauma on an individual, family, and community basis and how these coping mechanisms are affected by the current situation;

4.7 Check if a mental health policy and action plan exist and identify mental health personnel, potential paraprofessionals, and other related resources within the refugee and host communities (e.g., teachers, social workers, traditional healers, women's associations, community leaders, etc.), and external agencies;

4.8 Make recommendations for the development of a programme to respond to the needs of vulnerable groups and of the overall affected communities, taking into consideration the special needs of women and children especially for those who are alone and/or heads of household, or demobilised child soldiers.

RAMH TERMS OF REFERENCE (TOR)

1.   Because of the speed with which the RAMH needs to be conducted, it is important to establish a fixed set of standard TOR for the RAMH. Careful preparation for the RAMH is very important. These broad guidelines provide the framework that will enable the RAMH team to be activated immediately and to begin the RAMH as soon as it is authorized. These TOR must be negotiated in advance, particularly if more than one agency is involved so as to prevent confusion in the field.

Fundamental Issues

1.1. Who or which agency has requested/decided to carry out the RAMH;

1.2. Who will fund the RAMH;

1.3. What are the objectives of the RAMH;

1.4. Which government sector or UN agency or NGO is taking the lead role in the RAMH?

1.5. What is the role of the Ministry of Health (MOH) or its substitute and of each agency involved?

1.6. What is the mission of the RAMH;

1.7. What are the responsibilities of each person on the RAMH team;

1.8. What are the proposed time limits for the assessment;

1.9. What are the reporting requirements;

  (a) Content should cover the eight items mentioned in paragraph 4;

  (b) Ownership of the data;

---

[1] Data regarding this topic may be available in other reports on the conflict collected by UNHCR, UNICEF, UNFPA, OCHA, UNDP, WHO, NGOs and by local authorities.

"Rapid Assessment of Mental Health of Refugees, Displaced and Other Populations Affected by Conflict and Post-Conflict Situations, and Available Resources", WORLD HEALTH ORGANIZATION, Geneva, 2001

(c) Confidentiality of the data;
(d) Physical protection of the data in the field and after reporting;
1.10. What short and long term commitment is made by the organisations or governments participating in the RAMH to implement a mental health response.

Checklist of basic resources

2.   The following human and financial/material resources can help facilitate the RAMH.

Human resources:
1. Local principal collaborator/contact person;
2. Other local professionals (multidisciplinary team);
3. Translators;
4. Drivers;
NB: At least one of the local staff and especially the driver must know the security risks and the country/area visited.

Financial/physical resources:
5. Field communications equipment (especially for security reasons);
6. International and field transport;
7. Portable computers and related supplies.

PREPAREDNESS

Data Collection Team

Selection and training of RAMH Team

1.   Because of the urgency of the RAMH, it is recommended that a pool consisting of both local and international professionals be identified in advance. These prospective members can then be trained in the RAMH methodology. It is best for the RAMH team to be multidisciplinary, but of special importance is knowledge and experience in refugee mental health and in emergencies. Personal characteristics are very important, particularly the capacity for teamwork, for work under pressure and for mutual support. Because conflict can have unpredicted consequences and because experienced professionals are not always readily available, it is important to train a sufficiently large pool of team members, to ensure that adequate numbers are available at the time of an emergency. In each team at least one must be a professional experienced in working in crisis situations.

2.   The RAMH team needs to have basic information concerning the population, culture, religion(s), language, context of the conflict, conditions of flight, etc. before starting the assessment. This information can be prepared in advance for areas of the world where conflict is anticipated, and updated periodically.
3.   The RAMH must be undertaken during the emergency phase as soon as basic survival needs are met. Based on the characteristics of the conflict and the availability of team members, adequate persons from the pool can be selected and mobilized. One member of the team must be identified as the team leader and another as the secretary. Responsibility for other specific duties

----

"Rapid Assessment of Mental Health of Refugees, Displaced and Other Populations Affected by Conflict and Post-Conflict Situations, and Available Resources", WORLD HEALTH ORGANIZATION, Geneva, 2001

can be given to team members according to the TOR of the RAMH and to the situation. This provides an effective division of labour, as well as attention to each aspect of the RAMH. The size and possibly the composition of the team are likely to change as the RAMH moves toward the CAMH.

Care of the RAMH Team Itself

4.   Care of the RAMH team needs to be a serious concern throughout the RAMH. Team members can be exposed to accumulation of traumatic scenes, stories, difficult living and working conditions, and to bureaucratic challenges, to lack of security and to danger. Minimum periods should be reserved on a daily basis for rest, short regular recuperation periods for team-support sessions.

5.   Before sending the team to the field, information is needed related to the team's safety. This pre-deployment information can be obtained from government, UN agencies, national and international NGOs. Basic information needed:

   5.1. Security of the urban and rural areas, areas of military operations or other threatening situations;
   5.2. Security requirements and assets (regulations, clearances, laissez-passers for camps, safety jackets, helmets, etc.);
   5.3. State of roads, bridges, airports, availability of transport, communications, etc.;
   5.4. Access to the territory (road convoys, river and sea shipping, airlifts and airdrops, "humanitarian corridors", "windows of peace", etc.);
   5.1. Prevalence of endemic diseases, vectors, vaccines needed, etc.;
   5.2. Availability of medical treatment and evacuation plans/regulations;
   5.3. Presence of unexploded landmines, bombs, and artillery shells;
   5.4. Communication network;
   5.5. Procedures for international aid agreements;
   5.6. Rights and authorizations for movements of people and goods (international flights, transit, landing);
   5.7. Visa, customs regulations, clearance, number of photos needed, etc.;

6.   At the end of the RAMH a meeting of the team should be organised to process together their experience.

METHODOLOGY

1.   The RAMH depends not only on the discussions with and reports by governments, agencies, and others familiar with the situation. The RAMH team must visit and directly observe the refugee/displaced camps, and sites hosting other populations affected by conflict, including those most impacted, even in very remote areas. It is very important to include members of the affected communities in the assessment process. In a situation with important political, security, military, ethnic, and other problems, there is a risk that the data collected are unduly influenced by the opinions or by the biases of those consulted, or by written reports. Therefore, the RAMH team must remain independent, vigilant, and neutral in order to limit systematic biases.

Data Collection and Sources of Information

2.   **Work in the early days of emergencies is chaotic, and data collection during a RAMH may not advance in a step-by-step, logical fashion. Nevertheless, a good plan for collection**

"Rapid Assessment of Mental Health of Refugees, Displaced and Other Populations Affected by Conflict and Post-Conflict Situations, and Available Resources", WORLD HEALTH ORGANIZATION, Geneva, 2001

and analysis will lead to a more reliable report. **Enough time must be given at the beginning to identify the most adequate and relevant individuals to interview.**

3.   The RAMH uses a multifaceted approach, gathering information from key sources representing agencies of the affected government(s), UN Agencies, NGOs, local academics, researchers, and members of the affected and host communities. The assessment must cover all levels. Data collection must include central and peripheral levels – rural and urban – from national, and international sources. Populations in/from highly impacted areas should be given priority. Information can be collected from existing documents, interviews, and visits to the affected areas. Information collected from news media is important, however media information may be biased and needs to be cross-checked.

4.   It must be understood that any rapid assessment is a compromise between available resources, constraints and needs. Therefore, the margin of error inherent in the data collection must be kept as low as possible. Sensible, suspicious or inaccurate information must be cross-checked. For a number of reasons, is not always possible to consult with all the possible sources of information listed below. The higher the number of sources consulted, however, the better the quality and objectivity of the data collected. Therefore, critical thinking will be needed in order to select and access the most relevant sources of information.

Central and regional national authorities:
   4.1 Ministry of Health;
   4.2 Ministry of Education;
   4.3 Ministry of Social Welfare or of ad hoc Ministries (For example, "interior" and "security", "reconstruction", or "rehabilitation";
   4.4 Other ad hoc central district offices, local refugee offices, local UN administration, etc.;
   4.5 Other national, regional, and local administrative authorities;
   4.6 Regional/local security authorities;
   4.7 Refugee community;
   4.8 Non-state entities.

Representatives of agencies, associations, services, universities:
   4.9   Central UN administration in-country, if any;
   4.10 UN agencies;
   4.11 NGOs – international, regional and local;
   4.12 Religious groups, spiritual community and religious leaders;
   4.13 Indigenous/traditional healers;
   4.14 Cultural anthropologists, sociologists if any;
   4.15 Health and mental health professionals and relevant associations if any;
   4.16 Women's, youth, disabled, minority groups or associations.

Intersectoral sources:
(Note that information will be sought from and shared with other assessment teams).
   4.17 Physical health;
   4.18 Specialized mental health services;
   4.19 Rehabilitation centers for physically disabled;
   4.20 Pre-existing social welfare and services and newly introduced activities for:
      (a) Families: including family reunification, refugees, displaced, returnees, etc.;

"Rapid Assessment of Mental Health of Refugees, Displaced and Other Populations Affected by Conflict and Post-Conflict Situations, and Available Resources", WORLD HEALTH ORGANIZATION, Geneva, 2001

(b) Women: widows, survivors of torture/ rape, kidnapping, etc.;
(c) Children and adolescents: including unaccompanied minors, orphans, street children, children/adolescent head of families, and child soldiers;
(d) Survivors of extreme violence (rape, torture, abducted) and former detainees/prisoners during conflicts and their families, including released prisoners of war;

4.21 Other vital sectors: food, water, shelter, sanitation;
4.22 Education: primary and secondary school teachers, professors at universities, post secondary technical/vocational schools;
4.23 Cultural, youth, sports, and social groups: clan, village, camp, and community leaders, representatives of the elderly;
4.24 Police, army, and other local or international security forces.

Cautionary notes about data collection

5.   During visits to the affected areas, even careful observation may result in a biased impression. The area visited may be more or less severely affected than the rest. Therefore, quick generalizations must be avoided. In addition, the most severely affected persons are often the least visible; those injured or sick and those who have been most traumatized, avoid contact and are less accessible to visitors. Personal impressions and notes are useful, but these must be kept separate from the factual observations and data.

Field practical guidelines

6.   WHO or the agency responsible for the RAMH should make the initial contacts and preparations. This is best done with local counterparts.

7.   In the field, the RAMH team needs to introduce themselves and outline quickly the terms of reference and the method of the assessment. Avoid unnecessary jargon or acronyms. Be careful not to raise hopes too high. Treat everyone with respect. The best way to avoid being seen as a tourist, donor, or voyeur is to treat those met as valued colleagues. Explain what will be done with the information gathered. Avoid to take originals of documents from the site, make copies.

8.   Remember that staff working in emergencies has heavy workloads and difficult living conditions. They will stay behind; therefore, it is of utmost importance not to overload or expose them, their families or colleagues to additional security risks. It is important to carefully prepare questions to be asked, so that they can be presented in a non-threatening way. The RAMH team needs to openly express their appreciation for the good being done by existing initiatives (local and international).

9.   The RAMH team must adopt ethical behaviour and good citizenship. Working lunches/dinners are often necessary. But remember that meals, transport, and other expenses should not be imposed on field workers. Do not impose late evening meetings away from the residence of people, particularly if there are security problems. Remain alert to the security risks of travelling too early in the morning or late in the evening both for the RAMH team and for the community members with whom the team is meeting.

10.   Special attention is called to the fact that emergencies remain politically sensitive situations in which security is frequently a problem. The RAMH team must be sensitive to the consequences of

----

"Rapid Assessment of Mental Health of Refugees, Displaced and Other Populations Affected by Conflict and Post-Conflict Situations, and Available Resources", WORLD HEALTH ORGANIZATION, Geneva, 2001

their selection of people and organisations with whom they will be working. In addition, one should not underestimate the influence of the financial and material benefits provided to local staff during the field mission. Such elements can become a source of unnecessary pressure, which will eventually affect the quality of the information collected.

Coordination with additional organisations
11.   Numerous organisations are likely to be in the field responding to the emergency. The RAMH team must contact the most relevant to gain their collaboration and support and avoid duplication. Co-ordination and sharing of resources will produce a more complete and accurate assessment and save funds for direct services delivery.

12.   It is important to ensure that RAMH staff includes local community members in most phases of the RAMH assessment. Likewise, international NGO staff with the required knowledge of the situation can be called upon. This contributes to capacity building at each level of participation, and is likely to add to the validity of the data and improve future interventions and collaborations.

Precautions in analysing and interpreting data
13.   It is important to remember that information obtained from interviews is often biased by the interviewees' personal history, emotional condition, and intellectual capacity at that moment. There are objective and subjective biases. The way a person reports on actual events may be more or less accurate, introducing an objective bias. Objective biases may also result when individuals provide "official" information that may be deliberately inaccurate. It is difficult to distinguish fact from rumour, while in the chaos of a conflict official information can be tainted by inaccuracy almost as often as local gossip.

14.   Subjective biases result when individuals allow personal, cultural, ethnic stereotypes, or prejudices and expectations to affect their judgement. They also occur when individuals intentionally exaggerate the extent of damage or trauma to obtain emergency assistance for those they represent, or to protect the image of the agency or government they represent. These biases can be aggravated by those of the RAMH team.

15.   In emergencies, "hard data" are almost impossible to obtain. The lack or poor quality of information is in itself information. But comparing data and viewpoints from different sources can help to build a more accurate picture of the situation. Unofficial sources may be able to tell whether lack of data lies in the chaos of the situation, or the lack of support for mental health aspects among government or agencies, or other causes or a combination of the two.

16.   Difficulty in accessing certain areas may be the greatest constraint. Defining on the map the accessible areas, the "grey zones" about which little is known, and the "black holes" about which nothing is known will help to determine how much the situation is actually reflected by the collected data, and thus will indicate the quality of the assessment.

Common obstacles and possible sources of error

17.   Common sources of error may be logistical, organisational, or technical. The most frequent sources of error are listed below.

Logistical – Inadequate Resources:

"Rapid Assessment of Mental Health of Refugees, Displaced and Other Populations Affected by Conflict and Post-Conflict Situations, and Available Resources", WORLD HEALTH ORGANIZATION, Geneva, 2001

17.1. Transport and fuel problems;
17.2. Communications problems (at various levels);
17.3. Accommodation problems.

Solution: Develop as early as possible a checklist of needed provisions and resources, and adjust with flexibility according to availability in the field.

Organisational/Institutional:

17.4. The responsibilities of each team member are not well defined;
17.5. The team members have never met before;
17.6. Authorities, key decision makers, and possible donors in charge of the area(s) targeted for assessment are not informed and are not ready to assist or meet the RAMH team;
17.7. Key decision-makers and possible donors may also be under pressure to respond to political demands even before the findings and recommendations of the assessment are known, resulting in inappropriate assistance;
17.8. The assessment is conducted too late, or it takes too long, or it does not provide sufficient information;
17.9. Irrelevant information is collected.

Solution: Better preparation before leaving and better organisation in the field. Early contact and involvement of all relevant stakeholders (or agencies).

Technical:

17.10. Skilled and experienced professionals are not involved in the assessment;
17.11. Assessment conclusions are based on data that do not represent the true needs of the affected population;
17.12. Information received from field workers and official interviews is taken at face value, without cross-checking all sources.

Solution: Careful and continued monitoring of mission process and data collected.

Remember that situations may change quickly. Collect the most recent data and continue monitoring the situation when drafting the report. Depending on the situation, circulate and discuss preliminary conclusions while processing the final report.

Precautions for the RAMH in repatriation operations

18.   It is important to remember that the end of a conflict may increase distress for a certain time, due to the following:

18.1. News of deaths of family members, relatives, or friends may be learned during this phase;
18.2. Families returning to their homes may find that their home and/or other property has been looted or destroyed, or occupied by others;
18.3. There may be a return of demobilized soldiers, which can greatly increase tensions in the community, in particular if they their weapons.

Analysis

19.   During conflicts, the situation can change very rapidly. The analysis of data must be collected quickly and thoroughly, and the results made urgently available to decision-makers to draw the greatest benefit from the assessment. It is best for the analysis to use standardized categories of

---

"Rapid Assessment of Mental Health of Refugees, Displaced and Other Populations Affected by Conflict and Post-Conflict Situations, and Available Resources", WORLD HEALTH ORGANIZATION, Geneva, 2001

information as described in this tool. The analysis must be as specific as possible to ensure the best development of community-based, phase-specific programmes.

The RAMH Report

20.   The RAMH Report needs to be standardized in the same manner as the data analysis. It will consist of the same "chapters" as for the objectives. In addition, there will be at least four annexes to it:

    20.1.   **National mental health policy and other relevant documents, if any;**
    20.2.   **Other situational, health, or mental health reports, if any;**
    20.3.   **The List the active local and international relief agencies and the key persons;**
    20.4.   **The List of (with names of contact persons) local and international agencies involved in psychosocial projects; copies of such projects should be collected.**

21.   The report needs to be clearly worded. Decision-makers or staff of local, national and international organisations whose actions depend on the results of the RAMH may have little training in interpreting mental health data. Avoid technical jargon to permit rapid reading and decision-making, avoid presenting a voluminous report. Depending on situations, producing a detailed report before departure from a country might not be advisable. The complexity of the situation might require a few days of reflection to prevent hasty conclusions and decisions that might lead to damaging actions. It is therefore preferable to deliver preliminary conclusions and recommendations for immediate actions while waiting for the detailed report to be issued.

22.   In the report, give clear indication of the immediate priority needs and how to address them with community-oriented phase-specific programmes. The needs of the chronic mentally ill are to be distinguished from those resulting from the conflict. Make clear recommendations regarding the best approaches, strategies, and programmes. If possible, try to provide the worst and best-case scenarios and a contingency plan for the next 3-6 months, what will be the mental health priorities if the conflict continues or if a peace is reached.

Responsibility for the Distribution of the Report

23.   Distribution of the Report is the responsibility of the organisation or government that has undertaken it (see Terms of Reference, page 3).

"Rapid Assessment of Mental Health of Refugees, Displaced and Other Populations Affected by Conflict and Post-Conflict Situations, and Available Resources", WORLD HEALTH ORGANIZATION, Geneva, 2001

CONCLUSION

In conclusion, the RAMH is an important tool for the immediate assessment of mental health needs and resources in conflict and post-conflict situations. This tool can be used in both the emergency phase and in ongoing unstable post-conflict situations. The RAMH report will include recommendations for the development of a community-based, phase-specific, mental health programme. It will also describe available individual, family, and community strengths and human, financial, and material resources, including political support. It will provide useful cultural/ religious/ ethnic elements to be considered for both the refugee and other populations affected by conflict and host community/ies. Recommendations made in the report must aim at bridging emergency to longer-term actions and development. Finally, it is important to note that the RAMH is a first step to be followed by a more comprehensive assessment, when the CAMH tool is available.

The RAMH report will not contain a mental health project proposal but it will serve as a basis for its construction. The following project outline, being used by WHO and others, could be useful.

Outline of Project proposal

1. Background information on the conflict, on the forcibly displaced populations concerned and on the host community, environment, etc.;
2. Proposed project: outline overall perspective of location and duration of the project;
3. Objectives;
4. Activities, duration, collaborations;
5. Monitoring methods;
6. Qualitative evaluation (if possible also quantitative);
7. Reporting modalities;
8. Estimated budget.

Useful Bibliography

Ref: "Declaration of Cooperation: Mental Health of Refugees, Displaced and Other Populations Affected by Conflict and Post-Conflict Situations", World Health Organization, 2000;
Ref: WHO/UNHCR "Mental Health of Refugees", WHO, 1996;
Ref: Dr G. H. Brundtland, Director-General, World Health Organization, Editorial "Mental Health of Refugees, Internally Displaced Persons and Other Populations Affected by Conflict" in Acta Psychiatrica Scandinavica, 2000, Munksgaard, Copenhagen;
Ref: Petevi, M. "Forced Displacement: Refugee Trauma, Protection and Assistance. In Y. Danieli, N. Rodney and L. Weisaeth, (Eds) in International Responses to Traumatic Stress. New York: United Nations Publications, Baywood Publishing Co.

RAPID ASSESSMENT OF MENTAL HEALTH NEEDS AND AVAILABLE RESOURCES

	REFUGEES		HOST POPUL.	
	YES	NO	YES	NO
Data to be collected				
The data indicated below are needed for an effective assessment. The checklist is put in tables to help the RAMH team to keep track of the collection process. The answers should not be recorded on this form. These tables are to be used by the RAMH team leader or secretary to maintain an overall picture of which information was obtained by team members or by different teams. The section headings can serve as an outline for the RAMH report. Numbers/ estimates and other similar information must be described and reported with great caution to avoid over interpretations and misunderstandings.				
SECTION I. GENERAL INFORMATION ABOUT THE SITUATION AND THE CONFLICT **Description of the conflict, of the affected areas, of the populations and expected movements**				
1. Geographic and environmental (natural) characteristics of the affected area				
2. Previous conditions in the affected area; what was life like before the conflict; changes occurred due to the conflict				
3. Administrative and political divisions in the affected area				
4. Nature of the conflict itself				
5. Expected developments of the conflict				
6. Expected population movements - population movements that have already taken place				
7. Adequacy of security, types and degree of violence: Attacks, invasions into refugee camps, killings in affected areas, abductions, looting				
8. Basic survival situation and needs:				
(a) Morbidity, death rates, and causes (age, gender specific if possible)				
(b) Food supplies, recent food distribution, and future food needs				
(c) Supply and quality of water				
(d) Adequacy of sanitation				
(e) Other basic survival priority needs of the affected population				
(f) Situation of shelter and clothing				

Data to be collected	REFUGEES YES	NO	HOST POPUL. YES	NO
9. Economic aspects: employment or income generation activities, unequal distribution of resources and positions by ethnic, political, or other kind of grouping				
10. Community aspects: solidarity, ongoing political, ethnic, other tensions, problems with youngsters, other groups				
11. Education				
(a) Current education programs for the refugee / displaced community/war-affected community				
(b) Important problems for education generated by the conflict				
(c) Current roles and activities of teachers (if not employed in formal education)				
(d) Status of transport, fuel, communication, and other logistic necessities				

SECTION II. DESCRIPTION OF THE AFFECTED POPULATIONS

Statistics are not always available during a crisis. Therefore data collected on these aspects can be simple estimates. *Remember the different categories of affected populations and the variability within each of them: refugees, internally displaced, existence of old refugee groups/displaced populations, if the problem is not new, returnees, non-displaced war-affected populations, others.*

1. Estimates on population by age, gender, and vulnerability				
2. Orphans, unaccompanied minors, street children				
3. Children / adolescent heads of household				
4. Demobilized child soldiers, ex-soldiers, active soldiers, ex-"freedom fighters"				
5. Single mothers				
6. Survivors of torture, sexual violence				
7. Widows				
8. Elderly				
9. Chronically mentally ill: in institutions, in families, or elsewhere				
10. Physically disabled and developmentally delayed				
11. Average household size				

Data to be collected	REFUGEES YES	NO	HOST POPUL. YES	NO
12. Ethnic composition and place of origin of affected population (Where are they from?)				
13. Location of the affected population: type: camps, transit centers, besieged villages, towns; environment: rural, urban, desert, jungle, tropical; accessibility: easy, difficult, dangerous, etc.				
14. Mapping of the locations and estimated numbers of various types of the affected populations				
15. Location and number of those living with relatives, and local people in rural and urban areas				

SECTION III. MENTAL HEALTH NEEDS

Exposure of the population affected by the conflict to violence and to traumatic events and current camp life

	REFUGEES YES	NO	HOST POPUL. YES	NO
1. How sudden was the move?				
2. When and how refugees arrive in present locations? What have they gone through?				
3. Killings, executions, missing				
4. Ongoing /daily violence harassment: against whole populations or against women, or other groups				
5. Torture				
6. Sexual violence against adults or children				
7. Domestic violence, including child abuse				
8. Armed attacks, artillery shelling, bombing, etc.				
9. Separation of family				
10. Forced to perpetrate violence against their own family, community, nation				
11. Type of disruption of most important cultural and social rituals, family and community structure				
12. Abduction				
13. Imprisonment, detention in re-education/ concentration camps and other kind of settings				
14. Deprivation of food/water				
15. Epidemics with deaths				

Data to be collected	REFUGEES YES	NO	HOST POPUL. YES	NO
16. Breakdown of traditional family roles and support networks				
17. Ethnic, political, religious disputes				
18. Lack of privacy				
19. Disruption of status (e.g., economic decline, loss of power in the community)				
20. Extortion				
SECTION IV. CULTURAL, RELIGIOUS, POLITICAL AND SOCIO-ECONOMIC ISSUES FOR THE REFUGEES AND IDPs				
1. Community characteristics before and after the conflict - strengths - resistance				
2. Social structure; clans, tribe, ethnic				
3. Are there any psychological support structure and type of administration: civil, military (example: family, church, community)?				
4. Family structure: extended family, handling of financial resources, of family problems/hazards				
5. Economic structure: kind of production and management of resources at family, district/or camp and national levels				
6. Brief history of the host community or country, including conflict and disaster history				
7. Brief history of the relationship between host, refugee and displaced groups				
8. Sanctions/taboos about specific topics, traditions, rituals or social interactions: ex deaths, burial, mourning, rape, acts of revenge, justice, etc.				
9. Religious and spiritual aspects of host nation: ex. Are they similar to those of refugee community, are the relationships friendly in spirit of solidarity or very different creating or maintaining tensions and problems				
10. Emerging social structure and self-organization in the concerned community, existing activities				
11. Are there any emerging community leaders and what kind – political, ethnic, religious, ex-military, ex-freedom fighters?				
12. What kind of emerging social groups or associations, parties, etc. are there?				

Data to be collected

	REFUGEES YES NO	HOST POPUL. YES NO

SECTION V. BRIEF DESCRIPTION OF IMPORTANT CULTURAL ASPECTS

Describe how people deal with consequences of violence and trauma: individual/family/community levels and how these mechanisms are affected by the current situation

1. Is the society matrilineal or patrilineal?

2. Kind of religion/s and role of priests, traditional healers, kings, other community "authorities"

3. How did/does the community treat and consider people with physical illness and handicaps?

4. Ways conflict and disagreement are dealt with by people in the current situation

5. How are emotions/thoughts expressed? (For example, sadness, anger, happiness, suspicion, fear, attitudes, disagreement, intolerance, prejudice, etc.)

6. How did the culture/traditions of the refugee community consider and react to mental illness and problems? Has this changed as a result of the conflict?

7. Do people ask for help or for psychological support when they need it? If yes, how are they seen by their community?

8. How do people understand and deal with violence and suffering?

9. How do people deal with death, burial, bereavement and loss?

10. In the current context, are there any situations in which traditions and rituals can not be practised? (For example: for the missing, for the children born as a result of rape, for those who are buried on the way to exile, or when hiding in remote areas, in exile, or in the camps, etc.)

SECTION VI. MENTAL HEALTH POLICY AND RESOURCES
General information on mental health policy and action plan

1. Is there a national mental health policy on prevention, emergency response relief, and longer-term programs? Does it apply to asylum seekers, refugees, displaced, and other non-displaced populations affected by the conflict?

2. If this policy existed before the conflict, has it been adapted to the current needs?

3. Does a mental health operation plan exist? Is it being implemented? If so, by whom, where, since when? How can a copy of the plan be obtained? How does one contact the people in charge?

4. Is there a person in the MOH or in the designated body responsible for mental health activities?

Data to be collected	REFUGEES YES	NO	HOST POPUL. YES	NO
Mental health resources available in the affected and host communities				
5. Is there a data collection, dissemination, and updating system including follow up on the security, human rights violations, and other problems with an impact on mental health? Which organization is responsible for it?				
6. Were any other mental health needs assessments carried out? By whom? For what purpose? Were locals or refugees involved? Were the organisers/authors be contacted? How can the reports be obtained?				
7. Are there national mental health strategies addressing the emergency?				
8. Is there any national mental health personnel in the area of concern? If yes, what type and how many?				
9. Are there any mental health professionals within the refugee community, within the camps? What type and how many?				
10. How can these people be reached?				
11. What mental health training activities are available? By whom?				
12. What are the salaries of national health personnel? If a national scale does not exist, obtain minimum payment requirements, because it will be needed in the budgeting of the project which will result from the recommendations.				
13. What is the percentage of budget and the actual amount of money allocated to mental health by UN agencies, NGOs, government, others?				
14. Are there any international projects available to respond to mental health needs? If yes, obtain copies of projects and other relevant info.				
Resources, coping skills and behaviour strengthening at personal and community levels of reconstruction and functioning				
15. General resiliency and functioning of the community				
16. Does community show cohesion and solidarity?				
17. Is there communication between tribes, ethnic/political groups, the refugee, and host community (ies)?				
18. Do formal or informal educational activities, including extracurricular ones exist?				
19. Is there any support or self-help groups within the refugee community and or host support groups? (For example, between children, adolescents, adults, elderly, or between women and men, among the disabled, among women?)				

Data to be collected

	REFUGEES		HOST POPUL.	
	YES	NO	YES	NO
SECTION VII. CONCLUSIONS AND RECOMMENDATIONS				
Recommendations for an immediate and long term community-oriented mental health response based on the findings of the RAMH; the report should include most important facts among which the following				
1. Recommendations for immediate and long-term care of the most vulnerable				
2. Recommendations for immediate and longer term care of the most serious mental health problems of the overall population. What inter-generational activities, exchanges, support exists and what is needed?				
3. Recommendations for immediate and longer term capacity building				
4. Recommendations of immediate and longer term implementation of mental health programme				
5. Indication of available resources/ indication of required resources				
6. Provide from list of agencies involved (to be annexed) indication of possible collaborations				
7. Describe major obstacles – constraints, risks, assets for implementation of a mental health programme				
8. Recommendations in priority of the most cost-effective local interventions, external support and collaborations needed				
9. Existing activities and location (city contacts) of self-organization of the community must to be maintained or expanded as a significant power resource of the community				
10. Existing activities organized by the host community and local and international agencies to be maintained or expanded				
11. Ways to prevent breakdown of national services and local NGOs by excessive recruitment of local and regional staff or by introduction of wage discrepancies in salary scales by international agencies.				

End of the Tool

FEEDBACK FORM

for the TOOL
**Rapid Assessment of Mental Health Needs of Refugees, Displaced and Other Populations
in Conflict and Post-Conflict Situations, and Available Resources
WORLD HEALTH ORGANIZATION, Geneva, 2001**

After using the RAMH, please provide the following feedback to assist in revising the Tool to make it as useful as possible for the user in the field. Please print or write clearly so that your comments can be used. Please use the back of this sheet or attach additional pages if necessary. Thanks for sending it to:

**Ms Mary Petevi
Emergency Health Intelligence and Capacity Building
Department of Emergency and Humanitarian Action (EHA)
World Health Organization (WHO)
20, Avenue Appia
Geneva 27, SWITZERLAND
Tel: 41 22 7914232, Fax: 41 22 7914844, E-mail: petevim@who.ch**

In which situation and country/ies did you use this tool?

Questions to be added:

Material to be deleted:

How can the format of the RAMH be changed to be more effective?

What worked best about this tool?

What was most cumbersome about the tool?

What other suggestions do you have?

LIST OF PARTICIPANTS
INTERNATIONAL CONSULTATION MENTAL HEALTH OF REFUGEES AND DISPLACED POPULATIONS IN CONFLICT AND POST-CONFLICT SITUATIONS FROM CRISIS THROUGH RECONSTRUCTION
Geneva, 23-25 October 2000

Opening session

Chairperson: Dr David NABARRO
Executive Director, Director-General's Office, World Health Organization

SPEAKERS:

Dr Gro Harlem BRUNDTLAND
Director-General
World Health Organization

Ms Mary ROBINSON
High Commissioner
Office of the United Nations High Commissioner for Human Rights

Mr Frederick BARTON
The Deputy High Commissioner
Office of the United Nations High Commissioner for Refugees

Mr Pekka HUHTANIEMI
Ambassador
Permanent Mission of Finland to the United Nations Office at Geneva

Mr Hakan SANDBLADH
Deputy Director, Department of Health
International Federation of Red Cross and Red Crescent Societies (IFRC)

Ms Erin MOONEY
Special Representative, Dr Francis Deng's Office
UN Secretary-General's Office on Internally Displaced Persons

Dr Xavier LEUS
Director, Emergency Humanitarian Action
World Health Organization

Dr Benedetto SARACENO
Director, Department of Mental Health and Substance Dependence
World Health Organization

Dr Joop de JONG
Director
Transcultural Psychosocial Organization

Ms Mary PETEVI
Department of Mental Health and Substance Dependence
World Health Organization

PARTICIPANTS:

1. Dr Ferid AGANI
WHO Mental Health Assistant
Department of Neuropsychiatry
University Clinical Center
38000 Pristina, KOSOVO

2. Mrs Uju AGOMOH
Executive Director
Prisoners Rehabilitation and Welfare Action (PRAWA)
1A Bode Thomas Street
P.O. Box 2061, Sabo-Yaba, Lagos
NIGERIA

3. Dr Florence BAINGANA
Mental Health Specialist, Health Nutrition and
PopulationThe World Bank
1818 H Street NW, D.C. 20433
Washington, USA

4. Dr Ahmad BAKER
Professor of Psychology, Birzeit University
Jerusalem, PALESTINIAN TERRITORIES

5. Prof Constantinos BALLAS
Ministry of Health/KEEL
GREECE

6. Dr Helen BAMBER
Director, Medical Foundation for Torture Care
(Former Secr., Int Assoc. for Health and Human Rights)
96 Grafton Rd
NW5 3EJ London, UNITED KINGDOM

7. Dr Thierry BAUBET
Psychiatrist, Medecins Sans Frontieres
8 St Sabin 75011
Paris, FRANCE

8. Ms Lena BREMER
Director, Crisis Prevention Center
the Finnish Association for Mental Health
Simonkatu 12 B 13
FIN-00100 Helsinki, FINLAND

9. Dr Mustapha ELMASRI
Consultant Psychiatrist
Societe Algerienne pour Recherche en Psychologie
Villa No33 El Omrania
Dely Ibrahim
Alger, ALGERIA

10. Dr Suman FERNANDO
Professor, University of Kent and North London
Member of Mental Health Act Commission (UK)
20 Burghley Road, Kentish Town, NW5 1UE
London, UNITED KINGDOM

11. Dr Edvard HAUFF
Consultant Psychiatrist
Department of Psychiatric Research and Education
Ullevaal University Hospital
0407 Oslo, NORWAY

12. Dr Gerard A. JACOBS
Director, Disaster Mental Health Institute
University of South Dakota - SDU114
414 East Clark Street
Vermillon, SD 57069-2390, USA

13. Mr Ranjith JAYASINGHE
Chief Occupational Therapist, Mental Hospital
454/1A Dutugemunu Road
Colombo, SRI LANKA

14. Dr Joop de JONG
Director, Transcultural Psychosocial Organization (TPO)
Keizersgracht 329
1016 EE Amsterdam, The NETHERLANDS

15. Mr Noureddine KHALED
President, Societe Algerienne de Recherche en
Psychologie (SARP)
Villa No 33, El Omrania, Dely Ibrahim
16320 Alger, ALGERIA

16. Dr Anica Mikus KOS
Slovene Philanthropy
(Association for Promotion of Voluntary Work)
1000 Ljubljana, SLOVENIA

17. Ms Guiseppine LABELLARTE
Italian Psychiatric Organization
Stradella Carducci 5, 70124
Bari, ITALY

18. Dr Pirkko LAHTI
President , World Federation for Mental Health
Maistraatinportti 4A
FIN-00240 Helsinki, FINLAND

19. Dr Jean Claude METRAUX
Director, Appartenances (NGO)
Rue des Terraux 10, Lausanne 9, SWITZERLAND

20. Dr Richard MOLLICA
Director, Harvard Program in Refugee Trauma
8 Story Street, 3 floor, MA 02138
Cambridge, Massachusettts 02138, USA

21. Dr Edward NAHIM
National Coordinator for Mental Health, Ministry of Health
34 Ecowas Street
Freetown, SIERRA LEONE

22. Dr Flavio del PONTE
Senior Medical Advisor, Swiss Disaster Relief Unit
Federal Department of Foreign Affairs
Eigerstrasse 71, CH-3003 Bern
SWITZERLAND

23. Mr Francisco QUESNEY
Project Officer, Child Protection
United Nations Children's Fund
New York 10017, USA

24. Dr Jean-Pierre REVEL
Head of Project, International Committee of Red Cross
19, avenue de la Paix
Geneva, SWITZERLAND

25. Dr Bhogendra SHARMA
Medical Director CVICT
P.O. Box 5839, Bansbari-3
Kathmandu, NEPAL

26. Ms Beatrice STAMBUL
Psychiatrist, Medecins du Monde
19 Boulevard Chave
13005 Marseille, FRANCE

27. Dr Nora SVEAASS
Secretary General
International Society for Health and Human Rights
Urtegt. 50, 0187 Oslo
NORWAY

28. Dr Loes van WILLIGEN
Former Medical Director Pharos and
Honorary President of ISHHR
Foundation for Refugee Mental Health Care
Prinseneiland 11-II
1013 LL Amsterdam
The NETHERLANDS

Contact: Ms Mary Petevi
Technical Officer
Department of Emergency and Humanitarian Action
Cluster of Sustainable Development
World Health Organization

OBSERVERS (Permanent Missions):
Australia, Belgium, Canada, Cyprus, Finland, France,
Germany, Greece, Ireland, Italy, Japan, Netherlands,
Norway, Sweden, Switzerland, United Kingdom, United
States of America.

**OBSERVERS (Representatives of United Nations
agencies, international organisations and NGOs):**
United Nations Development Programme (UNDP)
United Nations High Commissioner for Refugees
United Nations High Commissioner for Human Rights
United Nations Children's Fund (UNICEF)
United Nations Population Fund (UNFPA)
Office for Coordination of Humanitarian Assistance
International Committee of Red Cross (ICRC)
International Federation of Red Cross (IFRC)
International Save the Children Alliance (ISCA)
International Organization for Migration (IOM)
International Catholic Child Bureau (ICCB)
International Rescue Committee
International Council of Voluntary Agencies (ICVA)
World Council of Churches   (WCC)
World Federation of Mental Health, Swiss Representation
World Psychiatric Association (WPA)
CARE International, Geneva
Center for Rehabilitation of Torture Victims, Greece
Red Cross Center for Rehab. of Torture Victims, Bern
Ms Liliana Urbina, WHO, Kosovo
Mr Franz Baro, Psychosoc & Psychol. Factors, Belgium

**The WHO REPRESENTATIVES of various
departments from Headquarters.**

SECRETARIAT of the Consultation:
Dr Benedetto Saraceno, Director, Department of Mental
    Health and Substance Dependence (MSD)
Dr Shekhar Saxena, Coordinator, MSD
Ms Meena Cabral de Mello, MSD
Ms Mary Petevi, MSD
Dr C. Mandlhate, WHO Regional Mental Health Adviser,
    AFRO
Ms Elmira Adenova, MSD
Ms Mylène Schreiber, MSD
Ms Roshni Fernando, MSD

Address: 20, avenue Appia
1211 Geneva 27
Switzerland

Tel: 41 22 7914232/ 7914939
Fax: 41 22 7914844
E-mail: petevim@who.ch

Index

ABOUT THE VOLUME EDITORS

GILBERT REYES, PhD, is a licensed clinical psychologist and the Associate Dean for Clinical Training at Fielding Graduate University in Santa Barbara, California. He has responded to several major disasters in the United States, including the September 11, 2001, attack on the World Trade Center. Reyes has also consulted with the International Federation of Red Cross and Red Crescent Societies on various projects and in 2002 co-authored that organization's training manual for community-based psychological support. He recently co-authored a training course for the American Red Cross on children's disaster mental health needs and is now collaborating with the Terrorism and Disaster Center of the National Child Traumatic Stress Network on the development of interventions for children in disasters.

GERARD A. (JERRY) JACOBS, PhD, is Director of the Disaster Mental Health Institute (DMHI) and a Professor at the University of South Dakota. He is active in field work, training, program development, and consultation nationally and internationally for the Red Cross movement and the American Psychological Association. He is a co-author of the WHO *Tool for the Rapid Assessment of Mental Health* and served on the Institute of Medicine Committee on Responding to the Psychological Consequences of Terrorism. He also works with the Asian Disaster Preparedness Center in psychological support training and program development.

ABOUT THE CONTRIBUTORS

FERID AGANI, MD, MA, is neuropsychiatrist, member of the Parliament of Kosovo, and assistant professor at the University of Prishtina. He is a leader of mental health reform in Kosovo. His main field of the interest is promotion of the human rights of the mentally ill people. Dr. Agani is a member of the American Family Therapy Academy, European Psychiatric Association, and International Society for Traumatic Stress Studies. He is co-director of the Kosovan-American university collaborative project, Kosovar Family Professional Educational Collaborative. Dr. Agani is also founder of the nongovernmental professional association, Institute for Mental Health and Recovery of Kosova.

PAUL BOLTON is Associate Professor in the Center for International Health and Development at Boston University and head of the Applied Mental Health Research Group (AMHR) located within the Center. Originally a physician by training, he has since 1988 worked with various NGOs in war, disaster, and development settings, either directly or as a technical consultant. His main areas of expertise are in cross-cultural assessment and the application of these methods to research and to project assessment, monitoring, and evaluation. Since 1999 he has focused his efforts on mental health and psychosocial programming.

EILEEN R. BORRIS, EdD, is a licensed psychologist and political psychologist who has worked for over 20 years in the areas of peace building, conflict resolution, and conflict transformation. She is currently the President of Division 48–The Society for the Study of Peace, Conflict, and Violence: Peace Psychology division of the American Psychological Association (APA). She has worked in regions of conflict around the world, which include the former Soviet Union, the Republic of Georgia, the Middle East, Nepal, Indonesia, Pakistan, India, and the Tibetan government in Exile. She serves on the Committee for International Relations in Psychology (CIRP) for APA. Borris received her doctorate in psychology from Columbia University, a certificate of advanced studies in communicative sciences from Johns Hopkins University, and a master's degree in special education from Columbia University. She is a member of the International Society for Political Psychology, Psychologists for Social Responsibility, and the Association for Humanistic Psychology.

ISMET CERIC, MD, PhD, is a professor of psychiatry at Sarajevo University and Senior Coordinator of WHO Mental Health Programs in Bosnia-Herzegovina.

YAEL DANIELI, PhD, is a clinical psychologist in private practice in New York City, a traumatologist, and victimologist. She is also Co-founder and Director, Group Project for Holocaust Survivors and Their Children; Founding President, International Network for Holocaust and Genocide Survivors and their Friends; and Co-founder, past-President, Senior United Nations Representative, International Society for Traumatic Stress Studies (ISTSS). Dr. Danieli integrates treatment, worldwide study, teaching/training, publishing, expert advocacy, and consulting to numerous governments, news, international and national organizations, and institutions on victims rights and optimal care, including for their protectors and providers. Most recently she received the ISTSS Lifetime Achievement Award.

SOLVIG EKBLAD is licensed clinical psychologist, PhD, and Adjunct Associate Professor in Transcultural Psychology at the Karolinska Institutet, and she is in charge of the research program Migration and Health at the National Institute of Psychosocial Factors and Health. She supervises a research group including national and international PhD students and is in charge of training courses on graduate, PhD, and postdoc levels. She has been consultant to several UN agencies and has co-chaired the International Committee on Refugees and Other Migrants, World Federation for Mental Health. She has written many articles and book chapters and has presented papers at international and national conferences.

SUZANNE FEETHAM, PhD, RN, FAAN, formerly held the H. H. Werley Endowed Research Chair at the University of Illinois at Chicago. Dr. Feetham has held clinical, research, and leadership positions in public health, academia, and health systems. Her career has focused on health care to underserved populations, including publication of an analysis of characteristics of effective family-focused, community-based interventions.

DZANA HUSENI, RN, is a psychiatric nurse at the University of Illinois, Chicago. Born in Bosnia to Kosovar parents, she works with mental health programs for Bosnian and Kosovar refugees.

VLADO JUKIC, MD, is the Director of the Psychiatric Hospital Vrapce in Zagreb, Croatia.

J. DAVID KINZIE, MD, is Professor of Psychiatry at Oregon Health & Science University and originated the Intercultural Psychiatric Program in 1977. He is still active in the program, and his caseload includes Cambodian, Somalian, and Latin American patients. After medical school he was a general physician in Vietnam and Malaysia, and after residency taught psychiatry at the University of Malaya School of Medicine. He currently directs the Torture Treatment Center of Oregon and the Child Traumatic Stress Center of Oregon. Dr. Kinzie has published over 100 articles and book chapters in the fields of Transcultural Psychiatry, refugee mental health, and post-traumatic stress disorder. He is a Distinguished Life Fellow of the American Psychiatric Association and Fellow of the American College of Psychiatrists. He serves on the Steering Committee of the Transcultural Section of the World Psychiatric Association.

YASMINA KULAUZOVIC is an occupational therapist at the University of Illinois at Chicago, and the project coordinator for the Coffee and Family Education and Support (CAFES) Program for Bosnian families in Chicago.

IVAN PAVKOVIC, MD, is co-founder of the Project on Genocide, Psychiatry and Witnessing at the University of Illinois at Chicago and designer of the nationwide plan for the reform of mental health services approved by the Croatian government. He is a Distinguished Life Fellow of the American Psychiatric Association and recipient of many awards, including the Bruno Lima Award recognizing his humanitarian contributions to psychiatric care in times of disaster. He has served the State of Illinois with distinction in several capacities, and is the former Director of the Department of Mental Health and Developmental Disability, former Chairman of the Dangerous Drugs Commission, and former Director of the Illinois State Psychiatric Institute.

RANDAL P. QUEVILLON, PhD, is a Professor and the Chair of the Psychology Department of the University of South Dakota. He is also a teaching faculty member of the Disaster Mental Health Institute. He specializes in rural community mental health, in psychoeducational and social support interventions, and in community issues of recovery from disasters. Dr. Quevillon has published in the areas of disaster management, mental health interventions in disasters, and aviation disasters. He has presented at many national conferences, often on topics related to community psychology issues and interventions in the wake of disasters.

DHEERAJ RAINA, MD, is currently practicing psychiatry at the Ashland Clinic in rural northwestern Wisconsin. He migrated from India for residency training at the University of Illinois at Chicago, where he met the coauthors with whom he collaborated in providing mental health services to Bosnian and Kosovar refugees, and in doing services-outcomes research.

JEAN PIERRE REVEL, MD, is currently a Medical Coordinator at the International Committee of the Red Cross, Geneva. He is a recognized expert in the management of emergency situations. Formerly, with the International Federation of Red Cross and Red Crescent Societies, he had overall responsibility for the development and management of the "Federation Psychological Support Programme" and "Humanitarian Aspects of Technological Disasters" (including nuclear accidents). Revel graduated from the School of Medicine, University of Lille (France) in 1975 and qualified in tropical medicine, public health, and epidemiology.

BENEDETTO SARACENO, MD, an internationally admired psychiatrist, is the Director of the Department of Mental Health in the World Health Organization (WHO). He has been a committed mental health reformer for over three decades, both in Italy and in the global arena. As a progressive voice for patients' rights and de-institutionalization, he has contributed to the reduction of the stigma associated with mental illnesses. Dr. Saraceno works closely with nongovernmental humanitarian organizations to promote greater awareness of the growing burden of mental illness around the world. He has recently worked tirelessly to ensure adequate and appropriate psychosocial support for victims of the Indian Ocean tsunamis.

DERRICK SILOVE, MD, FRANZCP, is the Foundation Professor of Psychiatry at Liverpool Hospital, Sydney, and member of the School of Psychiatry, the University of New South Wales. He is the director of the Centre for Population Mental Health Research, Sydney South West Area Health Service. He has a long history of clinical work, research, teaching and service development in the area of refugee and postconflict mental health. He is a board member of STARTTS, the torture and trauma rehabilitation service in Sydney, a Visiting Foreign Professor in Psychiatry at the Karolinska Institute in Sweden, and the technical advisor to the East Timor National Mental Health Program.

CHARLES D. SPIELBERGER is Distinguished Research Professor of Psychology and Director of the Center for Research in Behavioral Medicine and Health Psychology at the University of South Florida. He previously directed the USF Doctoral Program in Clinical Psychology. An ABPP Diplomate in Clinical Psychology and Distinguished Practitioner of the National Academies of Practice, Spielberger focuses his current research on anxiety, curiosity, and the experience, expression, and control of anger; job stress and stress management; and the effects of stress, emotions, and lifestyle factors on hypertension, cardiovascular disorders, and cancer. During 1991–92,

Spielberger served as the 100th president of the American Psychological Association.

STEVAN WEINE, MD, is Professor of Psychiatry at the University of Illinois at Chicago and Director of the International Center of Responses to Catastrophes, at the University of Illinois at Chicago. Weine is author of *Testimony and Catastrophe: Narrating the Traumas of Political Violence* (2005) and *When History Is a Nightmare: Lives and Memories of Ethnic Cleansing in Bosnia-Herzegovina* (1999). He was awarded a Career Scientist Award from the National Institute of Mental Health on "Services Based Research with Refugee Families."

MERITA ZHUBI, RN, is the Project Manager for the Tea and Family Education and Support (TAFES) program for newly arrived Kosovar families in Chicago. She also works in the Department of Psychiatry at the University of Illinois at Chicago.

ABOUT THE SERIES

As this new millennium dawns, humankind has evolved—some would argue has developed—exhibiting new and old behaviors that fascinate, infuriate, delight or fully perplex those of us seeking answers to the question, "Why?" In this series, experts from various disciplines peer through the lens of psychology telling us answers they see for questions of human behavior. Their topics may range from humanity's psychological ills—addictions, abuse, suicide, murder, and terrorism among them—to works focused on positive subjects including intelligence, creativity, athleticism, and resilience. Regardless of the topic, the goal of this series remains constant—to offer innovative ideas, provocative considerations, and useful beginnings to better understand human behavior.

Chris E. Stout
Series Editor

ABOUT THE SERIES EDITOR AND ADVISORY BOARD

CHRIS E. STOUT, PsyD, MBA, is a licensed clinical psychologist and is a Clinical Full Professor at the University of Illinois College of Medicine's Department of Psychiatry. He served as an NGO Special Representative to the United Nations, was appointed to the World Economic Forum's Global Leaders of Tomorrow, and has served as an Invited Faculty at the Annual Meeting in Davos. He is the Founding Director of the Center for Global Initiatives. Dr. Stout is a Fellow of the American Psychological Association, past-President of the Illinois Psychological Association, and a Distinguished Practitioner in the National Academies of Practice. Dr. Stout has published or presented over 300 papers and 30 books/manuals on various topics in psychology and his works have been translated into six languages. He has lectured across the nation and internationally in 19 countries, visited 6 continents, and almost 70 countries. He was noted as being "one of the most frequently cited psychologists in the scientific literature" in a study by Hartwick College. He is the recipient of the American Psychological Association's International Humanitarian Award.

BRUCE BONECUTTER, PhD, is Director of Behavioral Services at the Elgin Community Mental Health Center, the Illinois Department of Human Services state hospital serving adults in greater Chicago. He is also a Clinical Assistant Professor of Psychology at the University of Illinois at Chicago. A clinical psychologist specializing in health, consulting, and forensic psychology, Mr. Bonecutter is also a longtime member of the American Psychological Association Taskforce on Children & the Family. He is a member of organizations including the Association for the Treatment of Sexual Abusers, International; the Alliance for the Mentally Ill; and the Mental Health Association of Illinois.

JOSEPH FLAHERTY, MD, is Chief of Psychiatry at the University of Illinois Hospital, a Professor of Psychiatry at the University of Illinois College of Medicine, and a Professor of Community Health Science at the UIC College of Public Health. He is a Founding Member of the Society for the Study of Culture and Psychiatry. Dr. Flaherty has been a consultant to the World Health Organization, the National Institutes of Mental Health, and also the Falk Institute in Jerusalem. He has been Director of Undergraduate Education and Graduate Education in the Department of Psychiatry at the University of Illinois. Dr. Flaherty has also been Staff Psychiatrist and Chief of Psychiatry at Veterans Administration West Side Hospital in Chicago.

MICHAEL HOROWITZ, PhD, is President and Professor of Clinical Psychology at the Chicago School of Professional Psychology, one of the nation's leading not-for-profit graduate schools of psychology. Earlier, he served as Dean and Professor of the Arizona School of Professional Psychology. A clinical psychologist practicing independently since 1987, he has focused his work on psychoanalysis, intensive individual therapy, and couples therapy. He has provided Disaster Mental Health Services to the American Red Cross. Mr. Horowitz's special interests include the study of fatherhood.

SHELDON I. MILLER, MD, is a Professor of Psychiatry at Northwestern University, and Director of the Stone Institute of Psychiatry at Northwestern Memorial Hospital. He is also Director of the American Board of Psychiatry and Neurology, Director of the American Board of Emergency Medicine, and Director of the Accreditation Council for Graduate Medical Education. Dr. Miller is also an Examiner for the American Board of Psychiatry and Neurology. He is Founding Editor of the American Journal of Addictions, and Founding Chairman of the American Psychiatric Association's Committee on Alcoholism. Dr. Miller has also been a Lieutenant Commander in the U.S. Public Health Service, serving as psychiatric consultant to the Navajo Area Indian Health Service at Window Rock, Arizona. He is a member and Past President of the Executive Committee for the American Academy of Psychiatrists in Alcoholism and Addictions.

DENNIS P. MORRISON, PhD, is Chief Executive Officer at the Center for Behavioral Health in Indiana, the first behavioral health company ever to win the JCAHO Codman Award for excellence in the use of outcomes management to achieve health care quality improvement. He is President of the Board of Directors for the Community Healthcare Foundation in Bloomington, and has been a member of the Board of Directors for the American College of Sports Psychology. He has served as a consultant to agencies including the Ohio Department of Mental Health, Tennessee Association of Mental Health Organizations, Oklahoma Psychological Association, the North Carolina Council of Community Mental Health Centers, and the National Center for Health Promotion in Michigan. Dr. Morrison served across 10 years as a Medical Service Corp Officer in the U.S. Navy.

WILLIAM H. REID, MD, is a clinical and forensic psychiatrist, and consultant to attorneys and courts throughout the United States. He is Clinical Professor of Psychiatry at the University of Texas Health Science Center. Dr. Miller is also an Adjunct Professor of Psychiatry at Texas A&M College of Medicine and Texas Tech University School of Medicine, as well as a Clinical Faculty member at the Austin Psychiatry Residency Program. He is Chairman of the Scientific Advisory Board and Medical Advisor to the Texas Depressive & Manic-Depressive Association, as well as an Examiner for the American Board of Psychiatry & Neurology. He has served as President of the American Academy of Psychiatry and the Law, as Chairman of the Research Section for an International Conference on the Psychiatric Aspects of Terrorism, and as Medical Director for the Texas Department of Mental Health and Mental Retardation. Dr. Reid earned an Exemplary Psychiatrist Award from the National Alliance for the Mentally Ill. He has been cited on the Best Doctors in America listing since 1998.